GW01086905

Norfolk Record Society
Volume LXXV for 2011

NORFOLK RECORD SOCIETY

founded 1930

THE WORLD OF JOHN SECKER (1716–95), QUAKER MARINER

Edited by

ANDREW HOPPER

Norfolk Record Society

Volume LXXV for 2011

First Published in 2011
by The Norfolk Record Society

ISBN 978-0-9556357-4-8

Produced by John Saunders Design & Production
Printed and bound in Great Britain by
CPI Group (UK) Ltd, Croydon, CRO 4YY

Contents

List of Figures and Plates

FIGURES

PLATES

Between pages 22 and 23

Preface and acknowledgements

This project began in 2001 when I chanced upon the 'Autobiography of John Secker' while researching primary source material in the Norfolk Record Office for the Virtual Norfolk Project at the University of East Anglia. Since then, work on this edition has been intermittent and fitted around my teaching and research commitments at the Universities of East Anglia, Birmingham and Leicester. As a historian of the British Civil Wars, the eighteenth century has been refreshing new territory for me and in making this transition I am indebted to Richard Wilson, James Walvin and Peter Jones for their supportive advice. I am also grateful to Erin Bell and Sheila Wright for their expertise on Quakers and to Sylvia Stevens for permission to cite her doctoral thesis on eighteenth-century Norfolk Quakers, which included substantial work on Secker. I am very grateful to Norfolk's County Archivist, John Alban, for permission to publish the Secker manuscript in this series and delivering me a microfilm copy. I am also thankful for the assistance of his team of archivists at the Norfolk Record Office. I am obliged to Leon Doughty and Andrew Finch of the Virtual Norfolk Project for their digital photography and Clive Wilkinson for sharing his expert knowledge of maritime sources and ships' logs in particular. I would like to thank my illustrator, Louise Buglass for the family tree and map of Secker's voyages. I am also indebted to John Leech, the owner of Swafield Mill House in 2003, for a discussion of John Secker and his kind permission to take photographs and for providing an earlier photograph. I am also indebted to Ian Jackson, the librarian at Woodbrooke Quaker Studies Centre in Birmingham. Finally I would also like to thank the series editors, Paul Rutledge and Anthony Howe, for their careful reading of the text, helpful suggestions and additional guidance which saved me from numerous transcription errors. The responsibility for any remaining mistakes is mine alone. This edition is dedicated to my little son, Gilbert William Hopper in the hope that travels and adventures will enrich his life and widen his horizons.

Marc Fitch House, Leicester, 2006

Abbreviations

BL	British Library, London
EB	Encyclopaedia Britannica
IMD	René de Kerchove, *International Maritime Dictionary: an encyclopedic dictionary of useful maritime terms and phrases, together with equivalents in French and German* (2nd edn, London, c.1961)
NMM	National Maritime Museum, Greenwich
NRO	Norfolk Record Office, Norwich
OED	The *Oxford English Dictionary* Online
Oxford DNB	The *Oxford Dictionary of National Biography* Online
* *	Words which have been inserted
< >	Words which have been deleted
[ ]	Expansions of Secker's abbreviations
[italic]	Editorial comment within text

Editorial Conventions

Quakers disapproved of months named after heathen gods so they often referred to months by number. In many places Secker contents himself with referring to such months as 'month called July' and so forth, but in places, especially where he had copied from his earlier writings, he did refer to them by number. Although he was writing after the adoption of the Gregorian calendar in 1752, in some places he numbers months on the basis of the old calendar, in which the new year commenced from March, hence September being the seventh month, and October the eighth. Secker's punctuation has been modified especially by the removal of exclamation marks, often in the middle of sentences, with which he peppered the text. Modernisation of the spelling has been minimal and restricted to where the meaning of a sentence was affected. Secker's text was continuous so paragraphs have been imposed to make the text more digestible for the modern reader, along with the insertion of line breaks after each voyage. Where not given, the place of publication is London.

INTRODUCTION

The travel narrative of John Secker consists of two bound, manuscript volumes in the Norfolk Record Office. The un-paginated first volume[1] is the original in Secker's own hand, the binding of which is roughly stitched with string into a brown paper cover. It measures approximately 20 × 23 cm. The second volume, 'the Mason copy'[2] is a later, hard-bound, well presented copy made after Secker's death in 1800. The original starts abruptly with Secker's description of Rotterdam and concludes abruptly after naming his wife's siblings. This indicates that the beginning and end are missing and that only the portion that dealt with his seafaring years has survived. Ten folios, all of which were written upon, were deliberately severed from the end, leaving only stubs attached. On these folios, Secker had written about his life on shore after 1755, but they were removed, perhaps for personal reasons, as the narrative ends by discussing his wife's family. This transcription has been of the first, original volume, although because of this damage, additional passages at the beginning and end have been provided by the second, more robust volume.

Secker wrote his narrative soon after 1765, so it was written at least ten years after his retirement from seafaring.[3] He may have been partly prompted into writing by what Glyndwr Williams has called the 'Pacific craze' of public fascination with the South Seas that followed the conclusion of the Seven Years' War and embraced the famous voyages of James Cook during the 1770s.[4] His writing was guided by his memory, understandably imperfect at times, along with notes and sketches he made during his voyages, having begun keeping a sea journal while still a teenager [*ff. 5v, 8v*]. The narrative is written in a descriptive style, except for the daily account he provided of his passage round Cape Horn aboard the *Grand Tuscany* in April and May 1750 [*ff. 51r-57r*]. The intricate details and navigational observations in these passages suggest that he directly copied them from a journal he kept at the time.

By the 1760s it had long been fashionable for literate seafarers to write a journal of their voyages, but Secker did not intend his narrative to become a printed publication. If he had, being a Quaker, his manuscript would have

[1] NRO, Y/D 41/105

[2] NRO, Rye MS 71

[3] Secker referred to the Duke of Cumberland (d.1765) as 'then living' [*f. 75v*] and to June 1736 being 'ab[ou]t thirty years since' [*f. 12r*], suggesting he was writing in 1766 or soon thereafter.

[4] P.J. Marshall and G. Williams, *The Great Map of Mankind: British Perceptions of the World in the Age of Enlightenment* (1982), pp. 258–95

been sent for editing to the Morning Meeting in London.[5] Although 'the Mason copy' is in places slightly altered, the original volume appears to be wholly Secker's unedited work. At the time of writing, he had resettled into the Norfolk Quaker community, and it was largely for his friends and kinfolk among them that he wrote. He hoped to justify and vindicate his seafaring life and that his readers might learn from his navigation, travels and experiences. He was also compelled to record his deliverances to give gratitude to God and underline his Quaker credentials. Philip Edwards has observed that 'all voyage narratives are self-serving', with 'the record being adjusted, massaged and manipulated'. Secker's need to think well of himself was an important shaping factor.[6]

Secker mentioned in his will (see Appendix 2) several other works he had written, suggesting that he spent much of his later years in writing. These included a spiritual diary, a book of memoranda, and a 'Book of remarkable Dreams & Deliverances'. Having no children, he bequeathed them to his only brother, William Secker, along with his other papers, journals and charts of harbours in the Pacific.[7] William did not die until 1812, but in 1800, only five years after John Secker's death, his relatives made a copy of the travel narrative. This is the later 'Mason copy' which provides the passages missing at the beginning of the original and a brief conclusion at the end. It was entitled 'Memorandums collected and connected together in order to compile a short Narrative of the Life and Travels of John Secker written by himself, copied from the original Manuscript By Samuel Mason for D. Boulter 1800'. Mason was a Yarmouth Quaker,[8] whose wife, Phebe, was a daughter of Joseph Ransom of Yarmouth and therefore a niece of John Secker's wife, Phebe Ransom. Two notes at the beginning of Mason's copy read 'Rachel Boulter' and 'For Daniel Boulter', suggesting that this copy was made for Daniel Boulter of Yarmouth, shortly before Boulter's death in 1802.[9]

Like John Secker, Boulter was a nephew of John Sparshall and balanced his Quaker beliefs with a great interest in travel, natural history and geography. Both men attended the Quarterly Meeting at Norwich on 27 December 1786, and as cousins with overlapping interests, they were probably well known to each other.[10] A prosperous shopkeeper, Boulter opened a museum of 'Natural & Artificial curiosities' in Yarmouth market place in 1778. Boulter probably intended Mason's copy of Secker's narrative to be

[5] S. Stevens, 'A Believing People in a Changing World: Quakers in Society in North-East Norfolk, 1690–1800' (University of Sunderland, D. Phil. 2005), p. 257

[6] P. Edwards, *The Story of the Voyage: Sea Narratives in Eighteenth-Century England* (Cambridge, 1994), pp. 10, 188

[7] NRO, ANW 1795, Will 83, *ff. 118r-119r* (MF 350)

[8] Samuel Mason of Yarmouth, miller, is mentioned in the Minute Book of the Norfolk and Norwich Quarterly Meeting: NRO, SF 5, 20 June 1774 and 29 March 1780

[9] Stevens, 'A Believing People in a Changing World', pp. 65n, 67, 248n

[10] NRO, SF 6, 27 December 1786

displayed in this museum alongside his many books of voyages and travels that included works by Cook, Dampier, Frezier, Narborough and Shelvocke. The museum also exhibited artefacts obtained by Cook's voyages to the South Seas. Boulter handed over the museum to his nephew, John Boulter, in October 1794.[11]

The conclusion of Mason's copy remarked that Secker continued 'his Journal' after his travels ended, but that 'these having little variety in them, it was not thought proper to transcribe the remainder'. This suggests that Mason had seen the folios detailing Secker's life after 1755 that have since been lost. Mason's remark suggests that the intended readership for his edition of Secker's narrative now included the non-Quakers who visited Boulter's museum. Secker's detailing of his wife's relatives was omitted by Mason [*f. 87v*], as was his discussion of Joseph Peckover's death and 'Massa' Bell's Quaker ministry in the streets of London during 1753.[12] Secker showed much enthusiasm for Bell's preaching, referring to her as a 'faithful woman', furnished by God with 'wisdom, language & utterance, beyond all human ability' [*f. 83r*]. He also remarked that Joseph, 'son of our worthy friend Edmund Peckover of Wells' had accompanied her during her orations. Mason probably cut these passages because Quakers were becoming increasingly wary and hesitant about this sort of public exercise. In a recent thesis on Norfolk Quakers, Sylvia Stevens has noted that many Friends proved ambivalent towards Bell, despite her involvement in other respectable Quaker activities while in London.[13]

After its time in Boulter's museum, Mason's copy passed into the hands of the Norfolk antiquary Walter Rye, who donated it to Norwich Public Library in the early twentieth century. It was then transferred to the Norfolk Record Office on its establishment in 1963. The original was held by Yarmouth Borough Library until the early 1960s when it was transferred into Yarmouth Borough Archives by the borough archivist, Paul Rutledge. It then passed to the Norfolk Record Office when these archives merged in 1970.[14]

Secker's intended audience of family, friends and fellow Quakers shaped his narrative and influenced what he chose to omit. He admitted lapsing from his parents' Quaker morals while at sea, but insisted that these 'were never wholly erac'd, though much defaced by travel and bad company and

[11] NRO, MS 4415, A Short Narrative of the Life of Daniel Boulter, pp. 524, 527; *Museum Boulterianum: A Catalogue of the Curious and Valuable Collection of Natural and Artificial Curiosities in the Extensive Museum of Daniel Boulter, Yarmouth* (c.1794)

[12] Had Mason not cut Secker's original passage in NRO, Y/D 41/105, f. 83r, it would have appeared in NRO, Rye MS 71, pp. 245–6. Bell's preaching was described by J. Phipps, *A Summary Account of an Extraordinary Visit to this Metropolis in the Year 1753, by the Ministry of Ann Mercy Bell* (1754)

[13] Stevens, 'A Believing People in a Changing World', pp. 153–4, 248–9

[14] The editor is most grateful to Mr Paul Rutledge for supplying the provenance information in this paragraph.

too much liberty' [Rye 71, *p. 1*]. This falls short of the frank admission of another Quaker mariner, Edward Coxere, who recalled how he 'little considered the mercies we received, but took large liberty when ashore in drinking and sporting as the manner of seamen generally is.' Unlike Secker, Coxere had not been brought up among Quakers, having become one during his seafaring life. Perhaps this left Coxere freer to admit: 'I confess I was too wild, being left to my own range amongst other nations and people besides my own.'[15]

There are several awkward silences in Secker's narrative. He was sparing in mentioning the drinking culture that characterised seafaring life, and when he did so, carefully showed disapproval, as in the case of the customs officer at Al Mukhā (Mocha), who was 'greatly addicted to drunkeness and other bad practices' [*ff. 25r-v*]. He was defensive about his own drinking exploits, recalling that at the Cape of Good Hope 'we went to a wine house & got a bottle or two of wine amongst us, which made us full of spirits, though not drunk' [*f. 30v*]. If he was so abstemious, he would have stood out as exceptional among his shipmates.[16] He made no mention of the sexual excess notoriously associated with sailors fresh ashore after months at sea. His references to women were brief, usually confining himself to observations of their customs and appearance in the places he visited. He was also silent on his key role as a disciplinarian on board ship at a time when intimidation and violence were central features of maritime discipline.[17] His narrative may remain relatively free from exaggeration and distortion, but he had no wish to offend Quaker sensibilities by including subjects that were better left out. While his faith influenced his narrative heavily it did not overwhelm it or draw it fully into the genre of Quaker spiritual autobiographies. Although he repeatedly paused for accounts of his providential deliverances from danger, the narrative is driven more by describing travels and voyages than religious development. He was highly literate and his striking ability to organise his distant memories into a coherent, written form reflects how Quakers tended to be 'prolific writers of letters, diaries and meticulously-kept minute books.'[18]

Secker was born within four miles of the coast at Swafield mill, in North Walsham, on 20 June 1716. His father, Isaac Secker, a miller of North Walsham, married Hester Sparshall of Bradfield, at Lammas on 17 August 1715.[19] John's upbringing amongst a respectable, middling-sort family

[15] E. H. W. Meyerstein, ed., *Adventures by Sea of Edward Coxere* (Oxford, 1945), pp. 27, 33

[16] R. Davis, *The Rise of the English Shipping Industry in the Seventeenth and Eighteenth Centuries* (1962), p. 122

[17] M. Rediker, *Between the Devil and the Deep Blue Sea: Merchant Seamen, Pirates and the Anglo-American Maritime World, 1700–1750* (Cambridge, 1987), pp. 217–26

[18] A. Winchester, 'Travellers in grey: Quaker journals as a source for local history', *The Local Historian*, 21:2 (1991), p. 70

[19] NRO, MF/RO 320/6, SF 43 Births, Book 1010, p. 66; SF 42 Marriages, Book 1012, p. 51

endowed him with several advantages early in life. Firstly, he remembered being put to school at an early age, being taught to read, and borrowing the many books which fired his imagination to travel overseas. His education was probably in a school run by another denomination as there were very few Quaker schoolmasters in the county and no Quaker schools established on a long-term basis. Dissent had been long established in North Walsham, with records stretching back to the Compton Census of 1676.[20] These home districts of Secker's childhood delighted Daniel Defoe, whose description of the countryside between Cromer and Norwich praised the 'several good market towns, and innumerable villages, all diligently applying to the woollen manufacture.' Defoe found the countryside 'exceeding fruitful and fertile', with 'more tradesmen than gentlemen in it'. He concluded 'this part is so entirely given up to industry, that what with the seafaring men on the one side, and the manufacturers on the other, we saw no idle hands here, but every man busy on the main affair of life, that is to say, getting money.'[21] This image of a populous and mercantile region, relatively free from gentry control, satisfied Defoe's own preconceptions but suggests an environment conducive to Secker's aspirations.

When aged about eleven, Secker went to live with his mother's brother, John Sparshall, at Southrepps. Sparshall held a licence for Quaker meetings in his house and traded as a corn merchant and maltster at Yarmouth.[22] This move afforded Secker greater contact with the sea, and his parents, who opposed him becoming a sailor, procured him a trip on Sparshall's sloop from Yarmouth to Rotterdam. They probably hoped his romantic notions of life at sea would be broken by confronting him with the less glamorous reality. The life of a common seaman was ordinarily perceived by contemporaries to bring too much danger and hardship for too little reward; such a life was 'not, therefore, one which the son of the even moderately prosperous tradesman or skilled artisan would be encouraged to enter.'[23] The American Quaker, John Woolman, considered that fathers could not with good conscience apprentice their sons to the irreligion, licence and vice that he had observed to be endemic among seafarers.[24]

Yet Secker was not deterred by his parents and shortly afterwards became cook and cabin boy on another of Sparshall's vessels, mastered by Secker's cousin, Thomas Parsons. His family's Quaker principles were flouted by his subsequent desertion in 1732 to serve on the warships the *Namur* and the *Bonnetta*, and he did not write to them for a year. He fell away from Quaker practice, but maintained contact with his family by correspondence. On

[20] Stevens, 'A Believing People in a Changing World', pp. 34, 230, 232

[21] D. Defoe, *A Tour Through the Whole Island of Great Britain*, ed. P. Rogers (Harmondsworth, 1971), p. 95

[22] Stevens, 'A Believing People in a Changing World', p. 44

[23] Davis, *The Rise of the English Shipping Industry*, p. 114, 153

[24] F. B. Tolles, ed., *The Journal of John Woolman and a Plea for the Poor* (New York, 1968), p. 195

several occasions after 1738, he returned home to visit them. His family's Quaker network occasionally afforded him financial support and hospitality, aiding his subsistence during hard times between voyages. Despite voyaging far and wide, he became more integrated into this network as he grew older. When he retired from seafaring he returned home to marry a Quaker shopkeeper, Phebe Ransom of Ashill, at Swaffham, on 10 March 1756.[25] They kept her shop at Ashill until 1760, after which they moved to Holt, where they bought a house to run as a grocery shop. Trading as a grocer was a logical step for Secker, a man who had already spent years transporting the colonial, consumer goods that by the mid-eighteenth century had 'become sufficiently widespread to bring the spoils of empire to the level of every village shop'.[26] Phebe died at Holt, aged sixty-seven, on 24 November 1783.[27] Secker died at Holt, aged seventy-eight, on 20 March 1795. He was buried at Holt a week later.[28] In 1924 the meeting house and burial ground at Holt were sold and the building was demolished shortly afterwards. Two shops now occupy the site of John Secker's resting place, next to the Post Office.[29]

In addition to his family background, a closer understanding of Secker is established by considering the Norfolk Quaker community of which he was a part. The traditional historiography depicts eighteenth-century Quakerism as declining in vitality, with a 'dull, quiet, uneventful' image.[30] This depiction seems a little one-dimensional and is grounded upon a skewed comparison of eighteenth-century Quakers with the founders of the movement. It has been much influenced by the work of Rufus Jones, who found the missionary zeal and enthusiasm of Quakerism's seventeenth-century founders more attractive than the introspective and organisational concerns of their successors.[31] This image also neglects the regional differences and varieties of experience among eighteenth-century Friends. Its emphasis upon eighteenth-century Quakers channeling their energies into the internal discipline of their groups seems at odds with Paul Langford's observations that by the eighteenth century, despite being notorious for their exclusiveness, Quakers were becoming more 'active participators in an open society', and more successful in adapting themselves to business and commercial realities.[32] John Secker showed little sign of idealising his Quaker forefathers or looking back

[25] NRO, MF/RO 320/6, SF 45 Supplement, Book 1575, pp. 326–30

[26] L. Colley, *Britons: Forging the Nation 1707–1837* (2003), p. 69

[27] NRO, MF/RO 320/6, SF 45 Supplement, Book 1574, p. 1

[28] NRO, MF/RO 320/6, SF 44 Burials, Book 988, p. 6

[29] NRO, MF/RO 320/6, SF 44 Burials, Book 988, p. 6; D. M. Butler, *The Quaker Meeting Houses of Britain* (2 vols., Friends Historical Society, 1999), i, p. 442

[30] D. J. Hall, 'The study of eighteenth-century English Quakerism: From Rufus Jones to Larry Ingle', *Quaker Studies*, 5:2 (2001), pp. 108, 113, 116

[31] R. M. Jones, *The Later Periods of Quakerism* (2 vols., 1921), pp. 1–5

[32] P. Langford, *A Polite and Commercial People: England 1727–1783* (Oxford, 1989), p. 74

on a golden age, rather seeking to embrace and interpret the world as he saw it. The biographical approach that has been so characteristic within Quaker historiography might offer fresh challenges to Jones's thesis,[33] and it has been surprising that Secker was not subjected to academic study until the doctoral thesis of Sylvia Stevens in 2005.[34]

The Seckers were part of a well established Quaker network in Norfolk, whose numbers reached a high-point in the early eighteenth century. Michael Watts found evidence of twenty-two Quaker meetings in Norfolk at this time, with an estimated 1,690 adherents. This amounted to about 0.72 per cent of Norfolk's population. Although outnumbered by other dissenters, Quakers had more congregations than any other dissenting group. This tended to echo the national picture, where Quakers were less numerous than Presbyterians and Independents, but had developed a larger network of meetings, with a presence in every English county. Yet, as elsewhere in England by mid-century, Quaker numbers were in decline, with fewer births and marriages than deaths, and with 80 to 90 per cent of Friends having Quaker parents, as they became more concerned with convincing their own children than evangelising among non-Quakers. During the time of Secker's voyages there were roughly four hundred Quakers in Norwich and one thousand in the rest of Norfolk.[35] Their declining numbers were also due to a demographic trend among Quakers, of which Secker was a part, towards marrying later in life than the rest of society.[36]

Historians have tended to depict the eighteenth-century Quaker community as one of rising wealth and prosperity, with the emergence of many merchants, bankers, substantial traders and manufacturers.[37] This is partly owing to a focus on prominent Quakers, but many of the Quakers in Secker's home districts had middling-sort occupations, such as yeomen, millers, worsted weavers, grocers and shopkeepers. Several of them combined trade with husbandry. A few Quakers even became parish officeholders in Norfolk and on occasions it seems that enough of their non-Quaker neighbours were prepared to accept them in these roles. Secker's father, Isaac, acted as churchwarden at North Walsham alongside a non-Quaker soon after he arrived in town in 1715, indicating that the Seckers were not lacking in local status.[38]

During Secker's childhood his family would have attended the North Walsham meeting in a building amongst fir trees a mile outside town. The

[33] Hall, 'The study of eighteenth-century English Quakerism', p. 110

[34] Stevens, 'A Believing People in a Changing World', chapter six

[35] M. R. Watts, *The Dissenters: From the Reformation to the French Revolution* (Oxford, 1978), pp. 268–9, 285, 386–90, 509; R. T. Vann, *The Social Development of English Quakerism, 1655–1755* (Cambridge, Massachusetts, 1969), pp. 162–3

[36] Stevens, 'A Believing People in a Changing World', p. 274

[37] Watts, *The Dissenters*, p. 364

[38] Stevens, 'A Believing People in a Changing World', pp. 59–60, 202–3

brick meeting house now on the Swafield road was not built until 1772.[39] During his travels, he attended Quaker meetings in 'Sygamore Alley', Dublin [*f. 83v*] and the building used for the Yearly Meeting in Gracechurch Street, London [*f. 82v*]. His stated reason for his retirement in 1755 was that the master of his vessel had guns fitted on board, despite his 'being now principled against fighting' [*f. 83v*]. He had not always adhered to such Quaker principles and his increasing return to them in the 1750s contributed to his retirement from seafaring.

Secker's return to life on land and marriage to Phebe Ransom in 1756 reintegrated him into Quaker society. His local meeting was satisfied that 'good order was observed and ye marriage well conducted'.[40] From then until 1760, he diligently represented Swaffham at the Monthly Meeting held at Lynn[41] no less than twenty-two times, and on eight more occasions attended the Quarterly Meeting held at Norwich. When Secker and Phebe moved to Holt, the Lynn Monthly Meeting recommended the couple in a letter dated 4 December 1760. It declared that 'their lives & conversations were agreeable to the profession we make, and that they were in good unity with us as members of our society'. It added that Phebe had 'a gift in the ministry, in the exercise of which we had very good unity'.[42] Phebe's sister, Mary Kirby, was widely known for her ministry from about 1740, as were Phebe's brothers John Ransom of North Walsham and Joseph Ransom of Yarmouth.[43] Secker would have been able to compare his colonial experiences with local Quakers Edmund Peckover and Mary Kirby who had visited America in 1742–4 and 1758–60 respectively.[44] He may also have discoursed with his cousin, Joseph Sparshall of Yarmouth, whose botanical, naturalist and philosophical interests allegedly procured him the offer of membership of the Royal Society.[45]

Given that Secker had married into a family known for their Quaker ministry it is unsurprising that he assumed an important office-holding role in Norfolk Quaker Society. Although the minute book for the Monthly Meeting of Wells, Holt and Fakenham apparently does not survive for the period of his residence there,[46] glimpses survive of his participation in the

[39] C. Barringer, ed., *North Walsham in the Eighteenth Century* (North Walsham, 1983), p. 83; N. Pevsner and B. Wilson, *The Buildings of England: Norfolk 1: Norwich and North-East* (New Haven, 2002), p. 624; C. Stell, 'Nonconformist chapels in East Anglia', in N. Virgoe and T. Williamson, eds, Religious Dissent in East Anglia (Norwich, 1993), p. 18; Butler, *The Quaker Meeting Houses of Britain*, i, pp. 446–7

[40] NRO, MS 21,393/8, 6 May 1756

[41] The first Friends' Meeting House in King's Lynn dated from c.1700. A new one was built in New Conduit Street in 1774 and registered by Joseph Peckover of Wisbech in 1775: Butler, *The Quaker Meeting Houses of Britain*, i, p. 444

[42] NRO, MS 21,393/8, 4 December 1760

[43] NRO, SF 5, 30 March 1763 and 29 March 1780; NRO, SF 6, 31 March 1790

[44] NRO, SF 5, 10 May 1758 and 29 March 1780

[45] NRO, MS 4415, p. 531

[46] Secker's residence at Holt between 1760 and 1795 is not covered by surviving minute books: NRO, MS 21,393/3, 1738–1759; NRO, MS 21,393/4, 1797–1802

Quaker community. He was involved in drafting the testimony to mark the death of the eminent Quaker, Edmund Peckover at Wells in 1767. This testimony was read subsequently at the Norwich Quarterly Meeting on 10 May 1768. In 1770 he was appointed an examiner of the accounts of several monthly meetings held in Norfolk, while in 1774 and 1777 he was appointed to committees to audit accounts.[47] On 14 November 1767 he was among eight trustees of the meeting house at Wells,[48] and on 21 January 1774 he became a trustee for the meeting house at Holt.[49] His regular attendance at the Norwich Quarterly Meeting is given in appendix 4 and he was present on 27 June 1757 when this meeting declared it was 'apprehensive, that some under our Name both in this nation and in the Colonies abroad, are concerned for filthy Lucre's sake, in Dealing in Negroes.'[50] Considering his experience in the Caribbean and American colonies, Secker was likely to have been involved in promoting this declaration. The Yearly Meeting censured Quakers who engaged in the slave trade as early as 1727, and in 1783, it was Quakers who presented the first anti-slavery petition to Parliament.[51]

The next important context for understanding Secker's narrative is the maritime background. Linda Colley has recently led calls for maritime concerns to be reinstalled at the centre of eighteenth-century British history to destabilise notions of core and periphery and illustrate the diversity of Britishness. There can be few better case studies to implement this than Secker's narrative; he spent the best part of twenty-five years at sea and served on upwards of thirty-five vessels. He crossed the Atlantic sixteen times and also voyaged into the Indian and Pacific Oceans. His narrative voiced his identity, attitudes and beliefs so much because these had been confronted by new cultures, lands and ideas. His narrative addressed the multiple themes of religion, overseas cultures, migration, slavery, navigation, weather, maritime living conditions, commerce and cargoes, discipline and press-gangs, piracy, insurance fraud, imprisonment abroad and Jacobite exiles.

In many ways, Secker's seafaring life was highly representative of that of contemporary sailors. He first went to sea aged twelve or thirteen, confining his first voyages to the coasting trades. By his late teens he embarked on transatlantic voyages, with his longest voyages following in his twenties and thirties to India, St Helena and Peru. Then, like many of his counterparts, his last voyages reverted to the short-haul and coasting trades of his youth, returning to his home port of Great Yarmouth.[52] Like many others, Secker gave romantic reasons for first wishing to go to sea, including the desire 'to

[47] NRO, SF 5, 28 December 1774 and 24 September 1777

[48] Built in 1697, Wells Meeting House was replaced by a new building in 1783: NRO, MS 21393/51, 293 x 1; Butler, *The Quaker Meeting Houses of Britain*, i, p. 459

[49] NRO, SF 259, pp. 57–8

[50] NRO, SF 4, 27 June 1757

[51] Watts, *The Dissenters*, p. 479; Colley, *Britons*, pp. 352–4

[52] P. Earle, *Sailors: English Merchant Seamen 1650–1775* (1998), pp. 17, 20–5, 48–9, 185

travel into distant countrys and to see those strange things which I had read of' [*p. 2*]. Edward Barlow, another boy who went to sea at much the same age seventy years before, also recalled that he 'had always a mind to see strange countries and fashions'.[53] After his first voyages as a hired servant, Secker bound himself as an apprentice for three years to the Trafford brothers of Liverpool, merchants in the 'Guinea and Virginia trade'.[54]

Secker's integration into maritime life was facilitated by Yarmouth's status as a remarkable port. In the first two-thirds of the eighteenth century Yarmouth was prospering among England's most important ports.[55] In 1724 Defoe described Yarmouth quay as 'the finest quay in England, if not in Europe, not inferior to that of Marseilles itself'. He added that some of the merchants' houses looked 'like little palaces rather than the dwelling houses of private men'. Defoe saw Yarmouth as a place bustling with prosperity, remarking that the town's merchants cured forty thousand barrels of herrings in one season, and that Yarmouth's share in the coal trade between Newcastle and London had grown larger than any town in England.[56] Although Yarmouth declined in importance over the next fifty years, in July 1775, the American Quaker, Jabez Maud Fisher concurred that it possessed 'the finest Key of any in England', and that the town 'from the other Side of the River looks very pretty'.[57] Yarmouth controlled Norwich's seaborne trade and harboured vessels trading from the Baltic to the Mediterranean. Most of this commerce went through the ports of London and Rotterdam. Yarmouth offered a sheltered anchorage but the frequent silting up of the River Yare's mouth and the dangerous bar of sand and shingle that narrowed the town's outlet to the sea hindered further expansion. Yet by 1741 there were 2,123 houses in the town, suggesting a densely-packed population of between ten and twelve thousand inhabitants.[58] In 1744 Yarmouth stood in sixth place in a list of tonnages belonging to English ports. It imported iron, timber, bricks, canvas, linen, glass, wooden goods and shipbuilding materials from Baltic Europe. Yarmouth also imported lead from Hull, coal from Sunderland and Newcastle, and luxury goods from London. Its main export was woollen cloth, but the town also exported corn and malt to London and Ireland, along with coal and cured red herrings to Rotterdam.

[53] E. Barlow, *Barlow's Journal of His Life at Sea in King's Ships, East & West Indiaman & other Merchantmen from 1659 to 1703*, ed. B. Lubbock (2 vols., 1934), i, pp. 15, 60

[54] A full seven-year apprenticeship at sea was rare and shorter, three-year apprenticeships like Secker's were more common: Davis, *The Rise of the English Shipping Industry*, p. 117

[55] Davis, *The Rise of the English Shipping Industry*, p. 36

[56] Defoe, *A Tour Through the Whole Island of Great Britain*, pp. 89–91

[57] K. Morgan, ed., *An American Quaker in the British Isles: The Travel Journals of Jabez Maud Fisher, 1775–1779* (Records of Social and Economic History, new series, 16, Oxford, 1992), p. 36

[58] P. Gauci, *Politics and Society in Great Yarmouth, 1660–1722* (Oxford, 1996), pp. 257–8; J. D. Murphy, 'The Town and Trade of Great Yarmouth, 1740–1850' (University of East Anglia, D.Phil. thesis, 1979), pp. i-ii, 7n

Secker's last six voyages in 1754–5 were made from Yarmouth to Dublin carrying cargo belonging to Charles Le Grys, who was Yarmouth's largest maltster by 1760.[59]

Defoe claimed that Yarmouth's register of 1697 showed there were '1123 sail of ships using the sea, and belonged to the town, besides such ships as the merchants of Yarmouth might be concerned in, and be part-owners of, belonging to any other ports.' He also claimed that Yarmouth's seamen 'as well masters as mariners, are justly esteemed among the ablest and most expert navigators in England.'[60] Secker was well placed to take advantage of this environment and gradually became a self-taught navigator himself. His education and literacy was an immense benefit as merchant seafaring was increasingly a literate profession, especially for ships' officers who also required numeracy for navigation. Much could also be learned of navigation by observing the daily running of a vessel.[61] Like Barlow before him, Secker would have calculated latitude by observation and dead reckoning, and longitude by dead reckoning.[62] He was aided by books of navigation, charts and for a time, his Halley's Quadrant. Multi-linguistics were also invaluable to all seafarers, and he, like many others, learned foreign languages, including French and Spanish.

Many of the merchant ships on Secker's shorter voyages would have been 150 to 200 ton vessels, with crews of between eleven and fourteen men.[63] He did serve on several larger vessels and considered the privateer *Duke of Cumberland* a large ship with a crew of just thirty-four [*f. 41r*]. Secker's voyage on the *Defence* East Indiaman was among a crew of seventy-eight, on a larger vessel expensively built in a Thames shipyard and up to five hundred tons in size.[64] Yet by far the largest ship on which Secker served was the Spaniard, the *Grand Tuscany*, which Secker recalled at 'about 1000 or 1200 tun burden' with a crew of about 160 [*ff. 47r, 66v*].

Secker's narrative illuminates the interplay between the captains and crews of merchant vessels. Like many sailors, he developed a questioning and independent temperament that frequently vexed the captains and masters whom he served. Even as a boy, it was not long before he fell out with his first master, his cousin Thomas Parsons, deserting him at London for service on a warship after neglecting to attend a Quaker meeting [*f. 2v*]. Soon after he became servant to Lieutenant Smith of the *Bonnetta*, who

[59] The enterprising Le Grys leased land from Yarmouth corporation in 1759 to construct the town's first sea bath: Murphy, 'The Town and Trade of Great Yarmouth', pp. 15, 34–6, 55n, 70; A. W. and J. L. Ecclestone, *The Rise of Great Yarmouth: The Story of a Sandbank* (Norwich, 1959), p. 66

[60] Defoe, *A Tour Through the Whole Island of Great Britain*, p. 91

[61] Rediker, *Between the Devil and the Deep Blue Sea*, p. 87

[62] Barlow, *Barlow's Journal*, ii, pp. 334–7

[63] Rediker, *Between the Devil and the Deep Blue Sea*, pp. 86–7

[64] BL, Asia, Pacific and Africa Collections, IOR/L/MAR/B/647B; Davis, *The Rise of the English Shipping Industry*, p. 78

despite the kindnesses he showed Secker, was soon deserted by him at Shields in September 1733 [*f. 6r*]. His subsequent apprenticeship to the Traffords of Liverpool from October 1733 was cut short when he deserted their service on Madeira in March 1736 [*f. 10r*]. He left his next ship, the *John Snow*, in South Carolina in February 1737, 'on account of the captain's behavour which was none of the best'. He disliked him for bragging about cheating his crew of their wages, and for whipping a freed black man who had frustrated the captain's attempts to sell him into slavery [*ff. 17v-19r*]. In May 1739 he planned unsuccessfully to desert the *Defence* East Indiaman to join a French ship in the Red Sea [*f. 23v*]. In April 1746 he was sacked by his Yarmouth employers when the vessel he mastered for them failed to make sufficient profit [*f. 39r*].

Usually serving as chief mate from the 1740s, Secker fell out with several of his captains. Aboard the *Noble Ann* in February 1747, Secker was struck by the captain, whom he described as a 'very wicked abusive man', with 'a fierce fiery temper', and a tendency to beat his own crew. Secker recalled 'I obliged him to discharge me & pay me my wages' [*f. 39v*]. In April 1748 he complained that the captain of the *Duke of Cumberland* abdicated command when confronted with a French privateer, leaving Secker as his chief mate to resolve the situation [*f. 41v*]. He returned to this vessel as chief mate later that year, but fell out with its next captain, John Colwart, at Marseilles in February 1749, 'greatly owing to his son, a young, green impertinent lad, which accompanied him in the ship' [*f. 44r*]. After another argument with Colwart on 7 May 1749 Secker secured his discharge and pay [*f. 46v*]. He served as chief mate on his last vessel, the *Three Brothers* in 1755, whose master, Richard Smith, he described as of a 'hasty passionate disposition', with 'but little command over his tongue at such times', and 'wavering & timorous, in his friendship very inconstant.' [*f. 87r-v*].

Arguments between captains and mates on merchant ships were notoriously frequent. The chief mate was second in command, but was often the older and more experienced seafarer.[65] Their duties included commanding half the ship's company in four-hour watches, alternating with a watch drawn from the rest of the crew commanded by the other mate, or the captain. When in port, captains were often conducting business ashore, leaving the mate to command the crew and supervise loading the cargo. Chief mates often became focal points of a crew's opposition to its captain.[66] In 1701 a fifty-nine-year-old chief mate, Edward Barlow, believed that most of the merchant captains whom he had served 'care not how much or in what way they can get all to themselves, and care not what little other people get that are under them.' Barlow had much in common with Secker; both fell out with most captains they had served under as chief mates, both

[65] Earle, *Sailors*, pp. 161–3

[66] Rediker, *Between the Devil and the Deep Blue Sea*, p. 240

were assaulted at least once and discharged from service by their angry masters. Barlow disdained the youthful inexperience of his captains, resenting their incompetent seamanship and attempts to cheat the crew of their pay. Barlow described one captain as a 'knavish fellow' and another as 'young high-flown, conceited, proud, imperious, base and perfidious sort of a man'. He resented being questioned by one captain 'as though I could not tell how to hand sails, having used the sea six times the time he had.'[67] Experienced mariners would judge the seafaring competence of their officers; Barlow recalling that many of the English commanders in the Anglo-Dutch war of 1666 'were more fit to go commanders in some dung-boat than in a good King's ship.'[68]

By the mid-1740s Secker, like Barlow, was an experienced mate and navigator, with his own views on running a ship, and he clearly perceived many of his captains to be far less competent than himself. For all these reasons, he would have wanted to become master of a vessel. The advance in status from chief mate to master might treble a man's income and open the possibility of becoming a merchant himself. Yet to become a master required capital and a network of friends to invest and share the risk of ownership.[69] Like Barlow, when Secker got this opportunity, his fortune did not last.[70]

Nuala Zahedieh has contended that Quakers had 'extensive, well-organised communication links throughout the Atlantic world', which bestowed upon them 'conspicuous success in colonial commerce'.[71] Yet this success did not extend to Secker, who despite making several ventures of his own, and briefly mastering two vessels between 1742 and 1746, never made a fortune or became a merchant himself. However, his home Quaker network allowed him a comfortable living in which to retire, a luxury unavailable to many veteran mates who grew old at sea, remaining dependent upon wage labour.

Linebaugh and Rediker have argued that sailors brought to their ports 'a militant attitude toward arbitrary and excessive authority', and an 'empathy for the troubles of others'.[72] This comes through strongly at numerous moments in Secker's narrative, and even extended to members of out-groups such as the freed black slave ill-treated by Secker's captain [*f. 18v*], the 'poor Turks' scorned by the Portuguese, or the betrayal of the Turk merchant in Cagliari [*f. 45r*]. Yet whether such attitudes led Secker to develop a radical political identity of the kind that Linebaugh and Rediker believe existed among many sailors remains open to doubt.

67 Barlow, *Barlow's Journal*, ii, pp. 326–7, 339, 352, 355–8, 386–7, 529, 539–40, 543–4

68 Rediker, *Between the Devil and the Deep Blue Sea*, p. 95; Barlow, *Barlow's Journal*, i, p. 123

69 Davis, *The Rise of the English Shipping Industry*, pp. 84–5

70 Barlow, *Barlow's Journal*, ii, pp. 461, 463, 504, 507

71 N. Zahedieh, 'Economy', in D. Armitage and M. J. Braddick, eds, *The British Atlantic World, 1500–1800* (Basingstoke, 2002), pp. 66–7

72 P. Linebaugh and M. Rediker, *The Many-Headed Hydra: The Hidden History of the Revolutionary Atlantic* (2000), p. 214

Like all good seafaring journals, Secker's account of his wages, cargoes and ventures provides useful evidence for economic historians. The mate of a merchantman in Secker's day was paid on average £3 5s per month in peacetime and £4 8s in wartime,[73] sums consistent with his remembrances for many of his later voyages. Technological advances in shipbuilding during his day emulated the hull forms used earlier by the Dutch, thereby increasing the space for cargo and reducing the size of the crews required to sail them.[74] As Secker's narrative shows, merchant seamen endured cramped quarters, poor food, disease, disabling accidents, shipwrecks, pay arrears and the danger of impressment into the Royal Navy.[75] Highly skilled mariners such as Secker were especially vulnerable to the press, standing to lose their sea chests, months of pay arrears and all prospect of attending to their onshore affairs. By mid-century the navy needed forty thousand sailors to man its vessels, and it required experienced mariners like Secker, not novice landsmen.[76]

Quaker sailors faced further trials in their everyday seafaring lives. Edward Coxere remembered that he was unemployed for a long time because 'the name of a Quaker and not fighting shut me quite out of esteem' with prospective masters, and 'I became as one not fit to be suffered in a ship'. The faith of Quaker mariners brought them yet more problems at sea: drinking toasts, doffing hats to their captain, joining in shipboard services with swearers and cursers, or firing off guns in salute were all problematic for them. They might meet together for their own religious observances in silence and so provoke curiosity or resentment from their shipmates. Thomas Lurting's account of his deliverances and convincement recalled how when two men onboard 'refused to hear the priest, or put off their hats to the captain', they were soon derided as Quakers. Refusing to fight was also liable to antagonise captains and provoke them to violence against Quakers.[77] Sailors also had a reputation on land for drinking, swearing, whoring and violence,[78] pursuits repugnant to a committed Quaker. Indeed the New Jersey Quaker and anti-slavery campaigner, John Woolman, found a 'lamentable degeneracy' among seamen. He lodged among sailors in the steerage of the *Mary and Elizabeth* on a transatlantic crossing in 1772 and observed with regret how the youngest seamen were infected by the 'almost universal depravity among sailors'. He felt that crews were driven to excessive drinking by harsh working conditions, leading lives 'full of corruption and extreme alienation from God'.[79]

[73] Rediker, *Between the Devil and the Deep Blue Sea*, p. 306

[74] Davis, *The Rise of the English Shipping Industry*, pp. 58, 65–6, 71

[75] Linebaugh and Rediker, *The Many-Headed Hydra*, p. 160 [76] Colley, *Britons*, p. 65

[77] Meyerstein, ed., *Adventures by Sea of Edward Coxere*, pp. 88–90, 117; T. Lurting, *The Fighting Sailor Turned Peaceable Christian: Manifested in the Convincement and Conversion of Thomas Lurting* (1711), reprinted in L. Kuenning, ed., *Historical Writings of Quakers against War* (Quaker Heritage Press, Glenside, Pennsylvania, 2002), pp. 5, 12, 17 [78] Earle, *Sailors*, p. 13

[79] Tolles, ed., *The Journal of John Woolman and a Plea for the Poor*, pp. 190–206

Sailors' declarations of thankfulness to God for their deliverances at sea were a common feature of maritime narratives. The chances of a sailor dying in an accident at sea were fairly high. He might fall from the rigging, be washed overboard, or be struck by falling equipment. He might also fall ill as a result of suffering the thirst and malnutrition which often followed when captains put their crews on short rations to conserve supplies or save the ship owners' money.[80] Thomas Lurting's polemical account of his life at sea is full of his deliverances from death, while Edward Barlow thanked God for deliverance from his long captivity in the East Indies in 1674, and on several occasions for preserving him from shipwreck.[81] Yet Secker went to great detail in describing his deliverances, the accounts of which possess a mystical flavour in his discussion of dreams and visions.[82] Sylvia Stevens has recently argued that this aspect of his writing belongs to an eighteenth-century providentialism that circulated in manuscript form and has been under-researched by scholars. The idea that God would intervene directly in individual lives was still prevalent among some Quakers and Dissenters, despite becoming unfashionable by the late eighteenth century. Witness stories of dreams, deliverances and divine occurrences were of considerable value to such groups and remained a significant way of transmitting belief.[83] The importance Secker attached to such deliverances is observed by the number of times he paused his narrative to record them at great length.

In 1735 Secker passed out at the stench of noxious bilge water in his ship's flooded pumpwell and for a while was considered dead until revived by his shipmates. Secker considered he had been 'rekindled through the secret direction of his unsearchable providence' [*ff. 8v-10r*]. In 1736 he was preserved from drowning in the Golfe du Morbihan off Brittany until rescued by a French boat [*ff. 12v-13v*]. At the Cape of Good Hope in 1741, his boat was overturned in dangerous winds and he was again nearly drowned until a Dutch boat rescued him. He considered this another 'very remarkable deliverance' and pledged 'to engage a gratefull acknowledgement to the author of my life, as long as I have a being. He alone being worthy of praise who delights not in the death of a poor sinner' [*ff. 30v-32r*]. In 1745 he contracted a fever in Dublin, and his doctor abandoning him, Secker believed he would die. In his delirium, he dreamed he was met by an angel who told him that he would live. Then he beheld a vision of Hebrew writing in his room, which informed him how many years, weeks and days he would live. He considered that God had 'made way by his providence for my recovery

[80] Rediker, *Between the Devil and the Deep Blue Sea*, pp. 92–3; Davis, *The Rise of the English Shipping Industry*, p. 156

[81] Lurting, *The Fighting Sailor Turned Peaceable Christian*, passim; Barlow, *Barlow's Journal*, i, pp. 246, 248, ii, pp. 410, 553

[82] Secker also claimed that he observed 'a token of his death' two weeks before his father died in 1744 [*f. 34v*].

[83] Stevens, 'A Believing People in a Changing World', pp. 2, 157, 193–4, 281–2

according to the vision' [*ff. 36r-38v*]. Secker was later moved to leave 'a memorandum of this merciful deliverance upon record, in another place', probably in the 'Book of remarkable Dreams & Deliverances' he bequeathed to his brother. When he was afflicted with jaundice and the bloody flux at Lima in 1750, he declared his recovery was due to God blessing the remedies he took [*ff. 64v-66r*].

At some point in their careers, many sailors suffered imprisonment in a foreign port and Secker was no exception. He was twice captured by French privateers, in 1744 and 1748, between which dates French privateers captured around 1,600 ships.[84] In both cases his captivity was fairly brief, with exchanges arranged after just three months. A greater deliverance followed Secker's imprisonment in Chile and Peru in 1751. His sketches, observations and reputation as a navigator caused his arrest by the governor of Valdivia on suspicion of spying for the British government. He was threatened with burning by a crowd at Callao en route to his trial before the Viceroy at Lima. Although exonerated, he recalled that shortly before his arrest he dreamed that he was being crucified for a crime of which he was innocent, a manner of death for which he felt himself unworthy [*ff. 69v-72r*]. His last witnessing of providence came in describing his retirement from seafaring, which was prompted by his master fitting out the *Three Brothers* with guns. Secker recalled the ship was taken by a French privateer in the Irish Channel very soon after, without firing a shot [*f. 87v*]. Such cautionary tales were part of a Quaker urge to illustrate God's providence in upholding their testimonies against fighting; Edward Coxere recounts a similar story of the death of a prosperous Quaker master mariner, shortly after having his ship fitted out with guns.[85]

Secker's attitudes provide an empirical testing ground for Linda Colley's theories about a British national identity emerging from anti-Catholicism and Francophobia in the eighteenth century.[86] Eighteenth-century travel literature tended to 'reinforce native patriotism', while depictions of continental Roman Catholics as priest-ridden promoted comforting feelings of self satisfaction, independence and liberty among British Protestants.[87] Touring Italy in 1729, Lord Hervey remarked that to be Roman Catholic was to be 'economically inept: wasteful, indolent and oppressive if powerful and exploited if not.'[88] These preconceptions were reinforced by Secker, who frequently depicted an ignorant Catholic laity, downtrodden and at the mercy of grasping priests. Notions of British patriotism in Secker remain grounded in the perception that the British poor were better off than their counterparts in Catholic Europe and its colonies.

Secker considered that James II had 'abdicated the Crown' [*f. 3r*], and

[84] Earle, *Sailors*, p. 120
[85] Meyerstein, ed., *Adventures by Sea of Edward Coxere*, p. 102
[86] Colley, *Britons*, passim
[87] Langford, *A Polite and Commercial People*, pp. 506–7
[88] Colley, *Britons*, p. 35

as a beneficiary of the Act of Toleration of 1689, he remained distrustful of the exiled Jacobites. When questioned in French captivity in 1744, he claimed that he had been disdainful of Jacobite prospects, remarking that the English people well knew that Stuart pledges of liberty of conscience 'would last no longer than till they were established in their own way & had got a standing army, ready to suppress any opposition' [*f. 35r*]. This clearly marked a very British identification of a large, permanent military force with foreign, Catholic and undesirable styles of government.

In commenting upon Roman Catholic and Islamic societies abroad, like most travelling Englishmen, Secker was blending his pre-existing knowledge with his experiences. Yet his experiences themselves were coloured by assumptions, preconceptions and prejudices.[89] He considered the Portuguese inhabitants of Madeira lacked education largely because they were 'as much priest ridden as any people in the world'. After witnessing a procession of flagellants, he considered its participants 'slaves and drudges to superstition' and that Roman Catholicism on the island could be seen in 'its highest superstition & slavery' [*ff. 16v-17r*]. Likewise, he felt the 'poor bigoted' pilgrims that came to kiss the holy blood at Bruges were 'through the craftiness of the priest… fleeced of their substance' [*f. 36v*]. Yet his pity did not prevent him manipulating such supposed superstition to his advantage. He recalled how he and a comrade procured kindnesses from the Portuguese on Madeira by showing them the sailors' tattoos on their arms of Christ crucified, 'which they would embrace & kiss, calling us bon Cristianos, or good Christians & seem very fond on us; on that account' [*f. 11v*].

The tendency of the Spaniards in Peru to consider all Protestants not as Christians, but as heretics, was to Secker an 'impertinence which is too common in most Roman Catholick countreys' [*f. 64r*]. For this, he often blamed not the supposedly ignorant common people, but 'priest craft, the bane to civility' [*f. 67r*]. This reflects that by the mid-eighteenth century it was more acceptable for Englishmen to condemn foreigners for not adhering to enlightened forms of civility, rather than for their religion. Yet seventeenth-century suspicions died hard. Secker considered that the friars who operated the city hospitals at Lima threatened and cajoled the sick, Protestant members of his crew into turning Roman Catholic, and that when one Swede withstood their efforts 'he was not fairly dealt by' and died soon after [*f. 64v*].

When Secker was accosted by a friar in Lima for not kissing an image of a saint, he replied that he 'was an English man & a protestant' [*f. 63r*]. Yet his blend of hostility and pity towards foreign Roman Catholics, and his evident pride in his Protestant, English identity, coexisted uneasily with the strong sense of separateness still keenly felt among eighteenth-century Quakers, along with their equivocation about empires won by force of arms. Although he adapted himself well to the outside world during his seafaring

[89] Marshall and Williams, *The Great Map of Mankind*, p. 2

years, this was largely because he had fallen away from Quakerism. Writing his narrative in later life, he was under no illusions that Quakers were scorned by many of their countrymen [*ff. 83v-84r*]. In these ways the diversity of experience in his writings both support and raise questions regarding Colley's arguments, as they illustrate many differing aspects of maritime Britishness.

Secker's descriptions of many of his voyages can be verified with other primary source material to show that in most cases his memories and recollections held good. Several of his merchant voyages can be traced by using *Lloyd's Lists*. This was a newspaper for merchant shipping beginning in 1741 which listed the arrival and departure of merchant vessels from ports, named their masters, and published news of vessels lost or captured. Secker enlisted as chief mate on the *Duke of Cumberland* in February 1748, and his description of the vessel's lingering in the Downs prior to its departure on 31 March is confirmed by *Lloyd's Lists*.[90] The ship was taken by French privateers, but after a short period in captivity Secker returned to it, again as chief mate, in October 1748. Its departure from London in October 1748, bound for Marseilles, is also mentioned in *Lloyd's Lists*, as are several of his voyages in the *Three Brothers* between Great Yarmouth and Dublin in 1755.[91]

Other sources that illuminate Secker's recollections are ships' log books. These survive for several of the ships in which he served, including the *Namur*, the *Sunderland*, the *Defence* East Indiaman and the *East India Yacht*. Secker recalled that he enlisted on board the *Namur* in 1732 after a conversation in Wapping with its lieutenant, Sir Roger Butler. Initially, he was taken on board the *Sunderland* at the Nore on 22 June. The *Sunderland's* log confirms that after only a few days, on 26 and 30 June, two parties of men were transferred onto the *Namur*. Secker was among one of these groups and he correctly remembered that the *Sunderland* was functioning as a holding ship to distribute pressed men to other ships. Butler's own log on board the *Namur* also gives the dates between which he was enlisted: 'From Monday 19 June to the 11 July Employed in London to Procure Men for his Ma[jes]ties ship Namur.' Secker recalled that he only remained on board the *Namur* for six weeks before being discharged, during which time they sailed from Black Stakes in Chatham River to Gillingham. This is borne out by Butler's entry in the *Namur's* log on arrival at Gillingham on 12 August: 'Took in our moorings and unbent the sails, att ye same time the Commissioner came and Reduced the ships Company'. Butler's log ends on 21 August, supporting Secker's remembrance that Butler thereafter left the ship to command the *Bonnetta* [*f. 4r*].[92]

90 *Lloyd's Lists*, nos. 1286–1289

91 *Lloyd's Lists*, nos. 1345, 1347, 1348, 1994, 2003, 2034, 2051

92 NMM, ADM/L/N/5 Lieutenant's logbook for HMS *Namur*, 1731–3; ADM/L/S/511 Lieutenant's logbook for HMS *Sunderland*, 1729–37; ADM/L/S/512 Lieutenant's logbook for HMS *Sunderland*, 1731–36

More revealing is the log of the *Defence* East Indiaman which survives for Secker's long voyage to Al Mukhā (Mocha), Mumbai (Bombay) and the Malabar coast. It confirms his remembrance that they set sail at the beginning of November 1738 and even lists him among the crew.[93] He correctly recalled the surnames of the captain and supercargo, Thomas Coates and John Wallis, and that they arrived at the Cape of Good Hope in January 1739. The log also confirms his account of remaining at the Cape for two weeks. His letter home of 29 January 1739, that he recalled was conveyed back by a returning East India ship, was most probably taken by the *Beauford*, mentioned in the log as returning from Chenai (Madras) under Captain Stevens. However, writing so many years later it would be remarkable if some of Secker's dates were not wayward and the log records their arrival in Al Mukhā a full two weeks before Secker's claim of the beginning of May. The log also confirms the presence at Al Mukhā of the French ship from Pondicherry mentioned by Secker, while his comment on the unhealthy 'brackish' water [*f. 26r*] is borne out by an entry in the log for 21 April: 'sent the Longboat a shore for two Ton of water to boil our provisions in, the Mochas water not being good for Europians'. The log also confirms his recollection that upon leaving Mumbai they called in at Tillicherry and Cochin, and that they passed the island of Diego Ruis. The log also confirms their return arrival at the Cape of Good Hope on 4 January 1740, having 'got the Longboat out', and their departure after ten days, exactly as Secker described. It confirms his date for their arrival at St Helena on 27 January, and their departure thereafter on 10 July 1740, while its date for their anchorage in the Downs, 17 September 1740, is just two days after that given by Secker. The paybook notes his pay at £33–13s.[94]

Much of the detail given by Secker of his subsequent voyage under Captain Steward on the *East India Yacht* to St Helena is also closely supported by this ship's log. Secker's description of their encounter with Commodore George Anson's squadron in early December 1740 is reflected in the log and in the subsequent official account of Anson's circumnavigation.[95] As so often in his narrative, here Secker delighted in criticising the captain's mistakes. Writing with the benefit of hindsight, he remarked on his disagreement with the captain, recalling that Steward, in 'great consternation' [*f. 29v*] 'could not be persuaded but they were French men of war, and I as positive that they were Commodore Anson's squadron' [*f. 30r*]. Upon arrival at St Helena, a self-satisfied Secker claimed that when Steward

[93] BL, Asia, Pacific and Africa Collections, IOR/L/MAR/B/647B, Log Book of the *Defence East India Man*

[94] BL, Asia, Pacific and Africa Collections, IOR/L/MAR/B/647E, Pay Book of the *Defence East India Man*

[95] BL, Asia, Pacific and Africa Collections, IOR/L/MAR/B/645B; R. Walter and B. Robins, *A Voyage round the World in the Years MDCCXL, I, II, II, IV, by George Anson*, ed. G. Williams (1974), p. 50

reported these vessels to be French, 'the governour seemed to be of another opinion and rather laught at his conjectures' [*f. 30v*].

Secker may have been partly inspired to enlist for his voyage to the Pacific by the vogue for books describing voyages and travels in the South Seas, which was growing among the literate English public from the 1690s.[96] Jonathan Swift's *Gulliver's Travels* included episodes set in the Pacific and Daniel Defoe's *Robinson Crusoe* owed much to the story told by Woodes Rogers and William Dampier of the marooning of Alexander Selkirk on Juan Fernandez from 1705 to 1709.[97] Bartholomew Sharp's buccaneers had earlier unintentionally marooned a Miskito Indian called Will on Juan Fernandez between 1680 and 1684. This was also featured in accounts by Dampier and Ambrose Cowley, and was probably Defoe's inspiration for Friday.[98] The story of *Robinson Crusoe* became a bestseller stimulating interest in the South Seas and Secker himself indicated he was familiar with it as a 'feigned story' [*f. 33v*]. Perhaps, like Nathaniel Uring, another Norfolk Quaker mariner born a generation earlier than Secker, he disapproved of 'Falsities and Inventions' in 'the many Sea-Voyages and Travels lately published by Persons unknown, which are all made Stories, on purpose to impose on the World, and to get Money.'[99]

But perhaps the greatest draws on Secker's curiosity were the several publications that followed the conclusion of Anson's famous circumnavigation in 1744. This voyage was the talk of English dockyards for years to come. Many journals claiming to be written by men in Anson's crews were published and there were several bestseller editions of the official account first published in May 1748 to great public curiosity and acclaim. Although Secker left London for five years in October 1748, he cannot have been ignorant of this long-awaited official publication, which soon constituted a 'reasoned plea for the expansion of British overseas enterprise'. It included illustrations based on the sketches of coasts, harbours and ships drawn by Peircy Brett, one of Anson's lieutenants. Secker, even if only for his own curiosity, was soon doing likewise, perhaps spurred into action by Benjamin Robins's introduction, which lamented 'how very imperfect many of our accounts of distant countries are rendered by the relators being unskilled in drawing, and in the general principles of surveying'.[100] It is probable that Secker had harboured ambitions of voyaging to the South Seas for some time, but had found passages in suitable English vessels scarce. Glyndwr

[96] G. Williams, *Buccaneers, Explorers and Settlers: British Enterprise and Encounters in the Pacific, 1670–1800* (2005), I, p. 32

[97] Williams, *Buccaneers, Explorers and Settlers*, I, p. 52, II, pp. 115, 120; Walter and Robins, *A Voyage round the World*, p. 120

[98] Williams, *Buccaneers, Explorers and Settlers*, I, p. 115

[99] Edwards, *The Story of the Voyage*, p. 188

[100] Williams, *Buccaneers, Explorers and Settlers*, IV, pp. 289–312; Walter and Robins, *A Voyage round the World*, p. 15

Williams has concluded that from Narborough to Anson, British expeditions in Spanish South America were 'predatory and parasitic'.[101] A British South Sea expedition to survey the Falklands and Juan Fernandez had to be dropped for diplomatic reasons in 1749.[102] Understandably, the Spanish were so jealous guardians of their trade in these waters that if Secker were to journey there it made sense to enlist on a Spanish vessel.

On an individual level, Secker's voyages reflect that despite the importance of luxury manufactured goods imported from India and China in transforming British tastes, total imports from the Americas in the early eighteenth century were worth double the value of those from Asia. Likewise British exports to the Americas were worth four times those to Asia.[103] The cargoes of the vessels Secker sailed in were generally foodstuffs rather than manufactured luxury items. Secker's cargoes also included semi-luxuries such as coffee, tea, wine, spirits and tobacco, mainstays of a colonial economy that enabled the increasing British ascendancy in global trade. It should be recognised that individuals such as Secker played an important part in fashioning this process. For these reasons, Miles Ogborn has recently employed a biographical approach to restore human interest to the issues of early modern globalisation in historical geography.[104]

In 2002 J.H. Elliott called Atlantic history 'one of the most important new historiographical developments of recent years'.[105] An Atlantic or maritime perspective was central to British imperial assertions in the eighteenth century, and if contemporaries increasingly recognised that all parts of the world affected British commerce in some way, then there is no reason why historians should not. Secker's travel narrative offers an important new micro-history of this world from the perspective of one of its integral participants. Secker adapted himself to work on all kinds of vessels: native and foreign, East Indiamen, coasters, warships, privateers and merchantmen. His extensive writing in his retirement showed how he continued to engage with the outside world, balancing his wider interests with returning to life as a convinced Quaker. He provides historians with a rare glimpse of what a middling-sort, trading man from Norfolk made of the wider world. In future years, the study of more travel narratives such as this will enable historians to challenge the views of P.J. Marshall and Glyndwr Williams, who declared that 'we can only offer the vaguest conjectures about what, if anything, the great mass of the British population made of the world outside Europe in our period.'[106] The travel literature of the eighteenth century, of which

[101] Williams, *Buccaneers, Explorers and Settlers*, II, p. 126

[102] Williams, *Buccaneers, Explorers and Settlers*, I, pp. 51–2

[103] M. Berg, 'In Pursuit of Luxury: Global History and British Consumer Goods in the Eighteenth Century', *Past and Present*, 182 (2004), p. 132.

[104] M. Ogborn, *Global Lives: Britain and the World, 1550–1800* (Cambridge, 2008), p. 11.

[105] Armitage and Braddick, 'Introduction', in Armitage and Braddick, eds, *The British Atlantic World*, p. 4

[106] Marshall and Williams, *The Great Map of Mankind*, p. 1

Secker's voyages are part, also provides 'some of the most trenchant statements of the Enlightenment's view of man.' He used his narrative to address issues of cultural and racial difference but nowhere did he employ the terms 'savages' or 'barbarians', while his independent and questioning temperament remains attractive to modern readers. With his burial place now occupied by buildings, Secker's travel narrative provides a more fitting monument. It constitutes a life history with global ramifications. His employment on foreign vessels and the multinational nature of the crews serving alongside him stands as a warning against subdividing maritime or Atlantic history into 'neat national packages'.[107] Unlike conventional studies of Britain's Empire from the top down, Secker's world illuminates British identities and imperial experiences from the bottom up. We should remember that as an empire built upon its maritime trade, Britain relied upon its John Seckers just as much as its Horatio Nelsons.

[107] J. H. Elliott, 'Atlantic History: A Circumnavigation', in Armitage and Braddick, eds, *The British Atlantic World*, p. 235

Daniel Boulter,
From the Original in the Possession of H.Boulter Esquire

Plate 1 *Daniel Boulter (1848), the Yarmouth Quaker whose 'Museum of Natural and Artifical Curioisities' opened in 1778 and later held Mason's copy of Secker's manuscript amongst its collections. Dalrymple Collection, Norfolk and Norwich Portraits: Norfolk County Council Library and Information Service.*

Plate 2 *Swafield Mill, rear,* c.*1935, courtesy of John Leech.*

Plate 3 *Swafield Mill, Secker's birthplace, photograph by Leon Doughty.*

Plate 4 *Buxton Mill, home of John Secker during his youth, photograph by Leon Doughty.*

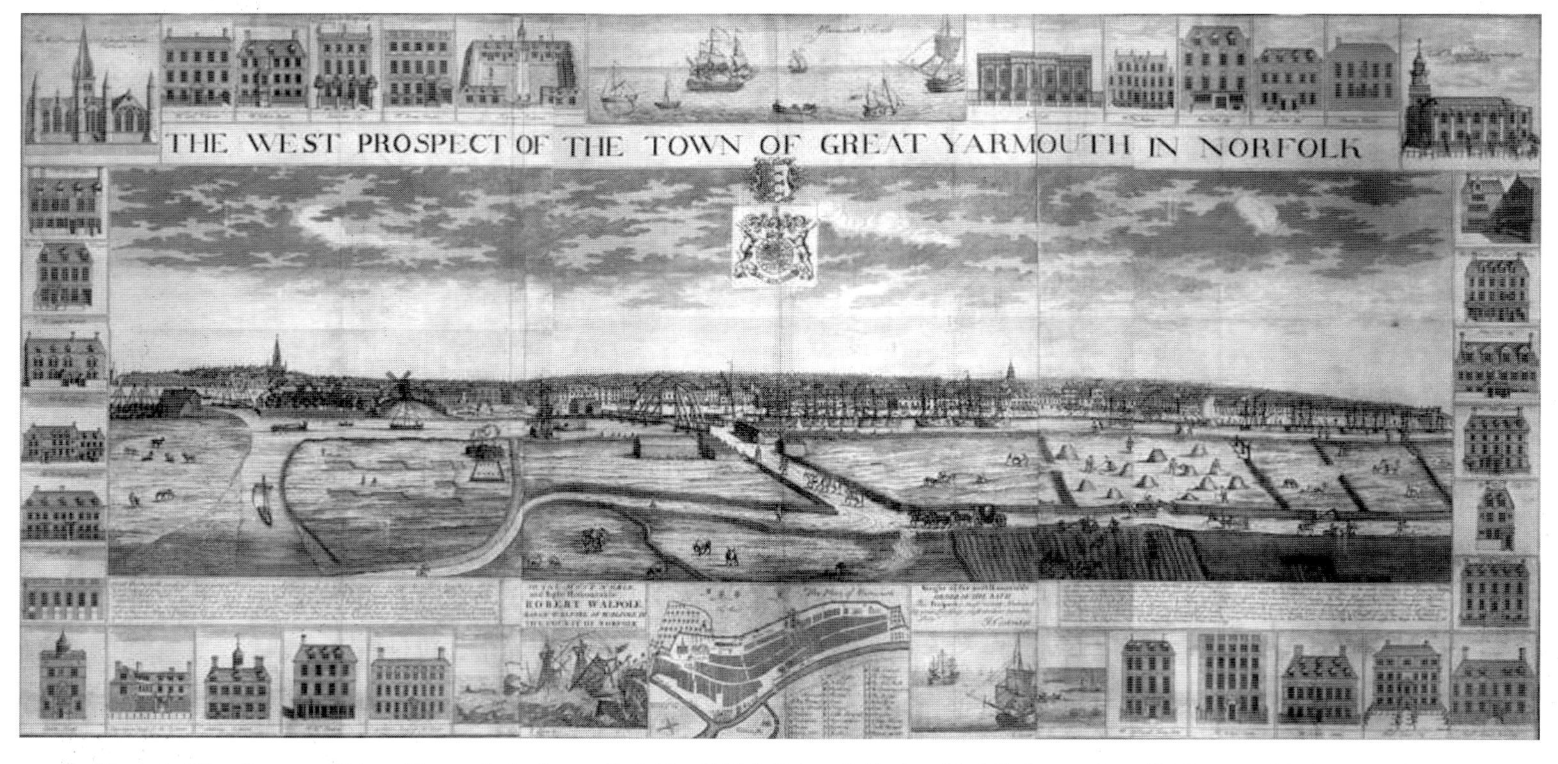

Plate 5 *West Prospect of Great Yarmouth, by James Corbridge (1724) Prints Collection, Norfolk County Council Library and Information Service.*

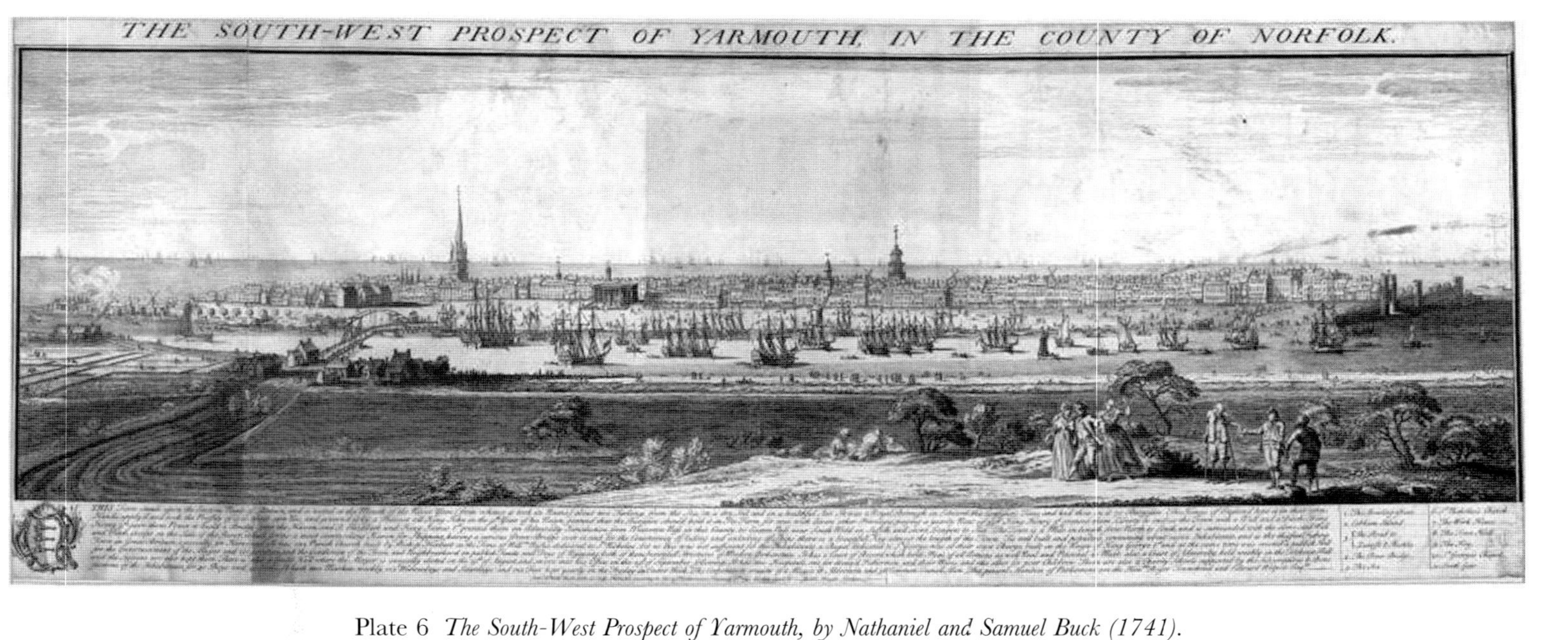

Plate 6 *The South-West Prospect of Yarmouth, by Nathaniel and Samuel Buck (1741). Prints Collection, Norfolk County Council Library and Information Service.*

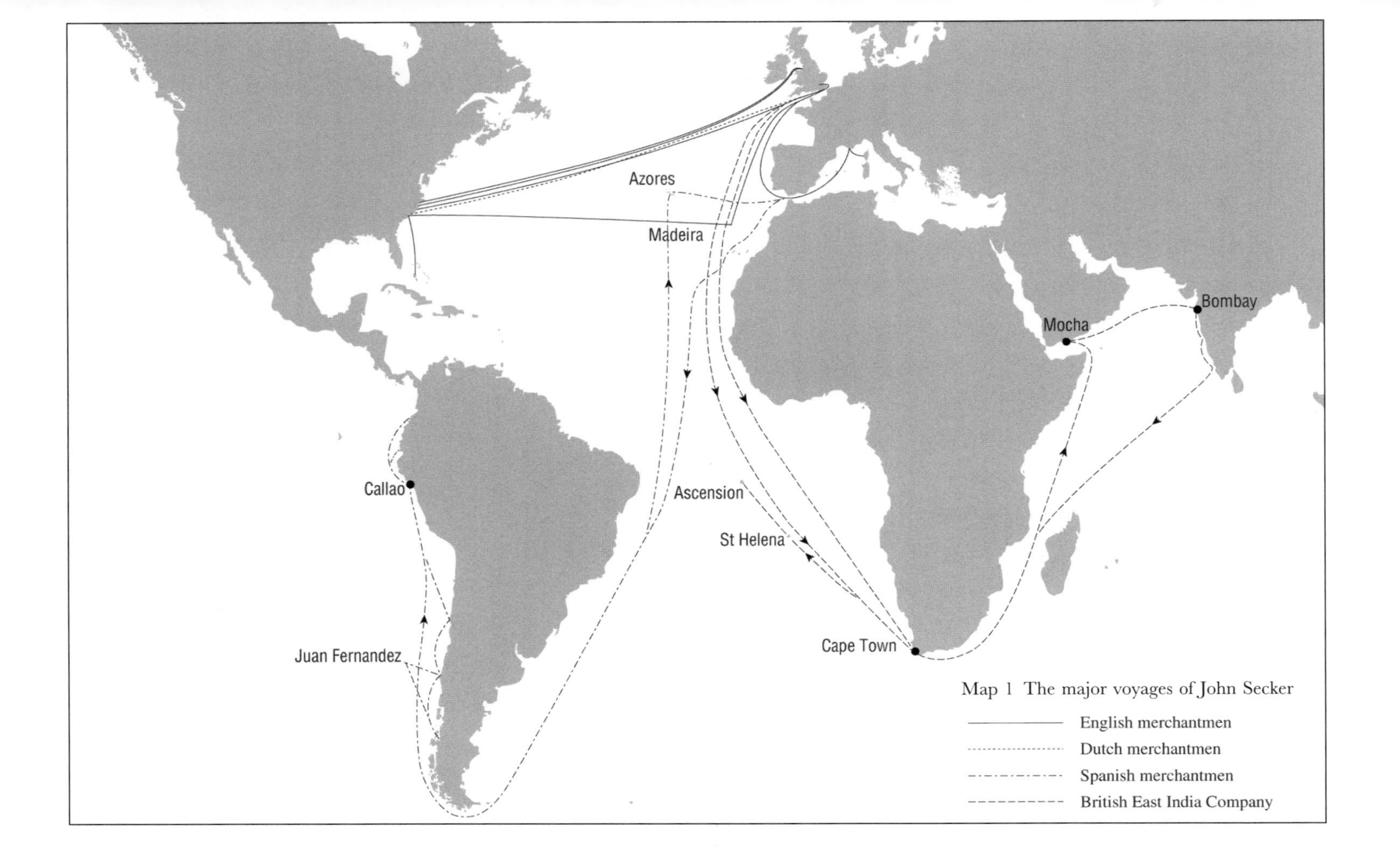

Map 1 The major voyages of John Secker

THE TRAVEL NARRATIVE OF JOHN SECKER

[NRO, Rye MS 71, *p. 1*] I was born at Swafield mill within the bounds of North Walsham, on the first day of the seventh month according to the present new style, or on the 20th of the sixth month by the old style in the year 1716. My father was by occupation a miller and both father & mother by profession of the people call'd Quakers in which way I was brought up and educated in my youth whilst with them, and those sober and religious principles imbibed by example and inculcation were never wholly erac'd, though much *defaced* by travel and bad company and too much liberty, which, is exceeding hurtful to youth for when there is none to be a check upon their conduct but *their* own conscience they soon stifle and get above that by repeated vanity and bad practices, till darkness cover their understanding and depravity their taste to that which is good and if the infinite mercy of God do not interpose and prevent, they stand open to all manner of evils, and are in the way *that leads* to destruction and down to the chambers of death.

But to return from this digression my father removed while I was young from Swafield to Buxton water mills at a town called Haverland[1] (commonly called Monge Mill). Both these removes were still further from the sea th*a*n where I was born. I was early put to school and having an opportunity of borrowing many sorts of books, I took [*p. 2*] a great delight in reading romances, travels and voyages, which had such a strong impression upon my tender mind that it seem'd to kindle a fire of emulation to travel into distant countrys and to see those strange things which I had read of: and I have often thought my reading so much in my youth of those books had a great share in that early propensity which appeared in me, to go to sea, for I would be making of ships and sailing them long before I had either seen the sea or a ship, when I was very young, which inclination increased with my years. When I was about ten years old I was put to a cousin, a farmer, named William Palmer to learn husbandry. I liv'd with him about a year and then went to live with an own uncle whose name was John Sparshall who liv'd then on a farm belonging to one William Barton esquire, at a town call'd South Rapes,[2] about three or four miles from the sea. This uncle of mine was a considerable corn merchant & maltster, both for the home & foreign trade, in partnership with one Richard Wright of Buxton.

After I had liv'd with my uncle Sparshall some time I had an opportunity

[1] Haveringland, 9 miles northwest of Norwich.

[2] Southrepps, 4 miles southeast of Cromer.

of seeing the sea & my inclination of going to sea and seeing foreign countrys grew stronger; as I had now the advantage to converse sometimes with seafaring men & such as had been abroad; which discourses were as fuel to the fire of emulation, already kindled in my breast, to see for myself. My parents and relations in general had a very great aversion to my going to sea, so that finding there was no likelihood of being assisted from them, I had once formed with another lad, a mason's apprentice [*p. 3*] at Thorpe, a design to run away together, he having also a mind to go to sea, and travel to some seaport town and seek a master to bind ourselves to sea. The time was fix'd, and I was to call him, which accordingly I did at the time appointed, but his heart failed him, and he dare not go with me, so that I was oblig'd to return back greatly disappointed, not having courage enough yet to venture alone.

My relations not being able to perswade me from going to sea, my uncle concluded to send me a voyage to Holland, in a small vessel which loaded malt for him, and was bound to Rotterdam; accordingly I was sent to Yarmouth and went on board the said vessel, being about twenty or twenty five tons burden, William Jolley master. Our passage over was a very fine one; but yet I was very sea sick; and the sailors laugh'd at me, and call'd me country *booby* and my answer was that when I got over sea sickness I should then be able to laugh at others in my condition. We arriv'd safe in Holland, & delivered our malt.

[NRO, Y/D 41/105, *f. 1r*]

While we lay in this place I had a great mind to see into the Jews' synagogue. Accordingly getting leave I went alone unto the Bombkeys where it stands & coming to the iron palisades stood waiting there a considerable time hoping to have seen, some English <gone> *go* in that I might have gone in with them, but saw none so did not go into the synagogue, but seeing a fountain spouting forth water in the yard and several Jewish boys playing about it I went to them. While I was looking on a woman came to the palisades & call'd to one of the boys & I perceiv'd by the boy's behaviour ask'd who I was & beckoned with her hand for me to come to her along with the boy which I accordingly did, he pulling me by my cloaths & making signs for me to go with him, we neither of us being able to understand one another. I followed them till we came into a yard & to the foot of a staircase which led up into a chamber the woman going up first stood with the door in her hand beckoning me up & the little boy pulling me by the cloaths. I went up, but with a good deal of fear not being able to understand their bussiness with me. After I was up the woman shutt too the door & I think lockt it; which increased my fear; but I endeavour'd to hide it as much as I could. There was another woman in the room besides she that I followed up & the little boy being gone down again, there was only the two women & my self lock'd into the room. They made signs for me to go towards the fireplace where there was some turf coals lying & they setting some empty pans there made signs for me to put the coals into the pans which I did & when I had fill'd them, I look'd to see if I had anything further to do; but one of the women went & unlock'd the door, for me to go down & return'd me thanks as well she could and thus ended the adventure that had afrighted me so much. I afterwards understood the reason to be; that this being the Jewish Sabbath they will not meddle with fire but gett any stranger to do it for them that they can, or good natur'd neighbour. This being my first voyage and first adventure I met with I have been the more particular about it. [*f. 1v*]

The city of Rotterdam is a very neat clean place, the houses well built & high: & keept extreamly clean both within & with out. The canals of water running up between every two streets up of which the shiping go to discharge their cargoes, lying most commonly before the merchants' doors, which is very convenient, the trading people knowing their interest, behave very civil to strangers but *the* common sort as in many other places are vulgar & morose. After having unloaded & ballast our sloop we sail'd for Yarmouth. In our passage home had very bad weather so that we lay'd too & drove most of the way over. I think I neither eat nor drunk very little for the space of forty eight hours being so very sick & dizzy; I stirred but seldom from under the master's cabin where I lay. Excepting once or twice I look'd up of the cabin scuttle[3] & saw the sea run so high, & the waves break on board so much that I was frightened to see it; besides the vessel being small had such a short & quick motion & tossed so exceedingly that I could hardly hold myself fast any w[h]ere but in my cabin. We drove over the sands in the night time; & was near being ashore before they perceiv'd it. Finding themselves in the roads[4] they let *go* an anchor & rode till the morning when the customhouse boat came on boards us & strip'd the master & men of their ventures leaving them but little which was of a great loss & disappointment to them. It being the custom at that time *that* the men who sailed in those small vessels had no wages but liberty to bring over what ventures they could purchase; which some times was pretty large, as it happened to be the case this time with us. But as for myself my venture was but small, I think two pound of tea & three [*f. 2r*] half stopes of brandy & cinnamon water for presents which the custom house officers would not take away from *me* so I carried them safe into the country & disposed of them according to my intent.

After I return'd from this voyage my eagerness seem'd damp'd for a little time, but I soon got above it & was as much for going to sea as before. It

[3] A scuttle was an opening cut through a hatch deck or bulkhead to provide access: *IMD*.

[4] The roads were areas of water where ships could ride safely at anchor, essentially an open anchorage affording less protection than a harbour: *IMD*.

happen'd I had a cousin whose name was Thomas Parson who had been master of a sloop out of Wells but failing; he and his wife who was sister to my Uncle Sparshall's wife came and staid at my Uncle Sparshall's a considerable time, he giving them their board. Though sometimes he would go to Yarmouth & make a voyage to Holland or London in some vessel loaded by my uncle & his partner & at his return come back again to our house. Till at last my uncle & his partner buying a vessel; put him in master of her & sent me along with him. I think this was in the latter part of the summer in the year 1730 and when I was just turn'd of fourteen. From this time till the year 1756 or latter part of 1755 I followed no other occupation but the sea being about twenty five years. I remain'd with my cousin Parsons till the spring of the year 1732 using the Holland & London trade & my station with him was cabin boy & cook; as is customary for boys in small vessels w[h]ere there is but one, to officiate in both places & indeed it is but a smokey greasy birth in any vessel but much more so in small ones; & I well remember I was none of the cleanest. We being in London in the spring of the year 1732 when a hot press[5] for seamen breaking out we lay there a considerable time. It was a customary thing with my cousin to take me with him on first days to Gracious street meeting[6] or some other; he being one of the people call'd Quakers.

It fell out so one first day that he being invited a shore to dinner did not take me with him [*f. 2v*] as usual but desir'd me to come ashore after dinner & go to meeting of my self. But lying alongside a Dublin trader where there was several boys, they persuaded me to get our boats sails & go asailing with them about the pool as tis call'd where the shiping chiefly lay, which I did and neglected going to meeting. My dear cousin not seeing me at meeting; & coming on board was soon informed of the reason. Upon which he threatened me much to aquaint my Uncle Sparshall & my parents with my bad conduct: & he being of a taunting temper & dwelling too long upon the subject raised such resolutions in my enterprizing breast that I was resolv'd not to go home to hear the issue of his complaints and from that time form'd a design of running away or leaving him which I soon accomplished in the following manner. The press continuing hot, we haled our vessel over to a wharf on Southwark side & sent our men to a relation's house named Kirby to hide away from the press & I, not being big enough to be impress'd staid on board the vessel to look after her, & cook the people's victuals & carry it to them. I would often go in amongst the press gangs as they went along the streets *in* hopes they would have prest me: but I being so small they took no notice of me. This strategem not taking, I set my head to work to enquire

[5] In a 'hot press' or 'sweep' only sailors with protections sanctioned by Parliament were granted immunity from impressment: P. Earle, *Sailors: English Merchant Seamen 1650–1775* (1998), p. 192; N. A. M. Rodger, *The Wooden World: An Anatomy of the Georgian Navy* (1986), p. 178.

[6] Gracechurch Street, a famous London Quaker meeting house.

whither it was not possible to enter on board *a man of war*. This I found by information practicable & accordingly went one afternoon round by London Bridge into that part of Wapping called St. Catherine's w[h]ere those men of war fitting out had their rendevouze. When I came there I went to one where the Namure[7] a second rate or 90 Gun ship was put up & while I stood reading the paper pasted up at the door to my great surprize my cousin Parsons came suddenly & unawares upon me; he first ask me whether I [*f. 3r*] was prest; which I answering in the negative he ask me whither I had entered, I told him no. When finding I was still under his subjection he began to make use of his stick but I took to my heels & run a little way from *him* in the way back again till I came to a wharf where I hid my self till he was past. I then return'd to the rend*e*vouze again; where falling to reading the paper <agan> *again* the landlord of the house coming to the door I ask him if he knew whither any of the ships wanted servants. He answear'd he could not tell for the lieutenant was not within but if I came again next morning by seven or eight a clock I might speak to him; this gave me some encouragement & I return'd on board directly. Late in the evening after I was a bed in my cabin; my cousin came on board and set upon me with his tongue but did not strike me. To all his remonstrations I made but little answere; being resolved to give him the slipe in the morning if possible. After he had said a great deal to me by way of expostulation he went ashore again to his lodgings; he lodging at the same house where the men keept.

Next morning I got *up* pretty early; my head being full of cogitations about the success of my enterprize. I having about eightpence or tenpence if I rem*em*ber right went to the nearest stairs & got a waterman's boy to put me over the water, for dispatch went directly to the rendevouze w[h]ere the Lieutenant Sir Roger Butler[8] was then hurrying the people to go aboard the tender[9] to carry the prest men down to the Nore.[10] By the assistence of the landlord I got to speak to him who told me I might go down if I would in the tender which was call'd the Royal Escape, being the vessel as tis said

[7] The Namur was built in 1729 and was rebuilt at great expense on several occasions thereafter: C. Wilkinson, *The British Navy and the State in the Eighteenth Century* (Woodbridge, 2004), pp. 73–4.

[8] Sir Roger Butler was a naval lieutenant from 1718 and promoted to a captaincy under Sir John Norris at Lisbon in 1734: D. Syrett and R. L. DiNardo, eds, *The Commissioned Sea Officers of the Royal Navy, 1660–1815* (Occasional Publications of the Navy Record Society, i, 1994), p. 66; J. Charnocke, *Biographia Navalis* (5 vols., 1796), iv, p. 261.

[9] A tender was a small vessel employed to attend a larger one, especially in taking ashore or bringing aboard passengers and stores: *IMD*.

[10] The Nore was a sandbank in the Thames estuary, extending between Shoeburyness and Sheerness, and the anchorage there was much used by the British fleet in the eighteenth century: *EB*.

King James made his escape in when he abdicated the Crown. He told me she would *go* down in about half an hour. He ask'd me whether I was a prentice. I told him I was not. He bid me make hast & get my things and go on board the tender.[11] Glad at this success I made the best of *my* [*f. 3v*] way to Tower stairs & agreed with a waterman's boy to carry me over to our vessel & take my things & me, and then carry me and them on board the Royal Escape tender, for all the money I had. Accordingly he carried me on board & I made what hast I could to put my bed & things in*to* the boat; being greatly afraid my cousin should have come on board & put a stop to my proceedings.

After I had got my things into the boat I lockt up the cabin & left the keys with the mate of another vessel we lay alongside of, telling him where I was going. We just got on board the tender in time; as she was getting under sail she sail'd down to the Nore & put us all on board the Sunderland,[12] a sixty gun ship which laid as a guardship at that time to take on board the emprest men; & to destribute them to their proper ships they were prest for. On board this ship I stayed several days till an oppertunity offer'd to put me & some more men who were prest for the Namure on board her who laid in Chatham river at a place at a place [*sic*] call'd Black stakes.[13] When I came on board her I was enter'd as captain's servant. This is a priviledge that the captains and officers of the king's ships have; each one according to their stations and the rate of the ship are allow'd so many servants for which they are allowed seventeen shillings and sixpence per month by the government, if in ordinary & if extra servants twenty one. These they get as cheap as they can; perhaps paying them forty shillings a year, the rest being all profit to themselves. While I was in this ship I mess'd with one of the boatswain's[14] mates whose name I think was William Crouch. Many of the *petty* officers & men took a liking to me, because I was obliging & willing to do any thing they set me about. Whilst most of the other boys would if they ask them to do any thing for them bid them do it themsel*ves* if not those they were oblig'd to wait upon. There being so [*f. 4r*] many of them; they corrupted one another.

[11] Butler's log book for 19 June to 11 July 1732 recorded that he was 'employed in London to Procure Men for his Ma[jes]ties ship Namur': NMM, ADM/L/N/5 Lieutenant's log book for HMS Namur, 1731–3.

[12] Secker was taken on board the *Sunderland* on 22 June 1732: NMM ADM/L/S/511 Lieutenant's log book for HMS Sunderland, 1729–37.

[13] The log book for the *Sunderland* states that it sent thirty and sixty-one men to join the *Namur* on 26 and 30 June 1732 respectively: NMM, ADM/L/S/511 Lieutenant's log book for HMS Sunderland, 1729–37.

[14] The boatswain was the officer of a ship who had the charge of the rigging and sails, whose responsibilities included summoning the crew to their duties, often with a whistle. The boatswain's mate was a petty officer acting as his assistant: *IMD*.

[15] The *Namur's* log records that the ship's company was reduced on 12 August 1732: NMM, ADM/L/N/5 Lieutenant's log book for HMS Namur, 1731–3.

After I had been about six weeks on board, the ship was order'd up to Gillingham near Chatham & we were paid off.[15] I received for my six weeks five shillings, sixpence of which I spent on board before I left the ship. I had but four shillings & sixpence to live on; & carry me up to London. But I going up with my messmates they were extremely kind to me, giving me victuals and pay*ing* my charges up; & took me with them to their lodgings when we got up to London & partly supported me there till I got a birth on board the Bonnetta snow. After being about two *weeks* at London; where I had been pretty much straitened for want of money my messmates inform'd me of a new snow[16] about to be launched at Woolwich & to be commanded by Sir Roger Butler, who was our second lieutenant on board the Namure & the same I first spoke to when I entered on board her. Accordingly I went down to Woolwich & spoke to the captain but he told me he had got all his servan*ts* but said he thought his lieutenant wanted one. I went to the lieutenant whose name was Smith if I remember right. He wanting a servant took *me* directly & that same night I think I went up with him in a boat to London where he bought me such things as I wanted & gave me some money to put in my pocket. This was a comforta*ble* exchange for my poverty in *so* short a time.

The next day we returned again to Woolwich. Shortly after the snow was launch'd & rigged with great expedition in order to convoy the king from Holland. After we were ready we sail'd for Helvoutsluyse[17] *with* the king's yatchs[18] under the command of Lord Torington.[19] After we arrived at Holland we waited some time before the king arrived at Helvotsluys from his German dominions. As soon as he came he going on board the Carolina [*f. 4v*] yatch we sail'd for England. In going out it proved calm, so that we got out our oars & row'd & I think after the rate of two miles & a half an hour. The yatch which the king was on board was in danger of being hove ashore by the swell so that all the other vessels sent their boats to tow her off. We in our vessel by order of Lord Torington rowing by the Carolina yatch saw the king standing upon her quarter deck[20] looking at us. This was

[16] A snow was a small ocean-going sailing vessel resembling a brig, sometimes formerly employed as a warship, carrying a main and foremast and a supplementary try sail mast close behind the main mast. It was among 'the typical ships of the middle decades of the eighteenth century': *OED*; R. Davis, *The Rise of the English Shipping Industry in the Seventeenth and Eighteenth Century* (1962), p. 77.

[17] The fortified town of Hellevoetsluis in the Netherlands was the traditional home port of the Dutch fleet.

[18] In this instance, a yacht was a vessel of state to convey persons of distinction by water: *IMD*.

[19] Torrington was first lord of the Admiralty from 1727: J. B. Hattendorf, 'George Byng, first Viscount Torrington (1663–1733)', *Oxford DNB*.

[20] The quarter deck was a smaller deck situated above the half deck and between the stern and aftermast, covering about a quarter of the vessel and used as a promenade by superior officers and cabin passengers: *OED*.

the first and last time to my knowledge that ever I saw King George the Second. The wind springing up fair we had a pleasant passage to the Nore; where after saluting the king with twenty one guns (a royal salute) we left the yatch & stood in for Sheerness.

From whence in a short time after we were order'd to Plymouth to join I think five more of the new built snows, there being one built in every king's yard after a new construction or model. We were order'd all of us here, that we might make a tryal of our sailing, to see which would sail best. When the wind & weather favour'd us we all of us sail'd out of Plymouth Sound right before the wind; having several of the old built in company with us. In sailing before the wind there was but little difference amongst us. After we had try'd several hours before the wind we hal'd upon a wind when all the old built except the Terible bomb ketch[21] were soon left a stern & *our* vessel & the Tryal, one of the new built, the two best sailors, there being little difference between us *&* her. We hove the log & found our vessel run when close hal'd upon a wind after the rate of ten or eleven miles an hour. After we had made sufficient tryal the commodore made a signal for us to give over & return each ship to her station before appointed. We in the Bonetta return'd to Sherness & went along side the hulk,[22] had our main-mast hoist out & shortened, being over masted.

While we lay alongside the hulk, a very remarkable [*f. 5r*] accident happened to one of our people; & because of its singularity shall give a brief relation of it & was as follows. The boatswain of the hulk being a Scotchman & this man his countrey man & perhaps intimate aquaintance, the boatswain of the hulk treating him, they set together all the evening drinking till both were intoxicated with strong drink. About nine or ten a clock the watch being *set* our people that were on board the hulk were all order'd on board their own vessel. Accordingly they came on board & most of them were gotten into their hammocks when the boatswain of the hulk & this man parted also, & took leave of each other. This man instead of coming on board went out of one of the hulks ports just astern of our ship directly over board. The quarter master who had the watch hearing something fall into the water, made enquiry whither all our people were on board, & being inform'd all were come on board but this man whose name was James. The quarter master suspecting it was him he heard fall over board sent on board the hulk immediately & finding by the hulk's people he was to come away from thence in order to come on board and was much in liquor & not being

[21] A ketch was a strongly constructed two-masted vessel (with its largest mast foremost) between 100 and 250 tons burden, often used as a bomb-vessel and equipped with mortars, or as a small coasting vessel: *OED*.

[22] An hulk was an unrigged hull condemned as unfit for seafaring, often used as a floating depot in a harbour: *IMD*.

to be found called the boat's crew up immediately to go in search of him. They took a lanthorn in the boat, being a dark night: and a strong ebb tide setting right out towards the Nore, they followed him keeping in the wake of the ship as near *as* they could. Till such a time as they were pretty sure, if he were alive, they must have past him, so were returning, concluding he was drownded. But in rowing for the ship by help of the lanthorn they saw his hatt floating upon the water and so in taking it up discover'd the top of his head even with the surface of the water swimming like dead log with out any motion. They got him into the boat & brought him on board, but he was senseless. They strip'd his cloaths off & put him into his hammock, & cover'd him up warm & in a little time he began to speak & recovering by degrees [*f. 5v*] his senses, but remember'd nothing of what had happened to him. After a long time he recover'd his for*mer* state of health. This was a very remarkable deliverance that a man should remain full half an hour, if not more, like a log in the water without any power to help himself, being so dead drunk. It was suppos'd the great quantity of strong liquor he had drunk resisted the water from entering his mouth & nose. For when he was brought on board he smelt so strong of spirits we could hardly beare to come nigh him.

After our mainmast was shortened & such other alterations as was thought necessary, we sail'd for our station on the north coast which was from Shields to Flamborough Head to guard the coast from smuglers. We lay most of our time at Shields where the men, all that chose it, had liberty to go ashore. The captain being purser,[23] had a considerable advantage by it in saving their provision, which was all profit to him. My master finding me honest entrusted me with his money or other valuable things & the keys of his trunks & chests, or what else he *had* under locke. I also had the cloaths he left off, made fit for me by the ship's taylor; which were almost as good as new he having I believe a pretty good estate; besides his lieutenant's pay which was about a crown a day. By which means I went as well drest as any boy in the ship & bore a considerable sway amongst the rest. My master also had a boat he bought for his own use & boys appointed for her to row him where he pleased when in a harbour. To these he gave caps. This boat I had partly under my command for my master's use & some times for my own in his name. I also had several priveledges in getting money, besides what he gave me himself for pocket money, so that it was a very agreeable place to me, without looking forward.

I remember'd while I belong'd to my master I had begun a journal of my life, mentioning my birth, parentage, my meeting with him & his kindness. After I had been so beset with poverty & want at London with many other

[23] The purser was a clerical officer required to keep the ship's books, crew and passenger lists, along with all documents relating to the cargo: *IMD*.

particulars. This I had hid up behind some books of his in his cabin & he in looking for something found it & after reading it carried *it* to the captain. They both seem'd greatly pleas'd with the simplicity of the stile & honesty of [*f. 6r*] the expressions & confession in it. My master return'd *it* me; telling me of his & the captain's approbation of it. But I was so asham'd and confounded, when I knew he had read it, that though he desir'd me to go on with it I wholy drop'd it. About the month call'd May in the spring of the year 1733 our snow was ordered to Spithead to join the fleet, fitted out for the Miderterenean. Here we arriv'd about the beginning of the month call'd June & the 23^d of this month I wrote a letter home to my parents; being the first since I left my cousin Pa*r*sons at London <late> something more than a year, & the seventh of the next month called July wrote home again. About the month call'd August the fleet not going up straits this year, we were order'd again to our station on the north coast & putting into Shields about the latter part of the month call'd September, my master & the captain being gone ashore to pay a visit to a country gentleman about seven or eight miles off.

If I remember right, my self & three more officer's servants took this oppertunity to leave the ship. This was a project I had long been forming, but wanted company to put it in execution; which now offering I took the advantag*e* of it, & happened in the following manner. The cook having beaten his boy pretty much that morning & the doctor & boatswain theirs sometime before, these three boys, being got together consulting how they should run away, I going to them and finding what they were after, offer'd to go with them & help to get them ashore also and there being no time to be lost we put it in execution directly having *got* such things as we could conveniently carry & put up with some of my masters dirty linnen which I wanted to carry ashore to wash. Having order'd my master's boat to put me ashore I ask'd liberty of the officers for the other three boys to go ashore with me for an hour or two, to get black berrys. Which being granted we four went ashore, but never return'd on board again. Being on shore I carried my master's linnen to his washer woman, and then we made the best of our way to New Castle which is about seven or eight miles & going over the bridge got to Chester Street[24] that [*f. 6v*] night late in the evening. Here we intended to have past the remaining part of the night but for an accident which put us to the scamper & oblig'd us to leave the town almost directly though late & we sorely tir'd with walking.

It fell out in the following manner. Some of the company telling some body that our ship was sail'd & we left behind; were going to London after her. This coming to the ear of a woman where our corporal work'd being a hatter by trade, she came to us to know wither it was true, being concern'd that the corporal should be left behind. As soon as the woman had been

[24] Chester-le-Street, co. Durham.

with us & heard the same storey over again she went home to acquaint them with it & we took to our heels as fast as we could, for fear he should <he> hear to the contrary & get us taken up. We traveled till meeting with a haystack *where we* took up our aboard till daybreak & then to the road again. In this manner we chiefly lodg'd, three nights *only* excepted, till we came to Warrington where we took water for Liver*pool*.[25] I cannot now recollect exactly the time, we were in traveling from Shields to Liverpool; but as we did not hurry our selves, but took our own time, beging our way through. <I think> it was near a fortnight when we left the ship we were, I think, all moneyless excepting my self: & my stock under sixpence. By begging we got either money or victuals sufficient to support us from day to day & we took but little thought for any further contingencies. We happen'd with several odd anventures [*sic*] upon the road, both with respect to ourselves and others, which I forbear to relate.

After we got to Liverpool we were advised & directed to make application to some merchants who *were* concern'd *in* shiping as we intended to bind ourselves apprentices to sea. Accordingly we apply'd to two reputable merchants named Traffords, own brothers & twins in partnership & great traders in the Guinea & Virginia trade.[26] To these we bound ourselves for three years apprentices & in the latter part of the month call'd October [*f. 7r*] or beginning of November 1733 sail'd from Liverpool in a ship named the old King George, Capt Tarleton[27] commander, for Virginia & Maryland. This ship was almost ready to sail when we came to the place & she carrying rigging and other materials for *a* new ship building in Virginia for the same merchants.[28]

[25] The slave and tobacco trade brought 'abrupt expansion' to Liverpool by 1740, with 435 ships sailing from the port in 1737, 33 of which were bound to Africa to embark black slaves for the 'Middle Passage': M. Rediker, *Between the Devil and the Deep Blue Sea: Merchant Seamen, Pirates and the Anglo-American Maritime World, 1700–1750* (Cambridge, 1987), pp. 43–4; G. Chandler, *Liverpool Shipping: A Short History* (1960), p. 26; 'D. Sam', *Liverpool and Slavery* (Liverpool, 1884), p. 137.

[26] Edward and Henry Trafford were bailiffs of Liverpool in 1739. In 1738 Edward lent the town £800 to construct a new pier. He was mayor in 1742 and lived with his sons Richard and William in King Street. Henry was treasurer of the corporation in 1721 and died during his mayoralty in 1740: G. Williams, *History of the Liverpool Privateers and Letters of Marque with an account of the Liverpool Slave Trade* (1966), p. 148; J. A. Picton, *Liverpool Municipal Archives and Records, 1700–1835* (Liverpool, 1886), pp. 18, 100, 142–3, 153, 157.

[27] The Tarletons were a very large Liverpool family, many of whom were merchants and mariners at this time: Liverpool Record Office, Tarleton Papers, 920 TAR; R. Stewart-Brown, 'Tarleton of Bolesworth Castle', *Cheshire Sheaf*, 3rd series, xxvii (1930), pp. 56–9; Picton, *Liverpool Municipal Archives*, pp. 45–6, 62, 202; Sam, *Liverpool and Slavery*, p. 119; J. A. Picton, *Memorials of Liverpool* (2 vols., 1873), ii, p. 95; F. E. Hyde, *Liverpool and the Mersey: An Economic History of a Port, 1700–1970* (Newton Abbot, 1971), p. 18.

[28] It was cheaper to build ships in the American colonies than along the Thames estuary, and by the mid-eighteenth century, half of England's merchant fleet was 'American built':

We were all put on board her. We also carried some hands for the new ship. We touch'd at Cork for to take in provisions, it being much cheaper than in England.[29] Here we also took in <Three> *4* Irish convicts out of Cork jail, having two before on board we brought from Liverpool. The crimes they told us they were transported for were as follows viz the two English convicts one a blacksmith an oldish man for stealing a hog's head, he said only in joke; but it prov'd in earnest to him. The other English man was a notorious offender being an old horse jockey,[30] stealing horses in one county and selling them in another & I think he said it was either the nineteen or twenty he was convicted for at last & was condemned to dye, but repriev'd for transportation. He was a stout bold man, middle aged; badly inclin'd and his narrow escape of the gallows seem'd to have made but little impression upon his mind towards a reformation. The three Irish told us their crimes were as follows: one being a shepherd to his uncle drove twenty of his sheep to a market & sold them, went off with the money & was catch'd. The other two were brothers, stole a pott of butter together and were apprehended in carrying it home. These three were youngish men & did not seem to be much rooted in evil but while I am writing this I recollect that there was another Irish convict an elderly man for stealing a cow, being four Irish convicts in all.

After having taken in our provisions we sail'd for Virginia run to the southward till we got into the trade wind.[31] Having fine pleasant weather & an agreeable passage of betwixt eight or nine weeks. During the passage the convicts had plotted to rise by getting the ship's arms into their possession & so to have run away with the ship, but was timely discover'd by one of the Irish convicts & they more strictly look'd after & confin'd the rest of the passage. The English horse jockey was the first proposer & instigator of the whole & the captain had been too indulgent in givinging [*sic*] them too much liberty, taking the said horse jockey out of irons & letting [*f. 7v*] him cook for the ship's company. Which gave him an opportunity of going into the cabin some times, where the arms were deposited & doubtless such opportunities to a man of his disposition & circumstance first gave birth to the temptation of seizing the ship to get his liberty. After an agreeable passage of between eight and nine weeks we arrived safe at Virginia; Capt. Tarlton being an old commander and one that he had often experienced the advantage of keeping to the southward till he got into the trade wind's way, when

N. Zahedieh, 'Economy', in D. Armitage and M. J. Braddick, eds, *The Britsh Atlantic World, 1500–1800* (Basingstoke, 2002), p. 61.

[29] Irish ports were popular places for English ships to cheaply reprovision before crossing the Atlantic: Davis, *The Rise of the English Shipping Industry*, p. 205.

[30] A horse jockey was a horse dealer, cheat or crafty and fraudulent bargainer: *OED*.

[31] A trade wind was one of the great aerial currents which form part of the general circulation of the atmosphere, governed by the distribution of pressure and keeping to a fixed track: *IMD*.

he sail'd from England in the winter quarter for North America. This he generally obtain'd about the latitude of the Canary Islands, some of which he generaly made as we did this voyage the island of Palmer,[32] then run down his westing till he approach'd the coast of Carolina where he was sure to meet with southerly winds to carry him down upon the coast of Virginia.

After arriving in Virginia we sail'd up Back river where the new ship was building in a creek call'd Harrison's Creek; & having landed the rigging & stores we brought over for her, the King George sail'd for Mary Land to purchase her cargoe of tobacco, leaving my self, some other lads & the men brought over for the new ship at Back river to wait her being launch'd, she not being quite finish'd when we arriv'd. After she was launch'd & rigg'd we sail'd up Potomack & enter'd Wiccomaco River in Mary Land, where we loaded with tobacco, walnutree & pipestaves.[33] Sail'd in the fall for England & arrived at Liverpool about the beginning of the month call'd December 1734 in the new ship call'd the two Traffords, Captain Langton commander.

Here I was turn'd over again on board of the old ship King George & sailed again for Mary Land in the beginning of the year 1735 or latter part of the month call'd March. Keept to the southward as before & had a safe agreeable passage being about nine weeks to the Capes of Virginia we sail'd up Chester river in Mary Land where we took in a cargoe of wheat (lying off Newtown) [*f. 8r*] for the island of Medera.[34] Sail'd from Maryland for the said island in the latter part of the month call'd October or beginning of that *call'd* November. About two or three weeks after we got to sea in a hard gale of wind our wheat shifted in the hold & laid the ship so much upon one side we could hardly stand upon deck. At the same time our ship being old & crazy made a great deal of water, & the wheat got into the pumpwell[35] & chok'd the pumps so that we were in great distress and in danger of perishing. But through the mercy & goodness of providence after much labour & fatigue we were enabled to righten the ship & stop the wheat from comeing into the pumpwell.

This great work done, we thought ourselves happy for several days being now able to take some rest when it was not our watch upon deck and also the gale of wind rather abated. But alas! This respite from trouble was but short before we meet with another disaster which swallow'd up all our

[32] La Palma, Canary Islands.

[33] Pipe staves were used in constructing pipes or casks for the wine and spirit trades. It was not unusual for loading a ship with tobacco in Virginia to take months, with sailors engaged in river navigation and loading hogsheads of tobacco, some of which weighed over 500 lbs: *IMD*; Earle, *Sailors*, p. 80; Rediker, *Between the Devil and the Deep Blue Sea*, p. 52; Davis, *The Rise of the English Shipping Industry*, pp. 285–7.

[34] Madeira.

[35] The pumpwell was a compartment or casing that extended from the ship's bottom to between the decks or the upper deck. It contained the pumps for removing bilge water: *IMD*.

golden hopes & brought a cloud of sorrow over the whole crew & happened in the following manner. After we had been *NB I was now in the nineteen year of my age* near a week free from the pumps choking; & the great fatigue of hoisting up the pumps to clear them; & drawing the wheat up in buckets out of the pump well & of trying every expedient that could be thought of to hinder the pumps from choking. But could find none that would do but by stopping up the limber holes[36] & hindering the passage of the water to the pumps that way. This answer'd with respect to the pumps but spoil'd a great deal of the cargoe by the water rising so high in the hold, having no passage to the pumps but through the crivises of the pumpwell where a grain of wheat could not pass, & having no occasion now to go down of the pumpwell as before, we keept the scuttle constantly laid over for fear *of* our cloaths tumbling down.

But on the fatal day when the following in the morning till noon & my trick[37] at the helm from ten to twelv*e*, the carpenter being in my watch, it was observ'd we were both uncomonly cheerfull. Our watch being out we went down into the steerage[38] & got our dinners. Which being over & the people turning in to their cabins as we call it [*f. 8v*] excepting the carpenter & my self. I keeping a journal, was upon my knees writing upon my chest. The carpenter sitting upon the side of his cabin just about to turn in (a sea phrase for laying down or going to their cabins). When the half hour being out the man at the helm cry'd out to try the pump as the custom then was to pump every half hour, when the people beginning to pump found the wheat come up again with the water. Which they acquainting the captain with, he instantly called to us in the steerage to know if the carpenter was turn'd in. He answering himself in the negative the captain told him the wheat was broke into the pumpwell again desiring him to go down & stop it in time. Whereupon the carpenter call'd to the cabin boy to light a candle & bring. Which being brought the carpenter went to the scuttle that openned out of the steerage into the pumpwell, took it up, & went down as usual, the boy holding the candle to show him light down. The poor carpenter going down in hast & without any dread of harm, did not feel the strong stench or deadly damp arising from the bilgewater,[39] being so long confin'd from the air, till he was at or near the bottom. When finding himself overpower'd with it, cry'd out 'help for God's sake! Or I am a dead man.' Striving to get up again & got his head just above the scuttle, so that the little boy got hold of his arm but the carpenter's senses & strength failing

[36] Limber holes were small circular holes in the vessel's structure near a deck or flat, designed to facilitate drainage: *IMD*.

[37] A trick was a period of two hours of duty for the helmsman at the wheel: *IMD*.

[38] The steerage was the division of the after part of a ship that is immediately in front of the chief cabin. In merchant ships it was generally the habitation of the inferior officers and ship's crew: *OED*.

[39] Bilge water was the foul and noxious water that collected in a ship's bottom: *IMD*.

him, he fell down again to the bottom, the boy being too weak to hold him.[40]

I being greatly frightened by hearing the carpenter cry out in such a manner and willing to help him with out any apprehension of the cause thereof, in the fright rise from my chest where I was writing my journal, run to the scuttle & jump'd down into the pumpwell (as the Cabin boy said) but I was no sooner down but feeling the deadly affect of the strong stench or damp so seize me cryed also out for help. Got up about half way; & fell down again senseless into the pumpwell where we both lay silent as if low dead. The cabin boy shrieking out alarmed the ship's company they be got out of their cabins calling the rest down from the deck as many [*f. 9r*] as could be spar'd, they all getting about the mouth of the scuttle leading down into the pump well consulted amongst themselves what was to be done for our preservation, but were some time before any of them dare venture down. Till one Edward MaccCollester an Irish young man offer'd to go down, if they would let him down with a rope & give him another rope to make fast to one of us & to be ready if he found himself overcome by the stench of the bilge water. That when he gave the rope he was let down with two or three sudden shakes they should haul him directly *up* which he accordingly *did* by that time he was about half way down, not being able to bear it any longer. This frighten'd & discouraged the rest very much, while we lay all the time they held their debates in that miserable condition without sense, & every time the ship rowl'd from side to side the noisome bilge water wash'd over us. But at length it pleased the gracious providence to give courage & presence of mind to the mate, who stuff'd his nostrills with tobacco & went down with two ropes as the other. Holding his wind as much as he could, & putting the rope about the first of us he met with, then got up again himself as fast as he could to get breath, without knowing who he had made the rope fast to. But the people pulling up as fast as they could soon found it was me but to outward appearance dead, my teeth set & fingers stiff.

But to return to the poor carpenter who was still lying in that dismal situation. After the mate had recover'd himself a little he went down again as before & slung the carpenter, who just as the mate was going down fetch'd a groan, which was his last & the first noise they *had* heard from either of us all the time we lay there. The carpenter being pull'd up they rowl'd him upon the chests & used such endeavours as they could in hopes he might recover but in vain, for he was quite dead & after keeping him a suitable time was hove over board. As to my self after they had rowl'd me upon a chest in order to get [*f. 9v*] the bildge water up I had swallowed down (& is the way they generaly use *with* drowning people if there remain any

[40] Part of a ship's carpenter's job was to search for leaks in a ship's hull: Rediker, *Between the Devil and the Deep Blue Sea*, p. 84.

symptoms of life) they concluded I was dead & laid me forth. But one of them laying his hand upon my breast felt a beating at my heart, upon telling of which some advised to get some drops out of the doctor's box, which being brought they apply'd them to my nose & rubb'd my temples with some, & soon found the beating at my heart to grow stronger and by a constant application a little while after perceiv'd breath to come up my nostrils & life in some degree to reassume its vigour and give motion to the body, which just before was like breathless clay without motion or strength. It having seem'd good to the infinite wisdom & mercy of a gracious god to preserve a small sparke of life in the body, which being rekindled through the secret direction of his unsearchable providence restored life strength and vigour to the body as before, but was wholly deprived of the rational faculty. Having neither sence or understanding, but fell suddenly into strong convulsions purging the noisome bilge water out of my mouth & nose; so that all that could get round me were not able to hold me after these convulsions ceas'd. I remained quite [*sic*] & still, but without understanding they put me into my cabin & keept a watch over me & keept me from starving by forcing open my mouth at times & pouring down some nourishment.

I think it was near two weeks before my senses began to come again, in the mean while the ship running to the southward we got into fine pleasant warm weather and the captain & people who were exceeding carefull of me & desirous I might live would bring me up, & keep me several hours in a day upon deck that I might have the benefit of the fresh air. This reviv'd me greatly & through the blessing of Providence restor'd me by degrees to my senses again, which came not all at once but was several days after I began to have a little understanding before I could make recollection or know the people, being full of confus'd ideas & wandering notions, looking for trees & other remarkable places that I had formerly known in the countrey [*f. 10r*] we came from, though now some hundred leagues distant from it. While I remain'd in that senseless condition & they watched me night & day to keep me in my cabin, they told me that some times they would let me get out of my cabin in the daytime to see where I would go, or what I should do, & that at such times I would go directly upon deck, & so to the ship side, straddling to go over board & also would look astern or towards the stern of the vessel, which the captain observing would say he looks after the carpenter. He will certainly dye.

When through the mercy & goodness of Providence my senses began to return I having very imperfect ideas of things for some time; so my talk to myself or questions I ask'd were very imperfect & unintelligible and the captain had given a strict charge to the people not to let me see them laugh, at any of my simple expressions. The first of my taking notice of knowing the people was in the following manner, being upon deck as usual at noon & the people being all up also upon deck, I look'd very earnestly at them for some time & thought within my self I miss'd some body I used to see; & after making some recollection in mind I very seriously ask them where the carpenter was, upon which they most of them burst out into laughter, asking me whither I remember'd what had happened to me. I told them nothing or to that effect, not being able at that time *to* recollect anything, but afterwards I could remember the carpenter being sat upon the side of his cabin, the captain calling to him, his calling to the cabin boy for a light and going with him to the pump well, the carpenter's calling out for help, my riseing from my chest where I was writing & going to the pumpwell, but could not remember any further. Only then that just as they pull'd me up out of the pump well, as I suppose, I began to come into knowledge again and saw things I cannot now describe, & was I suppose just as the spirit was about leaving the body. But being drawn up into the fresh air through the secret direction of a mercifull providence (being unprepared for that awfull change), I lost that sense again & remain'd in stupifaction as is before related till restor'd to my understanding as above.

Some weeks after my recovery we arriv'd at the island Madera an island belonging to the Portuguese where we was bound with our cargoe of wheat which we found much damaged when we came to unload. After our cargoe was out we took in another of wine for Jamaica in the West Indies with which she was to purchase another cargoe of sugar & rum for Liverpool, but I heard afterwards was lost in going home from Jamaica but the people saved. While we lay here myself & another young man one Edward MacColister of Dublin agreed to run away from the ship & go ashore amongst the Portuguese [*f. 10v*] which we effected in the following manner.

After *the* ship was loaden & ready to sail, we having wrought till late at night in making an end of stowing the wine & other preparatories for sailing. Next morning the pilot,[41] having been order'd to come on board early to carry us out of a place we lay moor'd in, call'd the Loo, before we went to sleep the captain order[ed] the oars to be taken out of the boat & laid upon the quarter deck over his head, as I suppose fearing least some of us should attempt to run away with the boat as being most of us prentices. I think as it was so late we were all order'd to go to sleep & no watch set as usual, but we two keept watch; but the Captain seem'd restless & could not sleep. Till just as the day began to dawn he got up & went upon deck & seeing the boat in her place, & all still & quite [*sic*] came down again & went to his cabin and shortly after began to snore, which I hearing went & acquainted the other lad & he getting up we went softly upon deck & finding by a shift of the current the boat to be swung towards the head of the ship, we put our

[41] A pilot was an individual with local knowledge of shallows, rocks and currents, and as such well qualified to navigate a ship over coastal waters and estuaries, or in and out of harbours: *IMD*.

things in & my companion getting into the boat to receive the oars as I was lifting up one of them, the blade being under some of the others, they slip'd off & made a considerable noise; which put me in a great fear least I should wake the captain & put an end to our enterprize. I laid down the oar softly again & slipt down into the steerage & listen'd at the cabin door, & found the captain sound a sleep by his snoring. Upon which I return'd directly upon deck, ha*n*ded a couple of oars into the boat, got in my self, loosed the boat & row'd softly away till we came abreast of the town, where attempting to put the boat ashore we were call'd to by a centinel from one of the forts, so was oblig'd to put off again least he should fire at us. We rowing along shore came abreast of another fort where we put ashore, & the boat off.

We went along shore, in order to put our project plan in execution, which was to go along shore for some distance & hide ourselves under the high cliffs till the ship was sail'd, we having carried our weeks alowance of bisket along with us for that purpose. But coming to a large fort that stood close down by the sea side on the eastern extreamity of the bay we found our passage stop'd & we could not get past that way. So was oblig'd to return back keeping a long by the town wall in hopes of getting into town. Accordingly after we had walk'd a little way by the wall we found a small door or wickett or more properly sally port[42] to relieve the centinels open where we got into the town, not seeing [*f. 11r*] any body, but went directly up a street which led out of the town to the foot of the mountains, we not seeing any body stirring in the town which prov'd greatly to our advantage as there would be no information given which way we went. We keeping along the road after we got out of the street it led us with a gradual ascent up the mountain amongst the vineyards.

After we had travel'd some considerable distance from the town & the sun being up we sett ourselves down & near the side of a large vin*e*yard, to refresh & rest ourselves & to consider how to proceed having so far been very successful in our escape & the land adorn'd with vineyards & other verdure with a serene sky & temperate air seem'd exceeding agreeable to us, who had been so long toss'd upon the great ocean, encountering such perils & dangers as is before related. While we sat thus consulting; behold providence open'd the way further for us in the following manner. There came into the vineyard we sat by a little boy & girl, brother and sister, about eight the girl & the boy about ten years of age. This little innocent couple came to feed their asses in the vin*e*yard after they saw us & seem'd to be a little afraid of us, being strangers. We call'd to them in their own language to come to us, which they did. We having got a few words of their language, while we lay in the harbour unloading & loading. When they came to us we

[42] A sallyport was an opening in a fortified place for the passage of troops when making a counter-attack: *OED*.

gave each of them a bisket, which as it was a rarity so they seem'd greatly pleas'd with them & very thankfull and we soon became familiar & aquainted as if we had seen one another before. They were both notable children; & we soon made them understand we were English & had ran away from an English ship then in the road. The little girl was so pleased with our company that she gather'd flowers and brought us.

I think after we had been an hour or two in the agreeable company of these two innocent familiar children there came another brother who was a man grown, who coming to the gate of the vineyard made a stop there, being suppriz'd to see two strangers with his little brother & sister. He call'd to them to know who those strangers were: they answer'd they were English: & he coming to us we gave him a bisket with which he seem'd pleas'd & the little boy & girl relating to him the reason of our being there having left a ship in the road which was to have sail'd that morning, setting forth as we had told *them* that the captain was bad to us. He seem'd to pity us; & contriv'd with another brother of his who join'd our company, who might be about twelve or fourteen years of age, to conduct us to a contrey seat where their father lived & had the manishment of it as an overseer for a captain of one of the forts who lived in town & was the owner of it. Accordingly this middle brother conducted us up to the house which was about two or three miles higher up the mountain.

As we drew near it, it had such a grand appearance that we began to be afraid to go too it, but through encouragement [*f. 11v*] of our guide we ventured and found it was not what it appear'd to be when we came at it. There being a great deal of art used to make it appear grand, such as large wooden frames painted & shaped like granadiers on horseback with all their accoutrements as also foot granadiers standing centry & upon the walls before the house. Faceing the ascent to the house there was portrayed the resemblance of soldiers of divers nations marching with their different colours in regiments, with several other curious devices I cannot now recollect. As we approach'd the house we pass'd through a long shady arbour framed by art & over grown with vines which made it extreamly pleasant during the heat of the day. When we came to the house the father & mother of the lad seeing two strangers coming with him seem'd a little supprizd at first till the young man had related to them the occasion & we coming up to them presented each of them with a bisket or two with which they seem'd greatly pleas'd & the old man call'd us into an out house where stood *some* pipes[43] of wine & gave each of us a good drink out of one of them telling us we might stay there safe, till the ship was gone if it was a week or more.

From the top of this house; & by the help of a telescope belonging to the captain, we could see the ships very plain in the road & distinguish our ship

[43] Casks used in the wine and spirit trades: *IMD*.

we left from the rest lying in the road ready for sailing; waiting only on our account. The captain having offer'd a considerable reward for *to get* intelligence of us but in vain, after having waited forty eight hours or more & search'd several houses in *the* town near where our ship lay & the most likely to conceal us & not being able to hear of us, sail'd for Jamaica in the West Indies.

While we remained at the country seat we diverted ourselves in the day time by walking up & down the neighbouring *hills* and looking about the vineyards, at night they put us into an out house & lock'd us up till the morning. I remember it was in the time of Lent, during which they live very meanly yet gave us to eat of such as they had, & we both of us having the figure of Christ crucify'd prick'd out upon our arme, and knowing their superstition, we would show them our arms, which they would embrace & kiss, calling us bon Cristianos, or good Christians & seem very fond on us on that account.

The third or fourth morning of our being there, going up as our custom was to the top of the house to look out for our ship, found she [*f. 12r*] was sail'd, upon which we concluded to go down that day into the town & to order it so as to enter the town while *the* Ave Maria bell was ringing at which *time* the people are most of them upon their knees at prayers, both in the houses & streets, & not so apt to take notice of who pass by. We accordingly tooke leave of our kind benefactors & descended the mountains loitering sometimes by the way, to make it evening before we enter'd the town. When we got near the first houses; going into town, we sat down till the Ave Maria bell began to ring then went into town & so through the streets to an house much resorted to by English sailors & I think were from New York.

Here we took up our quarters till we ship'd ourselves on board a snow formerly belonging to the west of England, but now to this island, the captain having run her out by taking up money on Bellomary from the Portuguese merchants. On board this snow we took in mamsey & Verdona wines, with sweet meats &c. for London & I think we two were to have forty shillings each for the run to London. We arrived at London from the island Madera about the beginning of the month call'd May in the year 1736. Wrote to my parents the 15th & again the 30th of the same month, agreed with *the* captain of the snow I arriv'd in call'd the John Snow, but the captain's name I forget, to go out with him again in the same snow at twenty five shillings 6: month; he was bound for France & Medera.

We sail'd in the month call'd June for Haverdegrace[44] loaden with tobacco w[*h*]ere arriving safe & discharging our cargoe we sail'd from thence in our

[44] The port of Le Havre in Normandy at the mouth of the River Seine.

ballast, bound for Vann[45] in Britany. Arriving in Vann River for we had not water enough to go up to the city by five or six miles, I think, that is to load there (though we often went up in our boat), we took in a cargoe of rye for the island Madera. The number of years elaps'd since my being there, & writing this account, will not admit of my giving much description of the place (being ab[ou]t thirty years since). After we were loaden; we sail'd down towards the mouth of the river, which open'd into the Bay of Biscay, where we lay some time wind bound. While we lay at anchor near the mouth of the river wind bound we met with the following accidents.

One day several of us went ashore with the captain in the boat to a French farm house to buy fowls, & having had a great deal of pastime on shore in running down the fowls & getting several sort of fruit, we return'd on board again & when we came alongside the ship the boatswain took the boat's rope for painter and made it fast over one of the short timber heads forward. After we that had been in the boat had handed the things we brought [*f. 12v*] on board, we quited the boat & went down into the forecastle to tell our comrades of our pastime on shore. Now while we were pleasantly relating our adventures on shore, the boatswain walking backwards & forwards on the deck by himself in the opposite side to where the boat lay, the wind blowing fresh, caused a short poppling[46] sea to run alongside by which means the boat snatching backwards & forwards upon the rope wrought it loose from the timber head where it was fast & went adrift. The boatswain, not hearing the boat jumble against the side for some time, went over on that side, & saw the boat driving a little way astern of the ship upon which he came running in a great fright to the forecastle scuttle asking if any of us could swim. But none made answere but myself who told him I could swim a little, he begged for god sake! I would come up directly & swim after the boat; for said he she is got but a little way astern, & may soon be recover'd.

I going up & seeing the boat was not drove far from the ship, thought I could easily swim to her; & so strip'd myself & went after her without further consideration of the danger (being always of a forward temper to do good if it was in my power). After I had swam some distance from the ship, I found the boat drove at a great rate & that I gain'd but little upon her. Therefore design'd to return back to the ship again, but in trying to swim back again found both tide, wind, & sea against me so that I could not get an end. And finding I had no remedy left but to gain the boat or dye, which I endeavouring to do used my uttermost efforts, by swiming with all strength, sometimes on my back, sides, & belly, in hopes to have come up with with [*sic*] the boat, but all in vain; for my strength was soon exhausted & the boat gain'd upon me as I grew weaker & weaker till unable to swim any longer, my strength gone, & all hopes of life over. And in just sinking in an

[45] Vannes, in Brittany, 65 miles northwest of Nantes.

[46] Turbulent or choppy: *OED*.

unprepar'd state into awfull eternity heard a great noise which revived that spark of life unquench'd in me by the suffocating waves which had swallowed me up all but the hair of *my* head which play'd a top of the waves as they toss'd me up & discover'd to the instruments of my deliverance (through the secret direction of that gracious Providence that watch'd over me in mercy) the wofull state I was in & their united voices was the noise I heard, which was a voice appointed by the great preserver of men for my preservation, sounded deliverance to my soul and rais'd a hope accompanied with strength & ability to lift up my dying eyes once more out of the water and saw a boat rowing towards me with [*f. 13r*] with all the speed they could, & as they approach'd me & saw me sinking joined their voices altogether in hallowing as loud as they could that if I heard them I might be strengthened so as not to sink down till they got hold on me, which they soon did & got me into the boat where I soon recover'd.

This wonderfull deliverance guided by the divine Providence fell out in the following manner. When I first went after the boat, neither the captain, nor mate knew anything of the matter, being in the great cabin; but the boatswain (through whose carelessn*ess* the boat got loose) watching me as long as he could see me. But at last, loseing sight of me & fearing I should be drownded, aquainted the captain & mate of it: who were very much concern'd for me, especialy the mate who was for stripping himself & swimming after me. But the captain told him if he went after me he would lose his own life & could not save mine, which prevented him from venturing after me. So concluding the boat lost & that I was drownded went down into the cabin again. But some Frenchmen belonging to a French vessel, which was laid ashore to clean her bottom, seeing our boat drive away & no boat go after her concluded amongst themselves to go with their launch or long boat and take her up that they might *get* something to drink. But did not know any body was swim*m*ing after her, till drawing near the boat they thought they saw a man drownding, my hair playing a top of the waves as the sea which was very rough toss'd me up & was the reason of their uniting their voices together, that if I heard them I might be encouraged from sinking quite down till they got hold of me. And this was the noise I heard when in the jaws of death & almost swallow'd up & which, through the mercifull asistance of divine goodness enabled me as it were to spring out of the mouth of this king of terors into the arms of life and mercy.

After the French men had taken me up they carried me on board my own vessel & tow'd the boat on board also, to the great satisfaction of the captain, mate, & ship's crew. And thus it pleased the Lord: to save my life in a wonderfull & unexpected way when all hope of life to me were lost, for which great & unspeakable mercy may my soul praise & magnify his glorious & worthy name & that for ever & evermore. Amen, amen! This great deliverance happened just as I was turn'd of twenty. [*f. 13v*]

After we sail'd from Vann River being bound for the island Madera, in crossing the Bay of Biscay, meeting with stormy weather & a great sea, we sprung a leak so that we could hardly keep our vessel free without pumps, & having but few hands were greatly fatigued & worn out; by pumping night & day, & fearing we should not be able to hold out till we reach'd the island of Madera, it was concluded to save our lives, the vessel & cargoe, to bare away for Lisbon as the wind then favour'd us, & it being also the nighest port we could go to with safety in our leaky condition. We accordingly bore away & soon arrived off the barr[47] of Lisbon, but the wind blowing strong out of the harbour & a great sea running upon the barr during the flood, as we were endeavouring to turn into the harbour, having hoist our boat out & vore her astern that she might be ready, if our vessel should founder before we could get in. Whilst we were busy in plying to windward, the boat broke lose from the stern through the carelessness of him who should have made her well fast. This put us into such a confusion, being already much dejected in our spirits with continual pumpings & fattigues accompanied with the fear of sinking that we could not recover *the* boat again, but the more we strove the further we were off for want of a steady conduct in this time of danger.

At last the captain thought of me, calling to mind; how I had swum after the boat before & adrest me in the following manner: Jack, strip yourself & swim to the boat & bring her on board. The boat being then to windward of us & the sea run high (occasion'd by a strong flood tide setting in against the wind which blew strong out of the harbour). Accordingly I strip'd my self & went into the main chains in order to jump into the sea & swim after the boat: but just as I was going to jump itt run through me in a very distinct & awfull manner that it was presumtion: that if I went at that time I should certainly be drownded. This stroke such a damp upon my spirits that I dare not venture, but came upon deck again & said I was afraid to go & there being none of the ships company besides myself that had courage to undertake it. Having now no other way left but to recover her with the vessel, which we soon did by our proceeding in a more prudent & steady manner (being somewhat [*f. 14r*] recover'd out of that fright which seiz'd upon us at first loseing her) & got safe into the harbour; & run her ashore in a suitable place by the direction of the pilot & got the leak stop'd. This I leave also upon record as a memorial of the divine goodness manifested in an extraordinary manner for the preservation of one of the unworthiest of his poor creatures!

When we arrived at Lisbon we found Sir John Norris[48] in the Britania (I think), a first rate with a fleet of men of war lying in the Tagus to protect

[47] A bar was a bank or shoal, usually at the mouth of a river, obstructing the entrance or rendering it difficult: *IMD*.

[48] From 1735 to 1737 Norris commanded the naval squadron at Lisbon to support Portugal against the Bourbon powers. Norris had also been captain of the 90–gun *Britannia* in 1703: J. K. Laughton and revised by D. D. Aldridge, 'Sir John Norris (1670/71–1749)', *Oxford DNB*.

the Porteguese from the insults of the Spaniards. Not withstanding which several of the men belonging to the men of war's boats were barbarously murthered on shore, till the Admiral gave orders for the boats' crews to go always arm'd ashore with pistols & cutlashes. This stroke an awe upon the murderers & preserv'd the men.

The city of Lisbon seem'd large & populous, but a bad govern'd dangerous place for a stranger to walk the streets by night in.[49] There being as I was told by a reputable inhabitant of the place <there being> a great many wicked lewd fellows, Irish & other strangers, who live wholly by robery & murder, who carrying a dagger under their cloaks conceal'd suddenly stab people as they walk the street & after wards take what they have if opportunity suits, if not leave them murdered without benefit to themselves. After our vessel was repair'd we took in several Porteguese gentlemen lately come from the Brasils, whose friends lived at the island Madera & so got passage with us for that island. When we were ready to sail, we were stop'd by a general embargo on all vessels on account of him they call'd the Black prince of Brasil being missing. Great search was made after him amongst the shiping lest he should make his escape & get to the Brasils. But after a while he was heard of and the embargo taken off the shiping, & we sail'd for Madera.

But as the voyage began with perils, so it continued. For about forty eight hours after we left Lisbon we were chas'd & boarded by a Barbary[50] cruiser[51] and being in the Porteguese service & the vessel belonging to them, had the Turks been able to make it out, we had been carried to Barbary & made slaves.[52] But having an English Mediterranean pass & hiding our Porteguese passengers away in the hold, & being otherwise very circumspect in our carriage, behaviour & language & also in our answers to their questions which [*f. 14v*] were some of them very subtile & crafty, but we being upon our guard by joint agreement they could get nothing from us which might give them suspicion that we belong'd to the Porteguese or was in their service.[53] When they run up along side our vessel they commanded us to

[49] Lisbon was notorious as a place where British naval servicemen jumped ship to find employment in maritime commerce.

[50] Barbary pirates, often operating from Algiers and Tunis, had captured over six thousand Britons at sea between 1660 and the 1730s, selling them into slavery in north Africa: see L. Colley, *Captives: Britain, Empire and the World, 1600–1850* (2002), p. 46.

[51] A cruiser was a vessel designed to cruise for long distances on open waters: *IMD*.

[52] In 1725 Daniel Defoe wrote that 'Not a sailor goes to sea in a merchant ship, but he feels some secret tremor that it may one time or other be his lot to be taken by the Turks': Earle, *Sailors*, p. 115.

[53] A consular report of 1765 claimed that one third of all trade carried under British colours in the Mediterranean was carried by Italians and others using forged passes in an attempt to outwit Turks and corsairs who granted immunity to British ships: P. Earle, *The Pirate Wars* (2003), p. 79.

hoist our boat out & come on board them with our pass, which we accordingly did; as fast as we could taking care to have none but English in the boat. When we came alongside <the> the Turks' frigate the mate went on board with the pass, where it was examin'd & found good as we soon heard from the Moor sailors, who repeated to us several times as we sit in the boat with our hearts full of fear Bon pass John, bon pass, which signify'd our pass was good. After they had keept the mate some *time* in examining him & asking sundry questions, they *kept him on board*, <order'd him in to the boat> one of their principal officers step'd into the boat with him making a sign in his hand for us to put off. This put us into a fresh consternation not knowing what it might mean, but when we came *on board found* it was only to beg something and ask the captain some questions. The captain gave him a few pieces of meat and some bisket, took a chart & shew him where abouts we judg'd ourselves to be, & what distance from the rock of Lisbon. Also call'd him aside & told him of a cruizer that was to sail in quest of the Moors the day after we sail'd. This had the desired effect, for as soon as he had heard it he was in a great hurry to be gone, & seem'd very thankfull to the captain. We carried him on board his vessel *& the mate return'd with us*; they wish'd us a good voyage and so we parted, with more satisfaction on our sides then when we met.

After we had got a considerable distance from them our passeng*ers* came out of their holes where they had laid conceal'd all the time of our examination, in great fear least we should have been made a prize. But now being out of danger; they put on the rodomentado,[54] drawing their sparders[55] & pushing them towards the stern, calling the poor Turks bad names & threatening how they would use them if they had them in their power. They being always at sworn war with the Turks & through a mistaken zeal, & false bigotry nourish up in their bosoms a perpetual hatred against them, esteeming them the enemies of Christ because they do not profess the Christian religion & judge they ought to be extirpated from the earth & indeed their spirits are too muchinctur'd with that belief; even towards them that profess Christianity if they descent from their superstition.

After this we met with nothing remarkable in our passage to Madera. Where we arriv'd safe & unloaded our cargo of rye took on board a ballace in [*f. 15r*] order to sail for the island Tercera to take in a cargoe of wheat and return with it to Madera. We accordingly sail'd for the western island and arrived safe at the island of Tercera which produces plenty of corne & wine. Their being according to report from the inhabitants a pretty deal of both sorts sent yearly to Lisbon from this & the other islands but Tercera is reckon'd to produce most corn, yet they are all or most of them fruitful but very mountainous but situated in a temperate climate from 36° 59 of latitude

[54] Rodomontade was vainglorious ranting, boastful, arrogant and inflated language: *OED*.

[55] Spada is the Italian word for sword.

to 39° 54 & west longitude from London from 23° 58 to 30° 55. The inhabitants are Porteguese: subjects to the King of Portugal. After we had anchor'd for some time off one of the principal towns in the island, we sail'd to another port of the island to take in our cargo of wheat & enter'd a bay where we had no shelter from the sea. But the wind blowing off the land we sent our water casks a shore to fill with water & began to take in our loading, but before we had completed it the wind shifted and blew into the bay so that we was oblig'd to slip our cable & run out to sea leaving our anchor & water casks behind, & the weather proving stormy & the wind likely to hold we stood away for Madera, but through bad management were in danger of perishing for want of bread & water before we reach'd the island of Madera, which happenned in the following manner.

After we had left Tercera & it was concluded to run for Madera we stood to the eastward till by the reckoning of the captain & mate we were in the longitude of Madera, then steering a south course to get into the lattitude they expected to have fell in with the middle of the island. I keeping a journal my own self was pretty certain we had not run far enough to the eastward & told the captain & mate so, but they were too positive in their own accounts to give credit to my estimation till they found by sad experience it was too late for after we got into the latitude of the island, & could see nothing of it: they to add to their error concluded we were to the eastward of the island and not withstanding all I could say to the contrary would stand to the westward in hopes of making the island. But after about forty eight hours or more standing to the westward in the lattitude of the island & not seeing anything of the island, the sky & horizon being clear & a western bank of clouds which had appear'd in the horizon for some days gone, which had been a deception to the captain & mate, they judging it hung over the island which is common in those parts of the world where the land is high & we [*f. 15v*] often in sailing near either the Western, Madera, or Canary islands or any other very high lands, discover first the tops of the mountains above the clouds before we can see the lower parts of the land. This deception as is before observ'd being remov'd, they were now but too certain that we had been running from the island instead of towards it & the wind, which had been favourable for us before to have stood to the eastward, now chop about into the eastern quarter against *us* & we had to beat to windward to recover the island, and having a pretty large sea as well *as* the wind against us it was not likely we should gain much in beating to windward, & having but little water & bread on board could look upon ourselves in no other light then being inn great danger of perishing for want of water & bread. This brought a general dejection upon all our spirits & made the times seem exceeding tedious & melancholy.

After having beat to windward some days & the wind like to continue we divided the whole quantity of bread on board in to equal shares. The captain and mate sharing equal with the rest, & our whole stock of water being but a piece of a pipe, we put ourselves to half a pint per man for twenty four hours. This small allowance we each of us put into *a* glass bottle and cork'd it up, putting a quill through the cork & suck'd now & then a little through the quill to moisten our mouths when almost dry'd up with thirst, & we having nothing to eat with our bread but salt Irish beef & salted baccaloe (cod fish cured with salt & dry'd) & which we were oblig'd both to freshen & boil in salt water. So that it remain'd so salt when cook'd that we were oblig'd to eat but very sparingly of it.

After having beat to windward I think about eight or nine days in this dejected situation it pleased God it prov'd calm & the wind sprung up at west in the night, & in the morning a little before sun rise as we were leting reefs out of our topsails[56] we saw the island of Madera very plain. So by our run afterwards computed it was at least twenty eight leagues or 84 miles from when we first saw it, we run all that day with a fresh gale westerly but could not get in with the island & in the night it prov'd little wind and the next morning calm, so that we hoist out our boat to tow our ship in with the land. It pleased providence to favour us with sight of a turtle lying asleep upon the water while we were towing the ship. Our boat cast off tow rope & row'd softly to the turtle & took it up. Which was very exceptable as we were now nearly out of both bread & water, & our cook made a most dilicious meal of it for us, which cheer'd our spirits [*f. 16r*] and fill'd our hearts with thankfullness. That night or the next morning we got into Fonchal[57] road where we were soon supply'd with such necessaries as we stood in need of. After lying some short time here we took in a cargo of wine for South Carolina.

But before I leave this place & this troublesome voyage, in which I was the nearest appearently: of being starv'd that ever I was in all my voyages & travels besides, I shall give some account of the inhabitants & their superstition. The island is pleasantly situated in a temperate climate. The body or middle of the island, being nearly in 32° 30 north lattitude and in 17° 20 west longitude from the meridian of London. Their long days in summer are about 14 hours 9 min: & their shortest in winter 9 *hours* 51 *min* that is reckoning from sun riseing to sun setting so that they are never much troubled with the extreamities of cold. Sometimes it is so temperate in the debth of winter that a person may go into the sea & swim, though at other times I have known the strong north west winds from the continent of America to prevail there accompanied with storms of haile, but this is but seldom & lasteth not long. The wind bloweth for the most part of the land especialy in the night time which is the security the ships have which ride in the bay

[56] In a square rigged vessel, the topsail was the single square sail set above the lower sail or yard, the uppermost sail: *OED*.

[57] Funchal, Madeira.

& road. But as soon as the wind blow out of the sea the large ships which ride in the outer road & bay too, if not moor'd in what they call the Loo, are oblig'd to slip their cables & run to sea & return again when the wind is favourable. For if the wind comes to the south & blow it soon raise a great sea, & some times drive the vessels ashore that happen not to be in a situation to put to sea, as it fell out to a vessel while I was there, who parted her cables & having no ballace in could carry no sail so drove ashore amongst the rocks & was breke to pieces in an instant, the people being taken out just before she strake by a Porteguese boat or they must all have perish'd. Through the temperature of the air, this island of Madeira is both healthfull & fruitfull, producing almost all sorts of fruits that grow in hot countreys, as well as those in northern countreys, but excede for wines; the soil in many places (being a mountainous island) *is rocky*, but yet thro the industry of the inhabitants by supplying those places with mould where tis wanting few places but precipices remain uncultivated & the surface of the south part of the island opposite to where we lay is adorn'd with an agreeable verdure.

The Porteguese are not reckoned so good in their morals as the Spaniards. (It being a common saying in those parts of the world that a Spaniard stript of all his good qualities makes a compleat Portegue) [*f. 16v*]. However I believe the prejudice of education is the chiefest cause of that difference which is *found in* their disposition towards strangers, especially, Protestants. The Porteguese being much more priest ridden then the Spaniards, consequently more prejudiced against those of other persuations & the Spaniards, though the best of the two, are greatly hurt thro the bigotry of religion. But to return, the Porteguese inhabitants of Madeira are as much priest ridden as any people in the world, this being like a little world by its self. The priest[s] here, bear a great sway over the people and the Roman Catholick religion is to be seen here in its highest superstition & slavery. For on their particular festival days when their processions go about the streets & numbers of penitents of almost all ages following them doing penance (as they are taught) for their sins. I shall next endeavour to describe the manner of their processions according to what I can now remember of them, having seen them in divers places besides this island of Madeira, as in old Spain & in the Southsea at the citties of Lima, Valparaiso, Baldiva, Guiaquil &c.[58] The manner then is on those festival days, when a procession is appointed & the penitents or devotees are to attend, they all meet at some particular or noted church from whence the procession is to go forth where all those of the clergy & religious orders who officiate in the procession marshal themselves into their proper stations, which they are to keep during the procession. All things being in order the procession comes forth as near as I can remember in the following manner.

[58] Lima is in modern Peru, Valparaiso and Valdivia in Chile, and Guayaquil in Ecuador.

First some of the clergy bare headed, with wax candles lighted in their hands singing; close after them come a representation of the birth of Christ, viz the Virgin Mary, with the child Jesus, in a manger and so in that manner is represented by image the most remarkable passages of his life, death, passion & ascension. These images represent each particular passage, being carried upon mens' shoulders, by themselves and with the clergy & others bare headed carrying each a wax candle lighted in his right hand singing hyms in Latin composed for that purpose & leave a small [*f. 17r*] space betwixt each representation that each passage represented may be the more distinct & observable to the people; who place themselves at their doors, windows, & in the streets to see them pass by, kneeling as each representation come abreast of them, saying such prayers at the same time as they are taught. The most remarkable things I can now recollect to have seen pass by in these processions is the Virgin Mary with the child Jesus in a manger. The Virgin Mary with the child Jesus in her arms I suppose when she with Joseph fled into Egypt to avoid Herod's cruelty. Christ with a crown of thorns upon his head & the blood trickling down upon his forehead. Christ after condemned bareing his cross to be crucified. Christ nailed to the cross & crucified. With several other things which I cannot now recollect. After all these follow the penitents doing their penance in different manners, some with their backs naked scourging themselves with a stick with several strings ty'd to the end & knotted till the blood run down their backs, some relation or aquain*tance* going behind & wiping off the blood at times with a cloth. Others with their bodies hard bound round with a rope or brambles & girted in, so that it must be very painfull to continue so long in that posture. Others with their arms naked & bound about in the same manner. Others again, going backward with one person to support them that they might not fall, having several sparders or long swords, with their blades crossing one another, & their naked points placed against their naked breasts lodging under their ribbs by the soft part of their body dinting in; & the weight of the other parts of the sparders & their handles supported only by their own hands clasp'd & held a little distance from their body. This is also a very painfull & severe punishment. Others again with their arms extended & made fast in that manner *a cross their breasts* to a stick so that they cannot draw in their arms. Another draging a large wooden cross after him as much as he can will pull along having some parts of it upon his shoulder, that he may bear the cross. Some lads & mere children with naked backs whipping themselves till the blood run down.

Thus these poor people are slaves and drudges to superstition & the will of their priests, being taught by them to believe that by performing these penances appointed them by the priests or their confessors & their absolution they are freed from their sins, though their hearts are not in the least chang'd from their [*f. 17v*] corruptions & the evil root still remain the same, ready to bring forth the same fruits again for which they have afflicted their bodies; the first temptation and opportunity depending upon being freed after the same manner again which is rather an encouragement to sin as they think they have it in their own power through penance & absolution to get free from their sins. But to return to the procession: after they have pass'd through the principal streets in the place, which generally take up three or four hours as they often stop for the penitents to come up & keep way with them & also to strike the greater awe upon the spectators, that they may behold them in a more serious manner. They return to the same church; ending where they began. The penitents have all of them a mark over their faces that they may not be known.

Being loaden with wine as is before mention'd for South Carolina we sail'd from Madeira about the begining of the month called January, & arrived at South Carolina as nigh as I can remember about the middle of that call'd February in the year 1736/7– at this place my self, the mate; boatswain, & most of the ship's company left the ship on account of the captain's behavour which was none of the best. And as we had often heard him telling the mate in a braging way over a bottle of wine that if his men had a year's pay due he knew how to make them run away & leave when he had a mind or words of the same import which made us think the sooner we left him the better & as my leaving had something singular in it, shall mention some of the particulars.

Before we left Madeira I had prevail'd with the captain to let me have two quarter pipes of wine for a venture which he readily let me have as I had pretty good quarters with him & he a better opinion of me then of any of the rest. I sold these cask of wine for forty pounds their currency, which then was accounted at seven hundred & fifty per cent, that is 7/6 currency equal one shilling sterling. So that the two cask fetch'd me about £5, £6 or £7 sterling. These I got on shoar & sold before I attempted to leave the ship. While we lay here waiting for our cargo of rice the colony of Georgye [*f. 18r*] was threatened with an invasion from the Havenna[59] by the Spaniards. On which occasion the government of Carolina fitted out two privat*eers* a snow & a schooner[60] to cruize upon the coast of Georgea & in order to man them, were oblig'd to press sailors belonging to the shiping.[61] I being on shore one evening with some others at an aquaintance house; & the press master with his gang & constables came in upon us unawares took us & carried us to the guard house & next morning guarded

[59] Havana is in modern Cuba.

[60] A schooner was a fore and aft rigged vessel, at this time usually with two masts, common in the coasting and fishing trades: *IMD*.

[61] Charleston in 1740 was dominated by slave-owners who owned very few ships and the colony was heavily reliant upon British vessels: Rediker, *Between the Devil and the Deep Blue Sea*, p. 55.

us down to the water side & put us on board of the schooner privateer. But my stay was but short, for at noon while the people were at dinner a merchant ship loaden for Bristol at the shift of the tide swung on board us & myself and several others, with an officer were order[ed] on board her *to* heave in some of her cable that she might swing clare of us. After we had hove in as much cable as was necessary every one of the people, both ours & the ship company, running aft to beat the privateer clare of the ship's stern as she swung.

I being behind the rest saw a fair opportunity offer to get down into the ship's steerage unseen & hide & told another so that was next to me, but he said we should be miss'd & that he & some others had agreed to run away with *his* boat at night. I finding he dare not venture run down the steerage alone and hungry crept out of my hole to the no small surprise of the mate & ships company who gave me some victuals & made me crawl back again out of sight for fear they should miss & come to seek me. But that panick was soon over for the privateer weigh'd anchor soon after & run down the river in order to hinder the people from getting either by swimming or running away with the boat. After it was dark they put me on board my own vessel [*f. 18v*] again, she laying ashore upon a bank where we had been cleaning her bottom.

But to delineate the spirit & principle of our captain I shall mention a perticular which happen'd at this time. We had a free negro on board we brought with us from the island of Madeira who had lived at Mary Land or Pensilvania. But going out in a ship from thence to Madeira he left her & turn'd Roman Catholic. Him our captain ship'd for our cook; our vessel belonging to that island. The man expected to return back again in the ship. But the captain would fain have sold him but he being a very notable and sensible fellow told those that came to buy him, that he was free & would not be sold, but would sooner dye then serve as a slave so that they dare not buy him & because of which he beat & whip'd *him* in a most sham*e*full manner. Howsoever at last being resolved to get clare of them, he put him on board the privateer snow, the captain of which taking a likeing to him, after his return from the cruize, made him overseer of his plantation which lay not very far from <Carolina> *Charles Town* where he lived very comfortable and well as he told me afterwards.

After our bottom was clean, we went to one of the wharfs in order to prepare for taking in our cargo of rice for Lisbon. But I having formed a design in my head to leave the ship now sought an opportunity to put in practice which shortly fell out in the following manner. There lay at the next wharf to us a sloop[62] one Captain Petty (who had a brother liv'd in London) who wanted hands, bound for the Bohemia islands.[63] Him I agreed with,

[62] A sloop was usually a single masted vessel with only one headsail and a short bowsprit: *IMD*.

[63] The Bahamas.

for £12 per month Carolina currency (that is thirty two shillings English money). At night when I intended to get my things on board the sloop there being now none left on board but my self & a New York lad who being gone to sleep, I was getting my chest out of the steerage, but hearing some body coming on board upon our plank I stopt & running upon deck to see who it was found it to be the captain. Who not suspecting any thing of the matter accosted me in a more particular & flattering manner then he had ever done before. Addressing himself to me [*f. 19r*] something after the following manner: 'Well Jack, then these have all left me but you & Davy. Well as long as you stay with me, I don't care for all the rest. They were a parcel of scoundrels', or some words to that affect. He order'd me to call Davy up & light a candle which was soon done, then taking a flask of Madeira wine out of his case set it upon the cabin table & would have me come and sit by him & drink with him: which I did. Then he began to promise me great things that I might not leave him. Telling me from that time I should be rated boatswain & have the same pay as the other boatswain that had left him & that after we had discharg'd our cargo of rice at Lisbon he should go to London where he was to have a new ship & I should be his mate. Also gave me directions how I should behave in my new post, that I should not make my my [*sic*] self familiar with the people but keep my self at a distance & when I had a mind might make free with his case of wine. These & many other things past betwixt us to which I answer'd but little except yes, & no, as they came in course. Thus spending the time till about one in the morning the captain took leave on me & went ashore to his lodgings, thinking he had with his promises secured me from leaving him.

After he was gone ashore & the lad gone to sleep again I got my chest & beding up, put *them* in the boat, & carried them on board the sloop I had ship'd my self in. Then brought the boat on board again makeing her fast as before. Going round by land myself to the sloop where I had a hiding place provided for me & a watch to give me warning when any body came they suspected. Next day when the captain went on board his ship & enquiring for the boatswain he was not to be found. & the captain telling the mate who came daily on board, though he was discharg'd & only waited for his wages, that he had made me boatswain the night before. The mate told him that perhaps being overjoy'd at my new post, I might go ashore to aquaint my comrades & was got up. This he said to screen the matter, for he knew where I was, I having aquainted him with my design. However after it grew near noon, & the captain very uneasy about me, he thought it was time to bring it out. The mate bid the lad [*f. 19v*] Davy look forewards & see whither my beding & chest was there, which accordingly he did & found them both gone. This stroke the captain with such surprise he knew not what to say or do, to think he should prefare me the night before & I should leave him so soon. He went on shore & search'd every house they could think of where there was any probability of finding me, but all to no purpose. They search'd also the shiping but could get no tidings of me. He also put me in the news paper offering a reward to any who could give information where I was, mentioning in his advertisement that I had run away with the boat, which was false.

About a week after the sloop I was in sail'd for the Behemia islands in the West Indies & was as near as I can calculate in the beginning of the month call'd March in the year 1736/7. After we got out to sea, we stood to the eastward as their manner is, till we reckon'd ourselves nearly under the meridian of the island bound to. Then endeavour to make a south course to run down the lattitude the first we arriv'd at was Harbour island, so call'd from the many excellent harbours. Here lives a few inhabitants whose chief employ is turtleing & cutting dye woods, mahogany & madera planks for the sloops that trade here. Here they eat sweet potatoes & casavy bread made of a root of that name, besides flour brought them by the traders. The weather here is very temperate & pleasan*t* and the *people* very civil to strangers & social amongst themselves. From this place we sail'd to another adjacent island call'd Eleuthera where we took in wood & sour oranges.

From hence we sail'd to the island of Providence where the captain's wife liv'd. Here he had a house & a new vessel upon the stocks building. At this island the governour of all the Bahama islands resides. Here is a fort & soldiers who complain very much of their poor living. Some years before I was here the soldiers belonging to this garrison being tir'd out with their confinement & bad living took an opportunity & seiz'd the fort & took possession on it, fir'd several guns at the governour's [*f. 20r*] house, then broke open the chests belonging to the officers, & took what they pleas'd & plunder'd the town. Afterwards seiz'd a vessel in the harbour & went on board her with their plunder designing to run down to the Havanna & surender themselves up to the Spaniards; & in order they might not be pursued took the sails from such vessels as was in the harbour. But after they got to sea they were most of them sea sick & I think but one which knew how to steer. After they were sail'd the inhabitants began to consult together about following them; & having secured *a sloop* which was loading at some other part of the island and having manned her with the officers belonging to the garrison & some of the inhabitants with fire arms they followed them & came up with them before they reach'd the Havanna. & soon overcame them, they being so seasick had little power to make resistance, & brought them back to Providence again, where the governour I think hung or strangled about twelve or fourteen of the ringleaders & afterwards their bodys were hung on gibbets as a terror to the rest & thus this tragical affair ended.

Having taken in our cargo *of* wood & fruit (that is sour oranges & limes) we sail'd for the island of Abaco & from thence for the island of Grand

Bahama to meet our turttlers, appointing to meet them at such an island agreed upon at a fix'd time. But before I leave the island of Providence I may just observe; this was the general rendezvous for the pirats after Queen Ann's war being an excellent safe harbour. Here they shar'd their plunder and refitted after their cruises upon the coast of North America or among the West India islands it lying convenient for them both. The manner of the inhabitants living is much the same as those at Harbour island, only this being the principal island, they have vessels come from New York & Boston with live stock, which is soon [*f. 20v*] bought up. When we arrived at Grand Bahama we waited some time for our turttlers. This is a low flat island, some parts barren & sandy, other parts woody with some large lakes of water where there resort great numbers of flemingoes and other fowls. Here is also great numbers of parrots both of which we shot & eat. The flemingo is pretty good eating but the parrot very dark coarse meat. Here, *we* dig'd two or three feet deep *in the sand* just above the wash of the sea & got good fresh water. Having taken our turtle on board we sail'd through the gulph of Florida for Carolina where we arriv'd about the 22 the month call'd April.

When we had discharg'd our cargo of turtle, fruit & plank & *I had* received my wages having been gone on our voyage about 6 weeks, I with my comrade a Scotch man who had left a Bristol ship & been with me in the sloop, ship'd ourselves in the Dantzick merchant Captain Powel belonging to Bristol, bound for Cows in the Isle of Wight & Lisbon. In our passage home we run *the ship* upon some rocks which lay about four or five Leagues of[f] Bermuda on the north east side, but the wind favouring us, back her off again with the sails, & next morning at daylight saw the island. It being in the night we ran upon the rocks, but receiv'd no damage. The captain was a right Bristol captain & pinch'd us pretty much in our diet.[64] Before we arriv'd at Cows though our passage was not very long, the scurvy prevail'd over all the ship's company, excepting my self, the captain & boatswain. So that when we came to an anchor in Cows road we were oblig'd to make a signal for hands from the shore to assist us & send our hands ashore who soon recover'd. We arriv'd at this place the 18th of the month call'd June in the year 1737, I being then just twenty one years of age. The captain altering his voyage contrary to our agreement we took the advantage to leave him.[65]

[64] Captains' control of sailors' diets provoked bitter resentment if the crew felt they were on short rations merely to save their employer's money: Rediker, *Between the Devil and the Deep Blue Sea*, p. 222.

[65] Sailors felt they had the right to renegotiate their terms of service if their captain altered the ship's course or destination from their original agreement: Rediker, *Between the Devil and the Deep Blue Sea*, pp. 109–10, 139.

I & my comrade the Scotchman beg'd our passage in a Palantine ship bound for Philadelphia, which put into Cows to take provisions & other necessaries on board; they had near four hundred passengers on board, which they took in at Amsterdam (if I remember right). These Germans commonly call'd Palatines[66] because coming out of a part of Germany call'd the Palatinate brought all their [*f. 21r*] families & substance with them in order to settle under the peaceable government of Pensylvania where they could enjoy the free exercise of their religion, undisturb'd by the Roman Catholick hierarchy. After we had taken such necessaries on board as was wanting, we sail'd from Cows about the beginning of the month call'd July. We were about three months upon our passage, which was a long & tedious one; near the lattitude of the Western islands we were becalmed near two weeks. It being in the month call'd August, was very hot & the great number of passengers throng'd us up so that it was very unpleasant being betwixt decks or in the hold. In the night many of the people would lay upon deck for the benefit of the fresh cooling air.

During this hot weather the small pox broke out amongst the children & carried off about twenty six or twenty seven, all of them dying which had the distemper. I not having had it myself was shy in coming near them when brought upon deck for air as they often were in the daytime, but after some time not finding any harm from them, the fear was taken away & when they dy'd I had a principal hand in tyeing balast to their feet & preparing for sea burial: & some times we have had three in an evening to bury. Our manner was as follows. After the deceas'd was sewn up in a blanket or sheet, or such as their parents thought fit & balast or shot fastened to their feet, they were laid upon boards, which had one end placed upon the gunnel of the ship, & being thus placed the captain generally read out of a Common prayer book the office for the dead; & when he came at that part, which mention earth to earth, ashes to ashes, dust to dust, we then lift up *the* inner end of the boards & the corps[e] slide down into the sea, feet foremost & is soon out of sight. The crys of the parents and the solemnity which death & interrment naturaly brings over the spectators render such times very affecting to those present.

I think about two weeks after the small pox ceas'd in the ship & we thought all was over; I fell down with it my self. At first I was down in my mind & greatly discourag'd; & believing as I had help'd to throw so many into the sea, my turn was now come to be serv'd so myself, their being none which had the distemper but dy'd of it. So that there was but little room for me who made the twenty seventh to [*f. 21v*] expect to escape. Howsoever, it so fell out through the goodness of a mercifull providence that I had the

[66] These German speaking people from the Rhineland constituted 'the largest continental contingent of migrants to North America in the eighteenth century': A. Games, 'Migration', in Armitage and Braddick, eds, *The British Atlantic World*, p. 39.

distemper very favourably, having but few, though the others that dy'd of it were extraordinary full even the bottoms of their feet. Mine came to the height in a few days as the weather was exceeding hot and the passengers exceeding kind to me, in giving me forcing things. For I was well respected by most of them, often giving them part of my allowance of water, when they were very thirsty and had none to drink. For several families had children under age that paid nothing, so had no allowance, which fell hard upon the parents when their own was shortened on account of the long calm & tedious passage. As we buried many children, so we had two born at sea during our passage. I think it was but about a week I laid by for the small pox. Our passengers were great singers of Psalms, which seem'd to be the chief part of their religious performances. This they generally practic'd morning & evening and their voices by constant practice affords an agreeable melody, yet have somewhat of the dolefull.

About the latter part of the month call'd September arriv'd at Philadelphia[67] where our live cargo was soon discharg'd. Those who were of ability to pay their own passagees [*sic*] soon went ashore with their things. The others which had not soon found masters & mistresses who agreed with them to serve so long a time according to their sex, ability & qualifications; & such masters & mistresses paid the captain their passages according to contract. The passingers after ashore are oblig'd of an appointed day to go to the court houses to promise fidelity to the English government. The ceremony is perform'd something after the following manner. They being assembled in the court house the preamble of their fidelity is read in their own language & they to show their assent all of them hold up their hands together as a token thereof. Here I staid & helpt to load the ship though not intending to go for England in her, having a desire with my comrade a Scotchman to go for Jamaica in the West Indies, but opportunity did not suit.

In the month of November I think we got our passage in *a* [*f. 22r*] New England sloop loaden with passingers & horses bound for South Carolina. During our passage we had rough stormy weather, being winter time; and a great deal of trouble both with our horses & passengers. One thing not unworthy of mentioning as it was the only one of its kind that I ever knew at sea; or caused by sea sickness. We had amongst other families of passengers one young man & a woman who seem'd newly married having no children. This young woman was so extreamly sea sick; that she was almost continualy vomiting or straining to vomit and though her husba*n*d did all he could for her, night & day, being very tender & kind towards her yet she was almost worn out when we arrived at South Carolina, & being oblig'd

[67] Philadelphia's population was around 13,000 by the 1740s and the Quaker influence in the colony was fading. A description of its trade and markets is given in Rediker, *Between the Devil and the Deep Blue Sea*, pp. 69–70.

to go again by sea to North Carolina where they were to settle. Her sickness being renew'd again by that passage, though short, it cost her her life. I being arrived at Carolina and not meeting with a voyage to Jamaica sail'd another voyage to the Bahama islands for turtle & fruit. A[f]ter our return, to Carolina; sail'd in a pettianger[68] up & down the river, bring*ing* wood from a plantation to Charles Town to sell. But being weary of that kind of life, though I was patron of the pettianger, as having nothing but new negros with me (excepting one or two) & they dull & hard to manage.

I left her after a few weeks and ship'd myself on board a Dutch ship call'd the Agatha, belonging to the Hope of Rotterdam,[69] which put in here on her way home from the Bay of Honduras, wanting both provisions and hands. In this ship I shipped myself by the run from this place to Rotterdam for eight pounds sterling. The captain was a Sweed, the chief mate[70] an Englishman ship'd in the bay, who left one Captain Samson belonging to Amsterdam upon some difference arising betwixt him and the captain. He that went out captain of the Agatha being an English man & dying in the bay this Sweed who was his mate succeeded him. In our passage from South Carolina to Rotterdam *we met with nothing very remarkable*, excepting in a hard gale of wind our water cask getting lo[o]se betwixt decks stove one against another by the quick & violent roleing of the ship. It being very hazardous to venture amongst them; yet we saved some which with an addition of some offer'd us by a vessel we met with at sea served us till we got in at Helvoetsluce.

We also after appro[a]*ching* the English land, met with another exercise from the captain's endeavour to lose the ship, by running her ashore. Some account of the reason of which (as I was then inform'd) is as follows. The former captain who dy'd in the bay, it seems carried instructions with him from Holland for that purpose; which this Sweed who succeeded him found amongst his papers after his death & was weak enough in his cups to give some hints of it to [*f. 22v*] his mate, who treasur'd it up in his memory to keep *guard* upon him well knowing if the ship was lost as he had no security he must lose his wages. When we got into the English Channel the captain would come upon deck in the night time when the mate was gone to sleep & alter the course several points in order to run the ship ashore. Which as soon done, & the sails trim'd some one or other would slip down

[68] A pettianger, pettiago or periauger was an open flat-bottomed sailing barge with decked ends and two collapsible masts, used in sheltered waters in the Americas and the West Indies: *IMD* and *OED*.

[69] The Hopes were a family of Scottish descent resident in London, Amsterdam and Rotterdam, who were becoming one of Europe's foremost banking dynasties in this period: of John Orbell, 'Hope family (per. c.1700–1813), merchants and merchant bankers', *Oxford DNB*.

[70] The chief mate was the officer next in rank to the master on a merchant ship, and the one upon whom command of the vessel would fall if the captain was killed or disabled: *IMD*.

& aquaint the mate, who would come upon deck and alter the course again. Upon which high words general ensued between the mate & captain who generally kept himself drunk long as his liquor lasted, he having sold logwood out of the ship in the bay to the Jamaica traders for rum & expecting to smother all by loseing the ship, which he had told the mate was insur'd in three insurance offices, London, Amsterdam & Hambrough.[71] Howsoever that might be through great care & diligence we brought her safe to Helvoetsluce, where we took in a pilot who carried us up to Rotterdam. & where, we had reason to believe; *we were* very unexceptable guests to the owners, who had rather heard of us at a distance then to have seen us so near. We had a great deal of trouble before we got our wages, being oblig'd to go three times before the states; being charg'd with assisting *the* mate to assault the captain and run away with the ship. But not being intimidated by the charges but standing stoutly on the mate's side, we at length clear'd up the point, got an order from the states to receive our wages & the mate also his.

After I had received my wages I went over in *a* vessel belonging to my Uncle Sparshall & Richard Wright, John Jermin master. After I arriv'd at Yarmouth went into the country to see my friends: having been absent about seven years, or rather more. I staid in the country the remaining part of the summer visiting my relations & in the month called October (& then the 8th month) about the 12th got a passage at Yarmouth for London; & on the 17th ship'd my self on board the Defence India man, Captain Coates[72] commander, bound for Mocha & Bombay, in the East Indies.[73] The 24th wrote home, & about the 30th rec'd an answer. About the first of the month call'd November, sailed for the Cape of Good Hope commonly called the Cape Bon Espearance, met with nothing very remarkable in our passage to the Cape, excepting loosing one man, who [*f. 23r*] having a rupture which the doctor putting up, it was thought he broke something within him for the poor man dyed shortly after.

We arrived save at the Cape, in the month called January; & the 29th wrote home by an homeward bound Indiaman; giving some descrip*tion* of the place. When we arrived at the Cape we found it the height of summer; all sorts of fruits being in perfection such as grapes, apples, pears, peaches, green pease & beans &c., the produce of that country, which lyes

[71] For the development of marine insurance in the eighteenth century, see: P. Crowhurst, *The Defence of British Trade, 1689–1815* (Folkestone, 1977), pp. 81–103.

[72] Thomas Coates (d.1747) commanded the Defence on this voyage, having served on four other East India Company vessels beforehand: A. Farrington, *A Biographical Index of East India Company Maritime Service Officers, 1600–1834* (1999), p. 159.

[73] The log book of *The Defence* East India Man lists a crew of seventy-eight men, naming 'John Seaker, seaman' as the forty-first: BL, Asia, Pacific and Africa Collections, IOR/L/MAR/B/647B.

in a temperate climate (in about 34° so south and 19° 36 east longitude from the meridian of London & is distant from London about 5200 miles). Their seasons are directly opposite to ours, they living on the other side of *the* sun, having it north at noon as we have it south. The inhabitants are Dutch and behave very civilly to strangers. We staid here about two weeks to refresh our selves, this place being blessed with all the necessaries suitable for the refreshment of seamen after a long passage at sea whether from India or Europe, having plenty of good beef, muton, fowls, greens, excellent wines & water. The Dutch East India Company have very *fine* gardens here, which yields plenty of choice herbs for their seamen; who are very subject to have the scurvy during their long passages so that sometimes when their ships arrive here the greatest part of the seamen are infected with it.

The land about the Cape is very mountainous, & subject to hard gusts & flows of wind, which rushing down between the mountains call'd the Table Land, Sugar Loaf & Lion's Rump with such violence sometimes as endangers the ships riding in the road. After staying here about two weeks & furnishing our selves with such necessaries as we stood in need of, we sailed for Mocha[74] in Arabia, meeting nothing very remarkable in our passage but what is common in sailing those seas. We saw several islands in the Indian sea, from some of which we smelt an agreeable fragrancy at several leagues distance. We had an uncommon large bate flew on board us, one evening near the coast of Africa, which was catch'd by some of our people. I think we were near three months on our passage from the Cape to the straights of Bablemandal[75] going into the Red Sea so call'd from an island of that name which makes the straights. [*f. 23v*]

We arrived at Mocha in the Red Sea about the beginning of the month call'd May. There we lay taking in our cargo of coffee & druggs about three months. During which time as I belong to one of the boats, I was often on shore; and had formed a design in my own mind, if opportunity had offered, to have left the ship, and gone with <with> the caravans overland through the deserts of Arabia into Turky. After having enquired of the Arabians I found it impracticable as no caravans went from that place. After this I planned another design to leave the ship & get to some other part of India where caravans might be met with, but this also proved abortive for want of opportunity, though once I seemed pretty near it, which fell out in the following manner.

A French country ship cruising down the Red Sea from India, bound for Ponticherry,[76] and anchoring about three miles from us, I formed a design to make a raft with deals[77] & in the night when all was asleep to have gone

[74] Mocha is now Al Mukhā in Yemen.

[75] These are now the straits of Bab al Mandab.

[76] Pondicherry is in southern India.

[77] Deals were slices sawn from a log of timber, to make planks or boards of pine or fir wood: *OED*.

onboard her, having got every thing ready for that purpose so privately as none on board had any suspicion of it. But the evening before it was to be put in practice, the ship weigh'd anchor & sailed away. As <it> there is a space of about thirty years from my writing of this, & my being there; I cannot give so good a discription of the place, as if the memorandum taken that voyage had not been lost. But I was robed of them & many others, by being taken a few years afterwards by the French.

The city of Mocha is situat'd upon the eastern shore of the Red Sea, but a few leagues within the mouth of it & lies in the lattitude of 14° 10 N & long: 44° 50 E^t^.[78] On the back of the city lies a barren desert extending far to the north and south. But over it to the eastward, is reckoned about seven miles to the foot of the mountains, amongst which lay many fruitful pleasant valleys, abounding with variety of choice fruits, gums &c the produce of Arabia Felix, or, Arabia the Happy, so called [*f. 24r*] because of the fruitfulness in all sorts of gums & other delicious fruits as well as the common necessaries of life. The coffee grows back in the country among the valleys & is brought down to the factory upon camels. About the town, or city of Mocha there is but little fruit grow[n], except in gardens, the chief of which is dates, though they have plenty of grapes and other choice fruits common to hot countreys sold in town. On the sixth day of the week which the Turks keep for their Sabbath, it was commonly their practice while we were there; after the governour came from the mosque or his place of worship, that the eunuchs exercise themselves upon a place before the governour's house, with their horses and spears according to the ancient custom of tilts and tournement, so much vaunted of in romance. Their manner of exercise is something after the following discription.

After the eunuchs are mounted upon their horses which are very nimble & active as well as their riders, having long spears in their hands, after prancing about the ground for sometime (the drums beating) the meanwhile; or hollow pieces of wood with skins nail'd over them imitating drums, the sound of which is rather doleful than musical. The foot soldiers are also drawn up with their match locks; two of the eunuchs on horse back single out themselves, like a challenge, the others making way for them; who gallop after one another in *a* circular course so that the pursued can always have his eye upon the pursuer. So that when he makes an offer to beare his lance, the pursued to avoid it, suddenly (though almost full speed) turn short round the otherway: at which they are very dexterous. Thus they keep pursuing one another; till he that is the pursuer gets an opportunity to cast in his lance, then he let it fall & a boy run and receive it. They also show other acts of dexterity on horsemanship, such as throwing a lance before them

[78] The mariner Edward Barlow provides another account of Al Mukhā in recalling his visit in 1697: E. Barlow, *Barlow's Journal of His Life at Sea in King's Ships, East & West Indiaman & other Merchantmen from 1659 to 1703*, ed. B. Lubbock (2 vols., 1934), ii, pp. 478–87.

when riding almost full speed, & catching it before it fall to the [*f. 24v*] ground with several other performances of the same kind, which, I cannot now particularize, by reason of the length of time since I was there. Howsoever they *are* extraordinary managers of horses, & also their horses are very beautiful in shape; & swift in running. I remember while we were there the principal officer of the customs, who sat at the gate to examine what goes in or out, was an English man turn'd Turk, which I have been told happened after the following manner.

He was butcher he [*sic*] of an English Indiaman & being on shore to kill for the factory, one of the mates of the ship entrusted him with goods to sell for him; which money instead of restoring to the owner; he spent & made away with on shore; upon which he was taken prisoner and confined under a guard at the factory, where they generaly keep soldiers sent on purpose from Bombay to guard the factory. & that they may appear the more respectable in the eyes of the Arabians, there is generaly one or two armed grabs,[79] with the second in command from the before mentioned place; which lay there till the European ship is loaden. It happened one day when the gentlemen belonging to the factory, were making a tour into the country for their diversion; which is custom*ry* for them to do, perhaps once or twice while the ship is loading. And what is remarkable, though there is so many fine horses in their country yet they will not let any but their own religion ride upon them in their country, but the gentlemen oblig'd when they make such a tour, all of them to mount upon asses, however great their station may be, which yields matter of laughter, sometimes to see them with their fine laced cloaths thus poorly mounted.

It was at such a time as is above mentioned, when the factory was left only with a *few* servants and soldiers, that <that> this man who was a prisoner, took [*f. 25r*] an opportunity to make his escape in the following manner. He seeing the factory gate open, & few people stirring, desir'd the centry to let him go to the necessary, which he not suspecting his design, readily comply'd with as at other times. But the man was no sooner at liberty, than he took to his heels running directly out of the factory quite into a large open place before the governour's house crying out as loud as he could for Mahomet. The Arabians directly flock'd about him; & carried him into the governour's house, where he was safe from being recover'd again by the soldiers of the factory. Thus for fear of being justly punished for his demerits he turn'd Mahometan, was circumcised & sent into the country till he had learnt the language & was instructed in their manner of worship & afterwards made chief officer of the customs attending the gate. I have many times discoursed with him, & he acknowledged to me that he lived in hopes that some time or other he should get an opportunity to make

[79] A grab was a large coasting vessel, drawing very little water, built with a prow, usually two-masted and most common in eastern waters: *OED*.

his escape from amongst them yet that to me seem'd not very probable as no European ship would chuse to take him away, making an advantage of his present situation; as by his means they got things ashore without pay[ing] duty, especially private ventures; for when the officers had anything to get ashore, they first would speak to him, & he would appoint the time he should be at the gate himself. So that when we carried any thing ashore, the other custom officers at the gate would carry unto him, who would just examine it, asking us who it belong to & so dismiss us, telling his partners it was something for the factory. & when he came to the factory the officers & supercargos[80] would give him wine to drink, which he would take a large draught of to the great surprise of the other Arabians, who would look on him with astonishment; being a thing strictly forbidden by the law of Mahomet.[81] But this man being greatly addicted to drunkeness [*f. 25v*] and other bad practices before he turn'd Mahometan, the virtue of his new religion, had not influence enough over him to better his morality. He told *me* he had three wives, a custom allowed amongst the Mahometans.

There was also a Dutchman who had turn Turk, by business I think a taylor. Him I saw several times but *not* understanding the Dutch language had no converse with him. I think he also told *me* there were one or two English men who lived up the country that had embraced that religion. For as I was told was the custom; when a Christian turn Turk, to keep him two or three years, from conversing with Christians; untill he has learned their language & is well established in their doctrine. While we lay here I saw some of the inhabitants from the western side of the Red Sea call'd Ethiopians, come over in their canoes to trade with the Arabians; some of them appear'd to me, to be of as deep & shining a black as some Japan work. We also catch'd the largest shark here, that as far as I can remember I ever saw any where: being tow'd or decoy'd along side by one of the Arabian cannoes employed twice a week to catch fish for the ship's company. The fishermen having catch'd a large fish; this over siz'd shark rise & swallowed it & the poor man being loth to loose his line kept playing with it while his partner paddl'd a long side the ship, upon which we slipped a rope with a running bowlin knot[82] down upon the fishing line, till we got it over the body of the shark & then hoist him on board, the carpenter standing upon the gunnel[83] ready with his broad axe to cut of[f] the tail, least he

[80] A supercargo was an officer whose business on board a merchant ship is to superintend the cargo and commercial dealings of the voyage, or an agent who superintended a merchant's business in a foreign country: *OED*.

[81] Britons who crossed over to live in non-Europenan societies often suffered from 'schizophrenia and isolation', as they gave up their old identity but were not fully accepted in their new one: Colley, *Captives*, p. 327.

[82] A bowline knot was made by an involution of the end and a bight upon the standing part of a rope. It did not slip or jam and could be cast loose instantly: *IMD*.

[83] A gunnel or gunwale was the upper edge of a vessel's side: *IMD*.

might damage the deck. After his jawbones were taken out & dry'd, they would slip over a stout man cloaths & all which considering how much they shrink in drying shews his enormous size. It is customary here also for the young women to go into the sea & swim. Another odd custom they have also here, that is in a morning to come down to the [*f. 26r*] sea side (so that the shore is lined with them) every one bring a little earthen dish with them, or something of that kind. This they dip into the sea & after having eased themselves wash their backsides: an eastern custom differing from Europeans.

Before I leave this place, it may not be amiss just to observe <that> that the great & allusive Being whose works are all established in wisdom & goodness, that he might *be* glorified & admired by the workmanship of his hands, has so ordered in his wisdom that the wind blow one half year up the Red Sea, & the other half year down, changing at a fixt time; seldom sooner or exceeding the time many days. This gives the ships from India bound up the Red Sea an opportunity of making their passage up the Red Sea while *the* wind is fair up & a passage down again when the wind shift, which they would not do if it was not for the shift of wind, the currant generaly setting with the wind. I saw some Arabian vessels building there, which are generaly sewn together with line made with cocoa nuthusks or strong grass or leaves of trees. Upon the quarters of some of them have shields & spears hung to make them appear the more formidable to their enemies; besides a small piece of cannon or two mounted.

While we lay here we buryed some of our hands, though this is not reckoned so healthfull a place as some, the water of the town being but brackish, & the place very hot. But the dews in the night though very great do not seem to be prejudicial, as in some places, for we generaly lodg'd upon deck for coolness & often lay uncover'd till wet with dew, yet I do not remember any of us receiv'd hurt there from. Some times in the night when the wind blew off the Arabian shore, it would come with such hot blasts fit almost to scald the face, the particles of air being so extraordinary heated by passing over the scorching sands of the desert which extends itself both ways as far as the eye can discern parallel with the Red Sea, making an horizon with the sky like the sea. But opposite to the city or town of Mocha it is counted but about seven miles to the foot of the mountains, where there is a well of good fresh water from which our factory was supplied by [*f. 26v*] camels. This well is called Moses Well, but from what reason or cause I know not, for tis some hundreds of miles higher up where the Children of Israel passed over.

Many have been the conjectures why this sea is called red, the water when taken up in a bucket is of the same colour as other water. Some has supposed it has appear'd so in some places from the reflection of some redish mountains. Other which seemes the most probable that it is occasion'd from a red sand at the bottom & coral rocks of which this sea is known to abound higher up where the water is shoaler.[84] The reflection of these at the bottom may very likely cause the water to appear redish to the eye. Howsoever what ever might be the cause of the first nomination; this we know that it is very ancient, from the scriptures.

About the latter part of the month call'd July or the beginning of that called August, having completed our cargoe & hired an Arabian vessel, which our supercargo loaded with rich gums, (I think the chief supercargos name was Wallis,) and some other things, also an Arabian horse which was made a present of by the governor, sailed for Bombay, which is situated in the lattitude of 19° 18 north & 73° 06 east longitude. I think we were about two weeks on our passage from Mocha to Bombay. Nothing that I remember happened remarkable excepting when we drew near the coast of Malabar we saw a great number of water snakes, a little before we came into soundings,[85] if I remember right.

After we arrived at Bombay island, we anchor'd in a large bay not far from the town and fort. The governor of this place is reckon'd the head governour belonging to *the* company, & has his residence in the fort which is strong & well built, the greatest part of the inhabitants setting aside the gar*r*ison are of that country. But the most reputable are the Gentu[86] merchants who are of a palish yellow complexion, & very faithfull & just in their dealings & are reported to hold some of [*f. 27r*] principles of Pathagoras, or the transmigration of the soul departed out of one body into another. For which reason tis reported they chuse not *to* take away the life of any thing least they should dislodge the soul of some of their friends or relations. Amongst the India black women there is some very beautiful, & well featured, & of an easy agreeable shape & gracefull carriage; their being nothing but the colour between them & compleat beauties. They most of them wear rings upon their arms & ankles, which according to their ability is either gold, silver, brass, white metal or horn, though here they do not wear nose jewels, as the women do in Arabia. At this place they build grabs & calivats[87] which are fitted out as vessels of war for the protection of the Companies trade, manned with Europeans & lascars that is country or black sailors, who generally do the working part of the vessel, & the Europeans the fighting part.

[84] A shoal was a place where water was of little depth, a shallow, a sand bank or a bar. Often exposed at low tide, it constituted a danger to navigation: *IMD* and *OED*.

[85] Sounding was to measure the depth of water by means of a lead line, particularly important when approaching a coastline: *IMD*.

[86] The most common term for Hindu among English travellers at this time remained Gentoo. Like many of his fellows, Secker reported a favourable impression of Hindu merchants on the Indian coast: P. J. Marshall and G. Williams, *The Great Map of Mankind: British Perceptions of the World in the Age of Enlightenment* (1982), pp. 19–20.

[87] A calivat or gallivat was a large boat used in the Eastern seas, having a triangular sail as well as oars: *OED*.

In those days there was a powerful pirate who lived upon the coarse [*sic*] call'd Angria whose grabs were very troublesome to the trading vessels that passed by upon the coast, but he is since destroyed. During the time we lay at Bombay one of our people met with a sad accident which happenned after the following manner. Our people having made a float, to scrub the ships the ship's [*sic*] bottom; after they had done, several of them got into the float to dress themselves. But one young fellow having a mind to swim a little more, went in again & swum round the ship to the other side, when taking hold of the entering rope in his hands & setting one foot against the side of the ship, as he was raising himself out of the water a shark came up & bit away his buttock; the poor young *man* feeling the shark take hold, in the fright pulled himself up in such hast[e], that the flesh broke out from the teeth of the shark, & hung down in large jagged lumps which were obliged to be cut off. He just got upon the quarter deck with the blood streaming from him where he fell [*f. 27v*] down, & the doctor was immediately called to his asistance who was obliged to cut away those jagged pieces of flesh which broke away from the shark's teeth. It was very dubious for some time whither *he* would recover or no, our doctor being afraid least that part call'd the popes eye was hurt. Howsoever he lived & before before [*sic*] we got home it was healed all to a small place, but he went a little haulting. I think I remember to have seen coaches drawn at this place by buffaloes, though it is also common for the gentry to be carried in palikeens,[88] or when carrying a large umbrello upon a staff which is held over their head, to keep the sun off them.

About the beginning of the month call'd September *we* left the island of Bombay, having one of the grabs for our convoy till we got past that part of the coast where Angria lived. The first place we touched at upon the Malabar coast after we left Bombay, was a factory belonging to us called Tillicherry, which lies in about 11° 42 north & 75° 25 east longitude. Our stay here was very short. I did not go on shore. The next place we touched at was Cochin a Dutch factory, which lies in about 9° 54 N° & 75° 55 east long. This seems to be a very good factory having a river & bar going in. A handsome town, with drawbridges & the river brought into the town for the conveniency of water carriage, after their way in Holland. At this time we were told they were building some vessels here, which were to be join'd by some vessels from Batavia, to go on an expedition against Angria who had taken some Dutch ships. From the place we sailed for Anjanga an English factory & the last on the Malabar coast, lying in the latt: of 8° 29 N° & 76° 25 east. The Companies fort & factory here, was reckoned to be a very compleat one. Here we staid but a few days, & then sailed for the Cape of Good Hope, leaving the Malabar coast about [*f. 28r*] the beginning of the month

[88] Palikeens or palankeen were covered litters or conveyances, usually for one person, used in India and other eastern countries, consisting of a large box with wooden shutters like Venetian blinds carried by four or six men by means of poles projecting before and behind: *OED*.

call'd October. I do not remember we met with any thing very remarkable in our passage excepting seeing several islands as Diego Roys, & Mauritius till we fell in with the coast of Africa not far from the Cape when we saw a large ship standing directly for us, under French colours, which gave us an apprehension that there might be a French war, having heard in India that it was expected, upon which, we hoist out our longboats, clear'd ship & prepared for defence. But being *an* healthy well manned ship everything was done with such dispatch it gave a show of our being a ship of force, and well mann'd. Which the Frenchman seeing, altered his course again & did not come nigh us to speak us. Our longboat being hoist out on the occasion, we towed her at our stern around the Cape into the harbour. And at that time being one of the longboats' crew, & my turn to be boat keeper, was order[ed] into the boat at first hoisting out: and was tow'd in her round the Cape into the bay or harbour of the Cape so that I could say truly I came round Cape Bona Esperance in a long boat.

We arrived at the Cape about the fourth of the month called January in the year 1739/40, staid here about ten days to refresh ourselves and then sailed for the island of St Helena, where we arriv'd the 27th of the same month. Here we found the Companies yatch from England, which brought news of war being proclaimed against Spain. Here we received orders to wait for convoy, and till the other ships from India join'd us. On the first of the month call'd May wrote a letter home to my parents, I think by a Swedish ship which put in here while we lay here waiting for convoy, beef being scarse by reason of a great mortality amongst the catle a few years before. We apply'd ourselves to catching mackeral, which are plentifull here all the year long, are rather smaller than [*f. 28v*] ours & are very sweet & good when fresh catch'd, but if salted & kept unwholesome causing those who eat them to break out in blotches. We also catch'd some albecores[89] & congo eels to help out.

This island lyes in latt: 15° 56 so[uth]: and longitude from London 4° 10 west, is reckoned to be in circumference about twenty or one & twenty miles. It is very mountainous, but lying between the tropicks it is always summer there. They can't produce any corn they say, because of the abundenc[e] of vermin which destroy it in the ground that is mice & rats, so have bread & flour from England by the store ship, the Company sending one every year, besides what they get out of other shiping which touch there. The inhabitants are English; or of English descent. Here the Company keep a governour & soldiers, the island being strongly fortified in all accessible places, either with forts or batterys. They likewise keep watch, & when any ship or ships are discovered they make signals by hoisting a flag upon an high hill & firing a gun or guns according to the number of ships in sight.

[89] A large species of tunny fish found in the Atlantic. Several were also caught by the crew on Barlow's voyage to Rio de Janeiro in 1663: Barlow, *Barlow's Journal*, i, p. 82.

Though the inhabitants can't raise any wheat, they raise cattle & fowls which they sell for necessaries to the garrison & shipping. They also grow a sort of yam or aderoot[90] which they eat with fish & flesh instead of bread. Of this root our ship's company eat to spare our bread. While we lay two of our passengers which we brought from India who had been soldiers in the Companies service dyed of the flux. It is customary here for the women who live back in the island when they come down to the garrison, whether it be to their place of worship, or upon other business; (being accustomed to go barefoot) to bring their shoes & stockens with them till near the town, & then sit down & put them on to enter the town with, being very curious of them as the stockens are perhaps either silk or fine cotton & the shoes fine sundry things more for shew than service. [*f. 29r*]

About the tenth of the month called July we sailed from the island of St Helena for England being in all fourteen sail, twelve sail of East India men, and two men of war *to* convoy us. We arrived in the Downs[91] the 15th of the month called September where the crews of most of the ships, as well as ours went ashore and left their ships on account of the press, traveling up to Lond[o]n by land. And by keeping in large companies most of them got up safe, amongst which number myself was one. But the Company of Directors stopped 40 shillings a man out of our wages for arms taken out of the ships & men hired to go up in our roomes. The 19th wrote home from London.

About the beginning of the month called October I again ship'd myself in the companies service for the Cape of Good Hope & St Helena in their yatch command*ed* by one Captain Stuart[92] at 45 – 6 per month. Wrote home the 4th upon to aquaint my parents with what I had done. Sail'd shortly after *to* Gravesend. From thence to the Downs & Portsmouth and the 12th dated a letter from thence to my parents; & on the 19th received an answere. On the 21st wrote again home. Shortly after this, we sailed from Spithead, in company with a very large fleet of men of war & transports, as well as merchant ships, who took the advantage to sail with the fleet; which was commanded by Sir Chaloner Ogle[93] going on an expedition against

90 A starchy, tuberous root cultivated for food in tropical and sub-tropical countries, where it takes the place of the potato: *OED*.

91 The Downs were an area of sea off the east coast of Kent between the North and South Foreland. They were a favoured anchorage in heavy weather and a gathering place for merchant ships en route to London.

92 Gabriel Steward the younger commanded the East India Yacht in 1740–1741, his first voyage for the company. He remained in the company's service until 1765: Farrington, *A Biographical Index of East India Company Maritime Service Officers*, p. 748.

93 Ogle won fame for his destruction of the pirate Bartholomew Roberts at Cape Lopez in 1722. Secker's remarks concerning the size of Ogle's fleet in October 1740 are quite pertinent: it numbered over thirty warships, including an expeditionary force of 8,000 soldiers: J. K. Laughton and revised by R. Harding, 'Sir Chaloner Ogle (1680/81–1750)', *Oxford DNB*.

Cartagena[94] in the Spanish West Indies. This was the largest fleet I ever saw together.[95] The sea appearing as if it was covered with ships not being able from the center of the fleet, to see to the extreames any way. We being a small vessel generaly kept under the admiral's stern and was taken little notice of. We accompanied the fleet until we arrived in the Bay of Biscay where a violent gale of wind separated us & most of the fleet: so that we saw but now & then a stragling ship afterwards.[96] The gale being over, we made the best of our way to the southward, and about the latter part of the month called November, we crossed the line.

And on the second of the month December fell in with Commodore Anson's squadron bound for the South Seas.[97] But not being certain at that time it was them, [*f. 29v*] and they as uncertain who we were, supposing us to have been a vessel dispatched on purpose by the Spaniards to carry the news of their intended expedition into the South Seas that they might be upon their guard in those parts. Therefore the commodore thought that the taking of us would be of great importance to their farther proceedings; by stopping the intelligence from getting there before them. Accordingly after they discover'd us which *was* a little after sun riseing in the morning, they immediately gave chase. We being to leeward[98] of them, saw them in the morning first before the sun rise. Being washing our decks, a lad that was handing water along said several times that their was clouds away with the sun riseing appeared just like rocks. Though I heard him I took little notice, knowing it to be customary in those climates just before the sun riseth & after the sun setteth to see the clouds form various representations, such as ships, towns, castles, islands & some time admirable to behold. Howsoever at length hearing him repeat it over so often I asked him where abouts it was; & as soon as I had cast my eye that way saw they were ships, & going up the shrouds told five sail in sight, upon which the captain was aquainted with; who coming

[94] Cartagena is now in Colombia.

[95] The East India Yacht's log book entry for 26 October 1740 confirms Secker's remembrance, recording that they departed in 'Company with Sir Chaloner Ogle and the Fleet in Number ab[ou]t 180 or 190 saill': BL, Asia, Pacific and Africa Collections, IOR/L/MAR/B/645B.

[96] The log book records they lost sight of the fleet on 2 November and that straggling ships were sighted on 5 and 8 November: BL, Asia, Pacific and Africa Collections, IOR/L/MAR/B/645B.

[97] Anson led a squadron ordered to raid and plunder Spanish interests on the Pacific coast of south America. His seven ships set sail on 18 September 1740, rounding Cape Horn in March-April 1741, exactly nine years before Secker did so. Although Anson's force suffered grievous losses, they burned Paita and captured a Spanish treasure ship. Returning across the Pacific, Anson was given a hero's welcome in London in June 1744. Anson's navigation and seamanship did much to inspire Secker: N. A. M. Rodger, 'George Anson (1697–1762)', *Oxford DNB.*

[98] Leeward was the side turned away from the wind, or sheltered from it, as opposed to windward: *IMD.*

upon deck was in a great consternation imagining them to be a squadron of Spanish or French men of war sent after Commodore Anson, & not the commodore himself as he had sailed from Spithead better than a month before us. They were about three or four leagues distant & about half an hour after sun rise we saw a smoke rise, as a signal for chase, & according we saw them all bear away after us. And we also supposing them to be an enemy bore away also, making what sail we could from them. The wind blowing fresh till about ten they gain'd upon us, till almost almost [*sic*] within gunshot, but the wind dying away towards the height of the day, we in our turn run from them our sails being [*f. 30r*] lighter & more suitable for light breezes than their heavy sails. Besides we had another great advantage over them we having but one mast & keeping right before the wind most of our sails were of service, while they being three mast ships, the sails only upon one mast would be of service. We had got the dispatches for the homeward bound India men with all letters on board done up in a sheet of lead ready for sinking, if they had come up with us. But our outrunning them put a stop to our fears. Howsoever it was a fatiguing troublesome day to us. We keeping almost constantly heaving water upon our sails to make them hold the more wind. About sunset the nearest ship was about two leagues distant I think from us, when they gave over the chase & lay too to wait for their company being seven sail in all: five men of war & two transports. We kept still running before the wind till near midnight where we down with our steering sails & hauled upon a wind.

Next day we saw nothing of the fleet. But at day break the day following we were gotten near the fleet again upon which we bore away right before the wind as before and by the wind dying away towards the height of the day from the heat of the sun, had the same advantage over them as before. And at sunset the headmost ships brought too for the rest for fear of separation. & we as soon as the night came on that we lost sight of them hauled upon a wind, least we should be served as before but we saw them no more. Our captain could not be persuade*d* but they were French men of war, and I as positive that they were Commodore Anson's squadron.[99]

We being now got clear made the best of our way for the Cape of Good Hope where we arrived about the fourth of the month called Jan[uar]y 1740/1. It being a little after harvest, fruits of all kinds being now ripe & in perfection. Their seasons being opposite to ours, they being on the south

[99] The log book of the East India Yacht and the official account of Anson's voyage both confirm Secker's remarks. Captain Steward's log recorded on 4 December 'I take them to be three of the 7 sail of French ships which we saw yesterday', while Anson's account states that his squadron chased the Yacht on 2 and 3 December: 'We were much chagrined at the escape of this vessel, as we then apprehended her to be an advice-boat sent from *Old Spain* to *Buenos Ayres*, with notice of our expedition. But we have since learnt, that we were deceived in this conjecture, and that it was our *East-India* Company's Packet bound to St. *Helena*.' BL, Asia, Pacific and Africa Collections, IOR/L/MAR/B/645B; R. Walter and B. Robins, *A Voyage round the World in the Years MDCCXL, I, II, II, IV, by George Anson*, ed. G. Williams (1974), p. 50.

side of the sun as we are on the North and Every day at noon the Sun is due north, as it is with us due south. At our arrival when the captain went ashore to the governour; I went with him to carry his commission. When the [*f. 30v*] captain told the governour by an interpreter of the squadron which had chased us in our passage to the Cape adding that he supposed they were French going to take the island of St. Helena. But the governour seemed to be of an other opinion and rather laught at his conjecture, not thinking it probable.

We lay here about two weeks, and I generaly steered the boat if no officer was in the boat who chose to doe it himself. While we lay here at anchor in the bay I met with the following accident and remarkable deliverance. Going ashore one day with our chief mate, who now officiated as captain, I think it was after we had dined on board being on shore we went to a wine house & got a bottle or two of wine amongst us, which made us full of spirits, though not drunk, the mate staying till within evening before he came to us to go off. The wind while we were onshore had increased, so as to blow extreamly hard, pouring down between the Table Land & Lion's Rump (two mountains so called) in such strong flows, as made it very unsafe for any boat to go off to the shiping. For which reason a Dutch vessel that was called the Commodore had struck her flagg as a signal for all boats on shore to remain there. But our mate coming down in hast, & we being all in high spirits got into the boat, which lying under the shelter of an high wharf; we felt but little of the wind; and we with as little consideration hoisted out whole sail, being a spritsail,[100] & being Englishmen paid no regard to the Dutch Commodore's signal but put off with our whole sail. After we got clare of the wharf we soon began to feel the strength of the wind but going before it for some time we did pretty well, the mate steer'd and I set by him having the sheat of the sail in my hand ready to let go if I saw need.

It was within evening & I think bright starr light in running off we passed under the Dutch Commodore's stern their people flocked to the stern to see us pass, no dought thinking we were either mad or drunk. The boat almost flying through the water after we had run some distance past the Dutch vessel I felt one of those violent flows of wind come down upon us, & finding the boat could not bear it, let fly the sheat. But the mate [*f. 31r*] instead of keeping the boat still right before the wind very imprudently in the strength of the flow, luff'd her up to the wind, which was so violent as it over sett the boat immediately. I finding the boat a going, gave a spring that I might not be whelped under the boat, and swam directly for our ship but having my clothes on, & also a thick pair of duck trowsers[101] on with cutlery ware in

[100] The spritsail was a quadrilateral sail extended by a spar reaching diagonally from the mast to the upper aftercorner of the sail: *IMD*.

[101] Duck trousers were made from a strong untwilled linen or cotton fabric, lighter and finer than canvas, often used for small sails and sailor's outer clothing: *OED*.

my pockets which I had carried ashore to sell but did not. The water being soak'd through my cloths & my pockets also full, I found I began to swim heavy. The sea also running high & breaking very much, the vessel still at a considerable distance from me made <me> *me* begin to fear I could not hold out till I got along side her. I also hearing the other people I had left calling one to another to get upon the boats thought it would be but for me to return & get upon the boat also. I accordingly swam back again towards the boat with that design, but when I came within a little distance of the boat, I chanced to swim right upon one who was drownding, & he feeling me catched fast hold about my neck with such a grasp as I could no way break loose his hold. While I was strugling to get clear of him it came very fresh into my mind that if I sunk down under water he would be obliged to loose his hold to get breath.

Accordingly I left of swiming & kept sinking down, striving at the same time with all my might to break his hold but in vain. And not being able to hold my breath any longer, was obliged to strike with all my might to get up to the surface again, & was almost gone when I obtained it, having swallowed a deal of salt water & was almost spent. But after treading water sometime & geting a little wind, he still hanging fast about my neck with his chin close to my chin so that when I got breath, he got breath also. Though then I knew not whether he was dead or alive not being able to speak to him. But was now sensible that I must either swim with him thus hanging under my belly till I got at the boat, or both perish together. But his hanging in that position was such a disadvantage to my swimming [*f. 31v*] that I could not swim above three or four strokes before I was obliged to tread water to get breath, he keeping my head continually under water while swimming. I also while treading water, directed myself a fresh for the boat and so in that manner by degrees, through the asistance of Providence I got to the side of the boat, where those upon the side of the boat asisted us, and helped him who was not so far spent as myself upon the side of the boat; and I also got on myself with their help.

After I was on I strip'd off my cloths & threw away least I should be obliged to take to swimming again. Those upon the boat's side who were able kept calling or hallowing out with united voices as loud as they could betwixt the seas which at times broke over our heads. Which voice reached our own vessel & put them in a great fright & confusion, not knowing what to do as they had no boat to asist us, but began to fire off guns in great disorder which alarmed an English India man who lay further out in the bay. They thinking there was a mutiny on board us double manned their longboat taking arms with them in order to quell it. But after they got on boards us with much difficulty the wind blowing so hard, they found it another matter and put off again to asist us but before they could get to us we were taken up by the Dutch Commodore's boat who hearing the guns firing, judged what the reason was & manned their launch & came & took us all up, not one being drownded, which was a very perticular & wonderfull mercy. As we were so long in that distressed condition in the night, and so much wind & sea, and besides him I saved, who being all the time about the masthead, & was a means through the orderings of providence to preserve the rest by balancing the boat upon her sides which otherwise might have rightened & threw them off; & he on the other hand by their weight on the side of the boat just kept the end of the mast out of the water, & his head just above so as to get his wind between the waves which generally broke over us all.

After we were carried [*f. 32r*] on board though I was in the worst condition of them all or had suffer'd most by taking in *a* deal of salt water & fatigue. Yet by taking some comfortable things & being putt to bed soon recover'd again, being then in the very strength & vigour of my age. After I recover'd in telling the young man whose life I was instrumental in saving, that had he laid hold of the wais[t]band of my trowsers, or almost any where but where he did how easy I could have swum with him to the boat. His answer was he thought of it but that if he had I should have unbuttoned my trowsers and swum out of them, letting him and them go to the devil. A very light & vain impression after so great a deliverance. Howsoever, I was sincerely glad that I was a means of saving his life. He was rather younger than myself. This very remarkable deliverance from death at a time I was so little prepared for it ought to engage a gratefull acknowledgement to the author of my life as long as I have a being. He alone being worthy of praise who delights not in the death of a poor sinner.

After staying here about two weeks, we took on board about twenty cape sheep[102] and sailed for the island of St. Helena, leaving Captain Stewart behind us. After our arrival at the island, provisions being scarc[e], the governour formed a project with the captain (now Galloway)[103] of sending us down to the island of Ascention, to catch turtle and fish & bring up for the shiping. Accordingly after a pretty deal of dispute between the captain & us concerning the intended expedition, which being kept as a secret from us we refused to go, it being rumour'd about that we were going back again to the Cape of Good Hope, & it being then winter time. But going before the governor he assur'd us we were not going to the Cape, but would not tell us where, so sent us on board with a file of musqueteers, who also asisted us to

[102] The ship's log records this cargo on 21 January 1741 and confirms Secker's memory of Dutch ships in the bay and a fortnight's stay at the Cape: BL, Asia, Pacific and Africa Collections, IOR/L/MAR/B/645B.

[103] The log records that Steward went aboard on 22 January 1741 'in order to Dispatch the yacht for St Helena under the care of Mr Robt Kellaway'. Robert Kellaway (d.1746) was a mate in the service of the East India Company: BL, Asia, Pacific and Africa Collections, IOR/L/MAR/B/645B; Farrington, *A Biographical Index of East India Company Maritime Service Officers*, p. 437.

unmoor & we imediatly sail'd for the above mentioned island of [*f. 32v*] Ascension, which lieth about 250 leagues almost NW from St Helena in latt'd 7° 20 south & longitude 13° 5 west from London. Being arrived at Ascension, we anchor'd in a sandy bay on the NW side of the island, the SE trade blowing directly off the land notwithstanding which there is generaly a large surf upon the beach which make it some time very difficult to land. When we went first on shore, we perceived by several tokens that there had been shiping very lately gone from the island we supposed the day before we arrived, as we found the fresh track of mans feet & an herb call'd pusley drop'd by the water side so fresh as to show it had been pulled but a little while. We found fresh graves with little wooden crosses stuck at the ends: we judged them to be homeward bound French India men, who often touch at this island especially in war time. We also found places where they had cooked for their sick, & some pendants or streamers flying upon the adjacent hills.

We employed our selves while here chiefly after the following manner. In that day time we *went* in shore with our boat where we catched with hooks & lines several kind of large fish which *we* split and salted down, four or five of us were put ashore to turn turtle in the night, they only going ashore in the night to lay their eggs. The turtle here are very large, some that we catched we computed to weigh 4 or 5 hundred weight. After we had turned what we could in the night; & drew them above the reach of the surf we left them till morning & then towed them off to the ship and hoisted them on board laying them upon a platform a top of the ballast. Our manner of acting on shore was to spread our selves along upon the beach & watch their coming on shore calling to one another for assistance as we stood in need of help, the fore part of the night being the chief time [*f. 33r*] of their coming ashore. The sea running so high upon the beach, & our pulling them through the surf to the boat drownded some & very much weakened the others.[104]

While we lay here myself & two more took a tour up the island, taking each of us a gun. In traveling up the island we saw large droves or companies of goats, but very shy & not to be come at but by stratagem, they being so often shot at by the French & others that toucht here. We also saw many pieces of nets & other contrivances which had been formed to catch them. We also saw several places where they had been diging to seek for water but with out success. On the plains & valleys we found a great plenty of the herb posley growing, which being a very wholesome & juicy herb the goats can very well subsist upon it without water, here being none to be found but in the rainy season. We saw abundance of sea fowl, and some of them so bold

[104] East India Company vessels were pausing at Ascension to revictual their vessels with turtles as early as 1671. Edward Barlow provides a similar account of turtle hunting on the island: Barlow, *Barlow's Journal*, i, pp. 200–1.

as to strike at our hats & other so tame upon their nest that when we approached them, instead of flying away, would pick at us till we got hold of them. In ascending a large mountain which is situated about the middle of the island, the top of which mountain is often seen above the clouds, being about two thirds up *more* we came to a precipice, above which there was a flat. When clim[b]ing up we saw several goats feeding within gunshot, upon which drawing back again undiscover'd my self & another got ready to fire at one, both taking aim at the same goat, firing as near as we could together. The ball from my gun stroke the ground just under its breast, but the carpenter's ball pass'd through the neck, upon which it kept rising & falling, not being able to run away, so that we got it, being a young one full grown and eat extraordinary well.

After we had kill'd our goat & taken out the innards, we left it and proceeded up to the top of the mountain, where we found a small cross erected, being if I remember right, the spung staff[105] of a gun stuck in the ground with something tied across. We also found a top of the mountain, & a pretty way down, by the moister of the clouds hanging about that it was covered with a long thick wirery grass, whereas the other parts of the mountain & island appear'd as if burnt up with fire [*f. 33v*] through the scorching heat of the sun. Except where the posley grow, as is before observed, there is scarse a green thing to be seen. I saw neither bush, shrub, nor tree; yet some of our people vouched they saw one or two small trees or bushes in some part of the island where they went. We having taken a view of the south side of the island from the top of the mountain & saw many flocks of goats feeding on different hills, we descended again, & took up our goat, carr[y]ing it by turns. The persons in company with me were the doctor & carpenter.

In descending the mountain we went down a valley which seem'd to be the direct nighest way to our ship. After we had gotten down some way the doctor, spying some goats feeding upon the side of a hill at some distance, left the carpenter & myself to try if he could shoot one & after some time, hearing the report of his gun the carpenter also left *me* to go & see if the doctor had shot any thing. Now being left alone I was almost accoutred in the *same manner* as is represented in the feigned story of Roberson Crusoe,[106] I having a gun, a goat, & a gallon cagg[107] with some punch in it, to carry & a difficult steep valley to descend, with some troublesome & steep precipices, where I was obliged to let my goat & things slide down & then seek out a place for myself to get down, which sometimes was both difficult and dangerous, & then return & take up my accoutrements again. In that manner descending the valley till about half down or better, when looking forwards I saw a great number of fowls in a flatish place below me,

[105] A spung staff was a kind of mob or swab, often made of sheepskin, for cleansing a cannon-bore after firing: *OED*.

[106] D. Defoe, *The Adventures of Robinson Crusoe* (1719).

[107] A cag was a small cask: *OED*.

right in my way down the valley, which being come at to my great surprize found two large basons of water where the *fowls* I saw had been drinking & washing. The discovery of this seemed the more strange to me, as it was generaly reported there was no fresh water to be found upon the island.[108] I was so elevated with their discovery that I fired off my gun in hopes that either the doctor or carpenter would hear the report & come to me that they might be eye witnesses, but they being out of sight & at some distance did not hear.

In examining the two places, I concluded that one might hold about an hogshead[109] & the other about a barrel and contained water from one rainy season to an other, these basons being worn or gulled out by the impetuous force of the water rushing down the valley in the rainy seasons & length of time & did not proceed from any spring they being one above another. The upper one when [*f. 34r*] full discharge into the lower one, & being partly shaded by the high mountain which lies on the southeast side of the valley, so that the scorching rays of the sun actes but part of the day in exhalation upon them. They remain all the dry season till rain come again to fill them up. But a man might perish with thirst in seeking for them before he found them, unless accidentaly led to them as I was. Yet I was not the first discovered of them, for I found lying by the side of the largest a tally of wood with a persons name cutt upon it and the date of the year, which if I remember right was the same year we was there viz 1740. This I took along with me; also emptied my cagg, by drink what I chose & pouring out the rest, & filled it with water that it might be a token of the truth of my assertion, which otherwise might not be so easily credited, as we seemed all to be prepossessed with an opinion from the report of others that there was no fresh water to be found as many had searched for it without success. I having filled my cagg with water took up my goat & gun again, & proceeded down the valley being much elated with my discovery.

When I came upon the plain near the waterside I joinned my companions & we went on board with our goat in the evening, being much fatigued with our day's perambulation about the island. In all our travel saw neither tree, bush nor shrub though some of our people said they meet with one or two trees or bushes in one part of the island where they rambled too, in hunting after the goats as is before mentioned. We having finished our business at this island, sailed with our fish & turtle for the island of St Helena, which lay directly to windward to get back to the island. But I think we were upon this expedition in the whole about five or six week & all to no purpose, the turtle all dying before we got there & the salted fish we carried there upon

[108] Edward Barlow noted of his visit to Ascension in 1671 that 'there is no fresh water upon it', except 'where some rain-water doth stand, which runneth off the higher land when it raineth': Barlow, *Barlow's Journal*, i, p. 201.

[109] A hogshead was a cask of capacity, varying according to the contents and locality: *OED*.

examination stunk for want of proper management. The 11th of the month called May 1741 wrote home.

We sailed for England with the fleet in the month called July and arrived safe at London in the yatch about the beginning of the month called October and wrote home to my parents the 3d of said month and about the 18th or 20th took the stage coach for Norwich, & [*f. 34v*] from thence went to Southrapes to see my parents after an absence of about three years.

Staid in the country this winter visiting my friends and relations. And in the spring 1741/2 went to Wells & sailed several voyages with my cousin Thomas Parsons in the Hull trade. Towards the latter part of this summer 1742, my uncle John Sparshall of Worsted & Richard Wright of Buxton his partner bought a vessel of one John Worsted of Yarmouth, and put me in master. In such station I continued using the Rotterdam, Amsterdam, London, & New Castle trades till the year 1744. When in the six month taking in a cargoe of coals[110] for Ostend at Newcastle, in my passage to that port from Yarmouth roades I was taken by a cutter[111] privateer[112] belonging to Dunkirk[113] & carried into that port, about the 20th of said month commonly called June, I being then about 28 years of age. About the fifteen of this month also my dear father departed this life in about the sixty second year of his age,[114] I having seen a token of his death about two weeks before his decease when at home before I went on this voyage in which I was taken.

Being carried into Dunkirk, I and my people were put into the common prison, but I myself soon agreed with the master of the prison for so much a week, so did not live on the king's provisions; being enabled to maintain myself, as I had the good luck to save my watch and money, in a very particular manner which I may just mention. We having defended ourselves for some time with small arms during a running fight of several hours, my mate and some of my men forsaking me, our firing almost ceasing, the privateer run up along side and boarded us. One of their men coming to me with his pistol cock'd held it to my breast & demanded my watch, but I telling him it was below. He I suppose not understanding me, went away, and I hurried into the boat & carried on board the privateer having my watch & money

[110] Peter Earle has claimed that the coal trade on the east coast of Britain was the largest single employer of English sailors in this period: Earle, *Sailors*, p. 6.

[111] A cutter was a one mast rig with gaff mainsail, stay foresail, jib and topsail, running or reefing bowsprit, and long housing topmast: *IMD*.

[112] A privateer was an armed vessel privately owned, controlled and officered, that was commissioned by a belligerent state to commit hostile acts against enemy shipping: *IMD*.

[113] Dunkirk privateers operated mostly in the North Sea, capturing coasters and fishing vessels. From 1744 to 1748, 137 vessels were captured and taken to Dunkirk: Crowhurst, *The Defence of British Trade*, pp. 25–6.

[114] Isaac Secker died at Southrepps on 7 June 1744: NRO, MF/RO 320/6, Registers of the Norfolk and Norwich Quarterly Meeting, SF 44 Burials, Book 1010, p. 166.

on board my own vessel, we running into Dunkirk road. Next day I told the captain if he would let me go on board my vessel again I would show him what things belong to me, which is the captain of the privateers own properly. He accordingly took me on board with him. We had no sooner entered the cabin but luckily for me the people on board who had made free with my liquors began to quarrel and fight over our heads, upon which the captain runninge up to apace them left me alone, though but for a little space. Yet I was not [*f. 35r*] idle having such an opportunity put into my hands but immediately went to the draw where my money lay & took it out, putting it into my trowser pocket, also my watch, which was gone down and had hung in a case in my cabin unobserv'd till now. This also put in my trowsers' pocket to accompany my money. Having now gained the point for which I had solicited so much to go on board turned myself to one of the lockers & began to search for a bottle of liquor, by which time the captain return'd not the least suspecting what I had done. I pulled out a cork and asked the captain to drink and told him something concerning my things, but not answering his expectation, which was to discover something hid. He soon hurried me on board the privateer from whence I was carried ashore to prison as is before related.

Not long after I was carried to prison I was conducted from thence to a perticular office where they examen prisoners concerning the cargo &c. While I was at this place under examination, I had the mortification to see one of the privateer's officers come in dressed with the best of *my* cloaths. After they had done with me I was reconducted back again to prison, where after about two weeks time I rec'd a bond of security by way of Holland for an hundred pounds for my liberty of the town. I accordingly came out of prison and lodg'd first at an English house along with some other masters who had the liberty of the town. I think I paid at this first place ten livres a week for my board & lodging, but having a mind to learn the French language I left this place & went to a creditable French house, where I paid twelve livres a week for my board & lodging. While I staid in this family I was introduced to be an instructor to Count Donay's secretary, who wanted to learn English & I wanting to learn French, it was an help to us both, & accordingly waited on him at appointed hour every day, he having providid himself with English & French grammars for that purpose. I also waited upon a captain in the army at his lodgings on the same account. Likewise went myself to a French school to learn the language so that I was not idle. Some time before I left the place I changed my quarters to a French ordinary, opposite to the nunnery of the rich dames or English ladies, there being two English nunneries the rich dames & Poor Clares.[115] At my quarters I paid but 7 or 8 livres a week.

[115] The Poor Clares were an order of nuns descending from the Franciscan order, and were founded in Italy, in 1212 by St Clare of Assisi: *EB*.

While I lodged here the father confessor of the English nuns over the way would some times send for me, when he had some other English or Irish priests come to visit him, and [*f. 35v*] would be very free in asking me many questions some times about religion & some times about politicks and I as free in answering those questions according to my judgment, which did not always please. But I being the king's prisoner was not so carefull of my words as otherways I should have been, I not intruding myself into their company, but they voluntarily sending for me to my quarters. The Pretender[116] & his party, asisted by the French were then enterprising an invasion in Scotland. I was often asked my opinion, whether I thought they might succeed or not in their attempt. I told them I believed they would not, though I believed there were many discontented people in the nation. Yet I did believe that those that were satisfied with the present family established upon the throne was much the greatest number & would be too powerfull for the malecontents though asisted from abroad. They would answer that if I knew the encouragement they had from all parts of England I should be of a different opinion. They told me they intended a liberty of conscience every where they came, supposing this would advance their cause much and gain upon the people. But I told them the English having had so much experience were not to be gull'd after that manner, well knowing that liberty would last no longer than till they were established in their own way & had got a standing army ready to suppress any opposition again*st* their proceedings or language of the same purport. Howsoever they were so confident of success that they had made promotion in the church; and this same confessor, who was born at London I think, told me he was to be Bishop of Carlile, which if it was the same man I heard afterwards he was exalted with an halter. After I had been a prisoner about three months, the secretary to Compt Donay who I asisted to pronounce & speak the English language, told me I should stay there no longer but he would get me a pass to return to my own country. Accordingly he obtain'd a private exchange of me & my cabin boy for a French captain before the cartel[117] was settled. He offer'd me the [*f. 36r*] choice whether I would go by Calais & Dover or by Flanders & Holland. I chose the latter & accordingly had a pass made for my self & boy to go by Flanders.

About the latter part of the month September left Dunkirk and went by water to Furnes;[118] from thence by land to Newport,[119] then belonging to the Queen of Hungary. After examination and staying the night, we proceeded for Ostend, walking most of the way upon the beach. I forget the

[116] The Old Pretender: E. Gregg, 'James Francis Edward Stuart (1688–1766)', *Oxford DNB*.

[117] A cartel ship was a commissioned vessel sailing under a flag of truce employed to conduct negotiations or exchange prisoners of war; a cartel ship was therefore legally immune from capture: *IMD*.

[118] Furnes or Veurne is now in Belgium.

[119] Nieuwpoort is now in Belgium.

computed distance but we left Newport in the forenoon & got there before night. Ostend was now garrisonned by the English. I think we staid about twenty four hours there to look a little about; & then took passage in a boat for Bruges where we staid several days to look about. While I staid here I went to one of their churches or chappels to see them kiss the holy blood as tis called. The manner of which is as follows.

When I came to the chappel (being accompanied with one to show me about) we ascended some steps into a sort of an entry which led into the chappel. In this entry stood several tables with wax candles lying on them for sale. In the chappel it self are many images of saints done up against the walls, and as it is customary amongst the Roman Catholickes each one to have their patron saint, so when any of them through devotion goes into this chappel to say their prayers they first buy a wax candle off the women in the entry, according to their ability; their being from a farthing upwards. Then lighting *it* at the table where the sellers keep a candle light on purpose before each of those titular saints. On the further side of *the* chappel there is a railed galery with steps up at each end, where several priests attend ready to present the holy blood to such as are inclined to sip it. That is the cup that it is kept in which seems to be partly of gold with some liquor contain'd in it much of the colour of blood. When they come at the foot of the steps which lead up to the gallery, they kneel an[d] ascend upon their knees. A priest presents the cup, they kiss the edge of it, putting some money at the same time into the priest's [*f. 36v*] hand.Thus through the craftiness of the priest the poor bigoted people are fleeced of their substance. I saw many other curiosities which I cannot now give a proper discription of.

While I stay here, part of the army came into their winter quarters, which I had also an opportunity of seeing. Having staid three or four days, we went in a scute[120] for Rotterdam. Soon after my arrival there I sent my cabin boy Stephen Abbott home to Yarmouth, staying behind my self in hopes of getting to be master of a vessel, which there seemed some prospect of at that time but it came to nothing. The 20th of the month October, I dated a letter to my Uncle Sparshall and sent by some of the shiping. In this letter I indeavour'd by expostulation to vindicate my conduct when taken by the French. After staying at Rotterdam I think *five* or six weeks, I got my passage for Yarmouth with a neighbour. Where I staid, (except now & then going into the country to see my relations) until the spring *1745* at which time I was put in master of a large snow belonging to Thos. Dawson & Willm Palmer, called the William & Thomas.

This snow being fitted out for sea, loaded with malt for Dublin & I think about the middle of the month called June we sailed, but the barr being bad

[120] Scute or scuit, a Dutch flat-bottomed river-boat: *OED*.

in getting out, we had like to have lost her, but with great difficulty & labour at last got her over the bar & into the roads. But by her striking so much she proved so leaky that we were obliged to *have* the Customhouse smack[121] accompany us to Harwich and to asist us with their people to pump. After we arrived at Harwich we laid her ashore & got her bottom caulked, finding the oakum[122] more or less started out of almost every seam. From Harwich we sailed by the flatts for the Downs but by the way had several of our hands prest by the She[e]rness man of war. In the room of which they gave us two Spittlefield weavers, who falling sick I put ashore at Deal and proceeded down the channel putting into Torbay, where we were joined by three London privateers and a north country snow bound for Dublin. The three privateers had engaged two large French privateers off Gurnsey, & lost their commodore who they brought in here to bury. They had all suffered pretty much in the engagement and, both French & English, very glad to leave one another.

After waiting here some days for a wind [*f. 37r*] we sailed in company with the three privateers who were going to the westward on a cruize, the snow bound to Dublin, with whom we agreed to keep company. And according did round the Lands End into St George's Channel, where we were separated by running from a French privateer (as we supposed) being chased by *a* vessel rigged something after the form of a Dutch hoy.[123] This vessel lay lurking under the land a little beyond the western extreamity of Mount's bay. And when we came a breast of her made sail after us, following us into St George's Channel; but the wind blowing very strong though fair, & we carrying a stiff sail, she could not come up with us, but towards night seemed to give over the chase. Yet in the night we met with another alarm, for our consort the north country snow, keeping a considerable way to the westward of us tho a breast, in the night fell in with a fleet of West India ships bound to Bristol. Which taking her to be a privateer fired at her to bring her too; but she returning the fire it caused a pretty deal of firing amongst *them*. And we being pretty near them, saw the flashes & heard the report of the guns upon which we hauled upon a wind & stood to the eastward not knowing what became of our consort till afterwards she arrived safe at Dublin. But being so long after ourselves, we supposed she had been taken. We having stood to the eastward for some time, till we had run out of sight & hearing of the ships which we then imaginned to be enemies. We tack'd & stood for the coast of Ireland, making the land next morning about

[121] A smack was a small, decked vessel with various rigs, often used for fishing or trading: *IMD*.

[122] Oakum was loosely twisted fibres obtained by untwisting and picking old hemp rope. Such fibres were often used as a caulking material to stop up the seams of wooden ships to prevent leaking: *OED*.

[123] The hoy was a small vessel, usually rigged as a sloop, employed in carrying passengers and goods on short coastal routes. Dutch hoys were usually ketch-rigged: *IMD*.

Waterford and also found our selves near a large Dutch ship bound for Dublin which we spoke with soon after. They told us they had been plunder'd off the Landsend by a French privateer, which we supposed was the same which gave chase to us. We both of us arrived same at Dublin I think the next day; but our consort did not arrive till about two weeks after, which *gave* us room to conclude she was taken. But the reason was the falling in with the land to the westward of the port of Waterford, & the wind proving contrary she could not get to the eastward.

While I lay at Dublin the small pox & spotted fever was very rife in the city & several of my people catched the small pox and after some time I fell down with a violent fever *my* self, & [*f. 37v*] was reduced so low by it as to be given over by the physician that attended me. And I fully believed myself I should dye. Yet the Lord was graciously pleased, when all hopes of life both to myself and others was given over, to raise & restore me again to health in a wonderfull manner. And though I have left a memorandum of this merciful deliverance upon record in another place, yet I shall just hint upon it here. Being reduced so low by the fever that they could not keep life in me, every little while fainting away, *one* forenoon the nurse which attended me being over fatigued with watching got the servant maid of the house where I was nursed to sitt by me, ready to raise me up when those fainting fits came, while she lay down upon the bed with her cloaths on to get a little sleep. The maid being accordingly placed upon a chair by the bedside to watch me, the nurse upon the bed asleep, one of those fainting fits coming on, the girl also by the bedside being fallen asleep, and none to assist me. I thought I died and my spirit left the body, which I saw lying dead upon the bed, but was hurried out of the room a great way; but felt a fear least it should not be well with me. After I had gone to my thinking a considerable way, an angel met me & said I should return to my body again & live, which was joyful news to me because of the before mentioned fear. Accordingly my spirit return'd, re-entered my body with a full assurance of life; as soon as my spirit had re-entered my body again I raised myself right up in the bed, which I had not strength to do before if I might have gained the whole world, shove something at the maid & woke her, & also woke the nurse upon the bed, teling her that I had been dead, &c but now I knew I should live & recover, & while I was talking to the nurse in this manner casting my eyes betwixt the fur curtains upon the head of a large chest of draws, where I saw wrote in Hebrew charac*ters*, which to that understanding then given me was as intelligible as English, that I should live from that time so many years, & so many weeks & days. I pointed to it & read it over to several times to the nurse and was sadly vext that she could not see it too, but she thought I was [*f. 38r*] out of my head, but my understanding was very clear & perfect. But the vision was wonderfull & only visible to myself. Yet the deep grounded assurance of recovery remained with me, but I soon fell into my old fainting way again and through excessive sweating the pores of my brain were so open, that they could not by sleeping doses compose me to sleep. But was almost in the state of a spirit without a body till Providence made way for my recovery which fell out in the following manner.

The next day I had a very strong desire after a drink of cold water, which the nurse was not allowed to give me. Howsoever I told the nurse that it was the custom in my country that when any body fainted they gave them cold water to drink & rubbed their temples with it. This relation prevailed with her to make a tryall with me, upon which she fetched a gorch of water from the college well, a noted place for cool water. It was brought in but a little while, before the eagerness I had to get some of it caused me to counterfit a fainting fit. Upon which the nurse fill'd a beer glass & rubbed some upon my temples, & put the glass to my mouth. Which I got fast hold of with my teeth swallowing some and spilling a part upon my breast in the struggle betwixt the nurs*e* and I, she to take it away, & I to drink it. I having got some, laid still for a while; but not being yet satisfied counterfited again and faired much in the same manner. But then was satisfied soon after falling a sleep & slept about two hours. In which time I dreamt I was in many places, & every where accompanied with two persons sprinkling cold water upon my face, & myself walked in a hoop slung round with bottles of cold water so that I thought I was so comfortably refreshed as if in paradice & what was still more remarkable, something was told me in this dream that while I could remember it, I could fall asleep when I would which staid or remained with me about two or three days, during which time I was so much refreshed & strengthened by sleeping, as to be in a fair way of recovery.

When I awoke out of sleep the poor nurse was watching by me, fearing I should never awake more and that she had killed me by giving me cold water to drink. I related to her what I had dreamt, where I could fall asleep where I would, showing her an instance of presently after, which was only to close my eyes, think upon what was told me, & I immediately fell into a sound sleep. Thus the gracious & holy one who desires not the death of a sinner made way by his providence for my recovery according to the vision. [*f. 38v*]

Having as before related, through the asistance of Providence got several days refreshment from sleeping, I began to get a strength and recover a pace, though I had still the yellow jaundice to a very great degree, nor could any thing the physician prescribed for me remove it. But my nurse hearing of a hattmaker in the city who had a family receipt for that disorder, & who cured a great many people [*but*] took nothing except a drink, according to the ability of the patient. To this person the nurse sent, carrying some of my urine. He undertook the cure & sent me a small quantity of greyish powder, which I took in a quarter or half a p[in]t of mild ale fasting. This medicine was so well adapted that the disease that generaly, in about a quarter or half an hour after it was taken, it wrought so effectually as to be felt in all parts of the body, fighting as it were against the distemper. This I took three times, & it cured me quite of that dreadfull distemper.

As the vessel had been detained a considerable *time* on my account, lying there at great expence and the people taking the advantage of having none to look after them were very irregular in their behaviour; selling several things out of the vessel. This hastenned me to get on board before I was well fit. Accordingly I sailed from Dublin for Milford Haven. I applied to Esquire Barlow for a loading of coales, but being disappointed I was obliged to go round to Tenby pier with the vessel, where after laying some time I took in a cargoe of Welch coals upon Sandersfoot beach.[124] And after clear of that place sailed for Yarmouth roads in the month called Jan[uar]y 1745/6, arriving in Yarmouth roads some time in the said month. But when we came off Lowestoft the land being covered with snow deceiv'd us in our distance. So that not hauling enough in for the land we were drawn by the tide into the mouth of a swash,[125] where we got aground, & lay for some time in danger of loosing the vessel. But the tide & sea at last forced her into the swash where she got afloat [*f. 39r*] again, and *we* run at the back of Cotton [Corton, near Yarmouth] sand into the roads. Where after we had anchor'd I went on shore, and it was concluded by the owners after some deliberation that I should go for London with my cargoe of Welch coals. Accordingly, when the wind suited I sailed & arrived at London about the begin[n]ing of the month called February. Here I lay till towards the latter part of the month called March (Welch coals being a drug.). When having discharg'd our cargoe & ballast the vessel I sailed for Yarmouth, and arrived there about the beginning of the month called Aprill *1746*. This voyage having been so long & unsuccessfull exasperated the owners so much as to turn me out of my employ (though it was not in my power to help it).

Being now out of business, & not likely to get an other vessel in town I sold off my household goods, sending some odd things into the country, & left a guinea for my dear mother. In the month called July, I went passenger down to Sunderland in hopes of getting a vessel, but was disappointed. Wrote home the first of the month called August, and shortly after got my passage for London arriving there some time in the said month. I took up my lodgings at the widow Helen Burns in Wapping, three doors below the sign of the Half Moon. The 19th of the month called September I received a letter aquainting me my sister Elizabeth Youngman's eldest *daughter* was dead. Which I answer'd the 6th of the month called October.

[124] By the early eighteenth century the coal exports of the Welsh ports in the Bristol Channel were expanding strongly: Davis, *The Rise of the English Shipping Industry*, p. 208. Saundersfoot is near Pembroke in South Wales.

[125] In this instance, a swash or swatch signifies a channel of water lying between sandbanks, or between a sandbank and the shore: *OED*.

Some time in this month shiped myself chief mate of a ship called the Noble Ann, belonging to Scarborough, Ralph Finch commander, bound to Virginia at four pounds per month.[126] We sailed from London the 4th of the month called November for the Downs, where we lay a considerable time wind bound. From thence we sailed for Spithead to wait for convoy (being wartime). On the 3d of the month called December wrote home from Spithead to my brother William Secker[127] & my dear mother taking my leave of them both, not expecting to hear from again before I sailed. We shortly after sailed in company with some other ships & a convoy for Virginia. We had I think about eight or nine weeks passage and arrived there in the month called February 1746/7 having met with nothing very remarkable in our passage, excepting the [*f. 39v*] captain, who was a fierce fi[c]ry temper, beat one of the people so much that he jumped over board, but was gotten on board again.

After we arrived at Virginia we sailed up James River as high as Warwick Town, within four or five miles of the falls. Here we took in our cargoe of tobacco. But when we were loaden or near it, the captain who was a very wicked abusive man, stroke me on some occasion which I resented so much, with his other bad behaviour, that I obliged him to discharge me & pay me my wages.

While I stayed here I went up to see the falls, which is very admirable, to see the whole river fall from steep rocks like a prodigious cascade, making a noise to be heard many miles. Being now at liberty, I passed some time away at different plantations as I went gradually down the river to get again amongst the shiping. I think it was in the month called August while I was up the freshes[128] that I saw the planters catch quantities of very fine herrings, which go up in large sholes as high as the falls to spawn. From which the inhabitants reap great benefit, several of them joining have large nets on purpose and during the season watch the sholes, & when observ'd drop the net around them in their canoes, & so drag large quantities on shore, where they are divided amongst those concerned. These they salt & keep for the winter for the use of themselves & Negroes. Towards the latter part of the

[126] Chief mates needed to be literate and competent navigators, able to take command if a mishap befell the captain. Secker's monthly wage of £4 compares favourably with the 25s per month usually allowed able seamen: Earle, *Sailors*, pp. 33, 43.

[127] William Secker (1725–1812) was born at Haveringland, co. Norfolk. Described as of Southrepps, he married Mary Allen (1716–1794), of Binham, at Wells, in 1749. He subsequently married Martha Jarvis (1738–1795) at North Walsham on 28 August 1795, and Esther Barber (1743–1818) at North Walsham on 17 February 1797. He died at Swafield on 9 October 1812, and was buried at North Walsham: NRO, MF/RO 320/6, Registers of the Norfolk and Norwich Quarterly Meeting, SF 43 Births, Book 1010, p. 70; SF 42 Marriages, Book 1000, p. 73; Book 985, p. 11; Book 1014, p. 93, SF 44 Burials, Book 988, pp. 15, 197; Book 989, p. 30.

[128] The freshes were the part of a tidal river and the lands adjoining it above the reach of the salt water: *OED*.

summer I got down to a town called Norfolk amongst the shiping. Yet before I proceed I shall just mention one thing forgotten in this place which I observed while up the freshes, where the land is fuller of woods & consequently in the summer season more hot & sultry. They being beyond the reach of the sea breezes, which blows into the bays & rivers nearer the sea, so that some times it has been so exceedingly hot & sultry that I have heard it reported the negroes have fallen down dead in the field at their work, and every thing seemed to languish. The air has been so hot & sulphureous, that the very birds have been silent. But Providence has provided a remedy for this evil. Which is, that generally after [*f. 40r*] some days of this exceeding hot weather there arises a sudden gust, or tempest which purges & purifies the air. This gust as they call it, is for the most part attended with a strong wind, violent thunder and lightning, and abundance of rain, the lightning many times split trees from the top to the bottom & as other damages, striking people & cattle dead & is exceeding terrifying especially when the sulphureous matter ejected from the cloud, with that undescribeable velocity which do the damage, is heard passing through the air, much resembling the shrill sound of a ball from a cannon. Also the violent redoubled claps of thunder seems to approach nearer & nearer as if coming down upon our heads. Yet these gusts or tempests so seldom last above half or three quarters of an hour before they are over, and then the cool & sweet refreshment of the air makes ample ameans for the former panick which the tempest caused. The creation seeming to be renewed out of its languishing to a state of rejoicing, the birds sweetly singing, & every thing extreamly pleasant & full of fragrancy.

Being got down amongst the shiping as is before mentioned, I in a short time after shipped myself chief mate of a new snow, built not far from Norfolk town, belonging to merchant John Hanbury of London. I think I was to have four pounds per month. The snow being launched & rigged, we took in a cargoe of tabacco for London and sail'd with a fleet & convoy (being war time) from Virginia about the 26th of the month called September. Our people being most of them such as had left other ships, were shipped by the run. But our captain, having concerted measures with one Captain Hunter belonging to the same owners, and the captain of the man of war very treacherously exchanged the men who had shipped themselves with us by the run for other men out of the man of war, which had been pressed out of Captain Hunter. Howsoever this unjust proceeding did not prosper, as will be observ'd in the sequel.

We were seven weeks & two day on our passage to Plymouth sound, being put in there by contrary winds, [*f. 40v*] and arrived there the 15th of the month called November, & the 16th wrote home. We sailed soon after for the Downs, and took in pilot at Margett[129] to carry us over the flatts.

[129] Margate in Kent.

But on the 2[d] of the month call'd December being *at* an anchor a little above Margett waiting for a wind to sail over the flatts, the captain having left us after the pilot came on board & was gone up in a hoy, a violent gale of wind came down upon us which drove several vessels ashore, also started our anchors so that we drove into shoaler water. And towards the latter part of the ebb our vessel stroke pretty much which scared the pilot & people to that degree that when the flood came in & floated her again they all with one voice cryed out to slip the cables & run for Margett Pier, the Pilot telling them there was water enough for us to go in. But I was very much against it, being afraid we should meet with some accident. But the clamour of the pilot & people was so great that I was oblig'd to consent, no perswasion being able to prevail; though I told them that I thought the heart of the gale was over & that I thought the sky look'd easier. But their apprehension of the vessel's bulging, if we waited another low water, was too great to be prevailed on.

Accordingly we slip'd over cables & run for Margett, but in running in the vessel took the ground, lost her steerage, & beat up against the end of the pier.[130] Where in about half an hour's time she bilged herself against the end of the pier & sunk. But we all got ashore safe upon the pier; soon after we were ashore the gale abated & became moderate. Next *day* we scuttled her and let out the water, nailed boards before the holes & daubed them up with clay. And at high water got her into the pier, having first lightened her by hawling some hogsheads of tobacco into, the pier head. But our whole cargoe was damaged, which was fit to make one think that the imprecatory wishes of the people so treacherously betray'd in Virginia had, had their effect.

Our vessel being repaired we took the tobacco on board again & proceed for [*f. 41r*] London, where we arrived about the 27th or 28th of the month called December. The 29th wrote home. We landed our tobacco at Deptford, where it was burnt to save the duty. After the vessel was discharg'd I received my wages & went and went [*sic*] to lodge at my old quarter the widow Burns in Wapping again near Union Stairs, three doors below the sign of the Half Moon.

On the 26th, called January 1747/8 wrote home again, & on the 18th of the month called February 1747/8 wrote home again to aquaint them I was ship'd chief mate of a large ship called the Duke of Cumberland, Captain Jefferson commander, bound for Leghorn[131] & Virginia at I think four pounds per month. This ship took out a letter of marque,[132] and I think 34

[130] Edward Barlow recalled a similar episode in 1668 when bad weather in Margate Road forced a ship to cut its mainmast, only for it to crash into Margate pier: Barlow, *Barlow's Journal*, i, pp. 140–1.

[131] Leghorn, now Livorno, is on the northwest coast of Italy.

[132] A letter of marque bestowed legal authority to fit out an armed vessel, to use it to capture enemy merchant shipping and to commit acts that would otherwise have constituted piracy: *OED*.

hands. I find in a letter of mine wrote home, that we expected to take in two hundred & twenty last of wheat, which *we* chiefly stowed in bags. After we were loaden we sailed for the Downs; and from thence again about the first of the month called Aprill 1748 in company with several other merchant men, bound to different ports.[133] We had a fair wind down the channel, but being deep loaden and a heavy sailing ship, our company left us.

On the fourth of the said month, being partly shot into the Bay of Biscay we saw a large ship in the afternoon, only under *her* courses or lower sails; but when we came abreast of her, she seemed then to veer & stand towards us making more sail. We judged her to be a cruiser, & saw an English ensign hoist, so hoped it had been an English man of war. In the night she came up with us, & fired at us to bring us too; which we return'd again, slinging our yards[134] with chains, & bore away right before the wind. Making a running fight towards midnight as she run under our stern to rake us, by some mismanagement they threw her up in the wind, lost her way through the water, & would neither veer nor stay, but lay a considerable time with her sails shaking in the wind. We took [*f. 41v*] this advantage to make what sail we could, hauling upon a wind in hopes of getting clear of them but in vain, though they did not come up with us any more that night, yet kept in sight.

On the 5th in the morning after day light, they having viewed our strength and we theirs; our captain said he would no longer make resistance upon which the charge was wholly t[h]rown upon me. I called the officers and men together & told them the captain had given up his charge, and desired to know their minds.[135] Whether they intended to defend themselves, or go to a French prison, telling them I was willing to stand by them as long as I was able, but if any of them lost their limbs in defence of their liberty it was not in my power to make them any recompence. Besides the force of the enemy was so much superior to ours. They seem'd at first pretty earnest for fighting, but after some deliberation & consultation amongst themselves the gunner I think, just as the privateer was running under our stern in order to fire into us, went aft & stroke the colours. The enemy immediately hailed us, demanding from whence we came & whether bound. After I had answered them they commanded us to shorten sail and keep under their lee, the sea then running too high to hoist a boat out. But in the afternoon the wind abating the sea fell; they hoisted out their launch & carried us on board the privateer. Puting hands on board the prize, keeping one of our hands, a Greek, to condemn her, they sent her away for Bourdeaux, where I think

[133] The *Duke of Cumberland*, with one Donaldson as master, remained in the Downs from 21 to 31 March 1748 before sailing for Virginia: *Lloyd's Lists*, nos. 1286–1289.

[134] A yard was a long, nearly cylindrical spar, tapering towards the ends, used for supporting and extending a sail: *IMD*.

[135] When merchant ships were endangered by privateers it was commonplace for officers to consult the crew on whether to fight, flee or surrender: Earle, *Sailors*, pp. 160–1.

she arrived safe, where such a cargoe was then very exceptable, as bread was very sca[r]se & dear at that time.

This privateer we were taken by, & were now on board of, belong'd to Grand Ville [Granville, Normandy], mounted 30 guns & carried according to information 360 men and was commanded by Dedesmain Hugen. Her pilot was an English man, an outlawed smug*g*ler. The privateer remained in her station, cruising in the bay three weeks after we [*f. 42r*] were taken several vessels more, the last prize a Dutch ship, from Suranam or Curaso.[136] We that were the principal officers eat & lodged in the great cabin with the captain and officers belonging to the privateer. When they gave chase to a vessel & came near her they generaly put us all down the hold. I was stripped of every thing but the cloaths upon my back. I think I had three guineas which I put into the waistband of my breeches & saved, my watch also by putting the chain in my fob I preserved till the latter part of the cruise when it was discover'd by an unlucky accident as follows.

My self two captains & a mate lying together upon our beds spread on the cabin floor, my watch got out of my fob in the night, & getting under a mate who lay next me & was quite ignorant of my having a watch, without any enquiry unthinkingly held it up in his hand in sight of the French officers supposing it had been drop'd from one of their hammock*s*. They handed it from one to another to look at but none own'd it so it was demanded of us whether it belong to any of us. Upon which I acknowledged to be mine upon which out of complaisancy it was return'd to me again, though I look'd upon it then as lost, unless we were retaken by an English ship of war.

After about three weeks from the time we were taken the privateer's cruise being out, they ran for the coast of France & landed us at Morlaix with the rest of the prisoners, amounting in the whole Dutch & English to about one hundred. Here we remained about 8 weeks, the princip*al* officers upon parole, the common people in prison. From hence we were traveled by land to Dinan another large town or city in Britany, about an hundred miles from Morlaix. NB: In going into Morlaix my watch was demand*ed* by the second captain & took from me. After we got to Dinan the officers had the liberty of the town, & the common people put in prison, but kept better than at Morlaix. The people here behaved very civil to us & we were allowed so much a day for [*f. 42v*] our subsistence.

After staying at Dinan above a month, towards the latter part of the month call'd June we were travelled down to a sea port called St Malo,[137] to wait for a cartel ship to carry us to England, which being arrived we

136 Suriname is in South America, and Curacao is off the coast of Venezuela in the Lesser Antilles.

137 Thirty-six prize ships were taken into Morlaix between 1744 and 1748 but St Malo remained the most notorious port for French privateers in the western parts of the English Channel: Crowhurst, *The Defence of British Trade*, pp. 15–16, 28.

embarked for Plymouth, where we were landed about the beginning of the month called July. And having got a pass,[138] several of us set out for London by land, being about two hundred & ten miles the nearest way. But we going by Bath & Wells, made it much farther. And not having money to defray our charges upon the road, we were obliged to ask charity, and some time got a bed to sleep in at night, other times slept in out houses upon straw or in the fields amongst hay. This happened in proportion to the charity we met with by the way, which we found grew less as we approached London the capital, having found the people most liberal in Devonshire, Hampshire & Somersetshire.

I got to London the 13th of the month called July 1748 after a great deal of fatigue, having suffer'd much in my feet, they being blister'd at the bottoms, and some of our company almost bare foot. And well they might, for by a moderate computation we had travelled in France & England above three hundred and fifty miles, chiefly on foot and but badly shod. The next day the 14th I wrote home to my brother William Secker acquainting him with what had happened, & of my arrival at London, also requesting him to remit me five guineas, being some part of what was left us by my dear father, who dyed without a will leaving four of us and my dear mother. Myself being the eldest son, yet I would take no advantage, (which the law gives to the eldest son), but desired it might be equally distributed amongst us, as being all children of one father & mother & equally near to them. Though too many take the advantage of the law where a will is wanting, yet it seems to me a little unnatural. I had accordingly five guinea remitted by a bill on Willet & Co. which I received (but paid one guinea away to a person who lent me one in France when in great need). He was master of a west country vessel & had credit from his [*f. 43r*] owners, and was also a generous man. I also received two presents, one from John Ransome, and the other from cousin John Sparshall. I think half a guinea each which was very acceptable at that time. I continued at London a considerable time before I got a birth, and on the 8th of 7th month September wrote to brother to remit me more money, which he did, I think three guineas also. John Ransome of North Walsham lent me five pound which I did not pay until I return'd from the South Seas.

On the 5th of the 8th month, October, ship'd myself chief mate with Captain John Colwart belonging to Scarborough in the Duke of Cumberland bound to Merseilles.[139] Loaden with wheat the 7th we cast off our moorings and warped down into Lime hole [*Limehouse*], where stopped alongside a Swedish

[138] This was an order from the magistrates exempting returning soldiers and sailors from the vagrancy laws and permitting them to beg.

[139] The *Duke of Cumberland*, with one Calvert as master, proceeded from the Downs to Cowes between 13 and 19 October 1748: *Lloyd's Lists*, nos 1345 and 1347.

ship, having received some damage from loaded colliers dropping up, by coming foul of us and carried away the thawrt bolts of both catheads[140] & broke the fluck[141] of our sheet anchor[142] which we sent up & got mended. The 11th having got a pilot we sailed down to Gravesend. The 12th sailed from Gravesend and the 13th anchor'd the Downs. The 16th being off the Isle of Wight & the wind scanting upon us, we put into Spithead. The 17th weighed & run into Cows road where we anchor'd in 8 fathoms. The 22d having got a pilot on board we sailed through the Needles, a passage so called going out at the west end of the Isle of Wight. We had in company Captain Alcock in a snow belonging to London & another snow, both bound for Merseilles,[143] besides several coasters.[144] The 23d about midnight took my departure from Start Point, allowing it to be in lattd 50° 7 N & in 3° 45 W from the meridian of London.

Having a fair wind & fresh gale the next day saw Ushant upon the coast of France, from [where] I took a fresh departure, allowing it lay in lattd 48° 30 N and in longitude 5° 0 W, from London. The 25th catched a woodcock, also sounded & found 59 fathoms Ushant E.S.E. about 7 league. The 26th spoke with three French West India men from St Domingo & Cape Francois, & had been three months upon their passage. We gave them the bearing & distances of Bell Isle in the Bay. Nothing remarkable (except in crossing the bay some hard gales of wind as customary) until November 7th, when [*f. 43v*] we saw the Rock of Lisbon. Here I found myself about ten leagues to the westward of estimation which I impute of having allow'd our ship more leeway when trying in the bay she made, she being a weatherly ship. Took a fresh departure from the route, & allow it to lay in lattd 38° 54 N and longitude from London 9° 50 W. The 10th of November or 9th month past Cape St Vincent with a fresh gale & pleasant weather. I took some sketches of the land as we ran along the coast of Portugal.

About the 12th before we had past Cape St Maria, the east or Levant wind set in strong against us. After beating to windward for some time and rather loosing than gaining ground, we stood over to the coast of Barbary where we met with a currant selling [*sic*] to the eastward. The 20th sailed

140 A cathead was a beam projecting almost horizontally at each side of the bows of a ship for raising the anchor from the surface to the deck without touching the bows and for carrying anchor on its stock-end when suspended outside the ship's side, furnished with sheaves at the outer end: *OED*.

141 The fluke or palm was the flattened end of an anchor arm which bites into the ground: *IMD*.

142 A sheet anchor was a spare anchor, the largest on board and kept ready for use in emergencies: *IMD*.

143 The *Duke of Cumberland* sailed from Cowes for Marseilles on 22 October 1748 exactly as Secker recalled. Accompanying them were Captain Alcock in the *Petersburg Packet* and Captain Willson in the *Middleburg Packet*, both also bound for Marseilles: *Lloyd's List*, no. 1348.

144 Coasters were vessels specially designed to engage in the coasting trade, usually between ports of the same country: *IMD*.

through the straits of Gibraltar, the 21st were abreast of Malaga, the 27th saw the little island of Alboran, from which I take a new departure: and allow it to lay in lattitude 36° 10 N & long 3° 50 W from London. The coast of Spain from Malaga to Cape Legate is very mountainous & the tops of the highest of them called the Granadas always covered with snow & upon some of those high mountains grow many trees which they call Mountain *Pine* which is used in building of shiping and is reckoned very durable; not much inferior to our English oak for lasting.

December the 3d saw the islands of Ivira & Fermentera,[145] the 4th saw the islands Majorca & Cabrera, the 8th anchor'd under the Laire of Mahon[146] in 20 fathoms water, in company with the Crown man of war, Captain Cockburn, an English 40 gun ship. He also spared us about a tun & a half of water, which we were in wants of. The 10th the *wind* coming fair we weighed in order to sail for Merseilles, taking a gentleman passing out of the man of war, who intends to go from Merseilles to Leghorn. Found by a good amplitude the variation of the compass to be 18° West while at anchor under the island of Minorca or Port Mahon. About this forenoon were abreast of the harbour of Port Mahon, when the Crown man of war entered the harbour. At noon took my departure from Cape Mola the northernmost point going into Mahon harbour and allow it to lay in latt 40° 2 N° and 4° 25 E long from London the 11th having lost sight of the island, met with a hard gale of wind northerly which split our mainsail, so that we bore away [*f. 44r*] for Minorca again and run under the Laire of Mahon where we mended our main sail. And the 13th of December made sail again for our intended port. Took my departure again from Cape Mola, and the 17th arrived at Merseile having had a favourable passage both for wind & weather, in crossing the Gulf of Lions a place so much noted for hard gales of wind, & a dangerous breaking sea. The same day we arriv'd in the bay, the captain and gentleman passenger went ashore to get products. About 8 the same evening a pilot carried us into the bason.

We remained here until the 8th of the month called February during which time discharg'd our cargo of wheat & ballast'd the ship. The captain & I also had several fallings out while we lay here; greatly owing to his son, a young, green impertinent lad, which accompanied him in the ship. I shall next endeavour to give some description of the city of Merseilles before I leave it, which is situated on the NW side of the bay bearing its name. It has a very good mold[147] capeable I believe to hold more than 300 sail of ships in safety, and is accounted the best in the straits. Here is very little rise or fall of the water, but what is occasioned by winds, which at times blow very hard from the snowy Alps, betwixt the W and N° and in winter very sharp

[145] Ibiza and Formentera are in the Balearic Islands. [146] Mahon on Minorca.

[147] A mold or mole was a large structure of masonry, often serving as a breakwater on its outer side while offering facilities on its inner side for loading and discharging ships: *IMD*.

& cold, when in that quarter. The adjacent country affords an agreeable landskip from the bay being variegated with hills, valleys & plains, intermix with gentlemen's country seats, which are most of them whited over and adds to the beauty of the prospect. The country is fertile in wines the chief of their growth.

The city of Merseilles is pretty large and compact, and in peaceable times is certainly a very brisk place for trade; but at the time when we were there, it had not that appearance, being just after the war. The houses are indifferent well built, and a great number of them whited without side. Their churches no ways excells that they needs any particular description, but are without & within much like other Roman Catholic churches in France. [*f. 44v*] The streets are in general narrow, and very disagreeable to pass in a morning, and not very agreeable to pass any time in the day, especially to strangers. The inhabitants empty their chamber pots out of the windows in the night, they having no other conveyance; and the scavengers are not very neat in performing their duties of keeping the streets clean, so that in a morning they stink intolerably. The inhabitants are a mixture of varies of nations but the chief tongue amongst the vulgar or common people is ordinary Italian. The gentry speak chiefly the French tongue. The gentlemen & merchants make a grand appearance upon the Exchange. The women dress much after the French mode amongst which are some beauties. As in all places wine is cheap both red & white, and some is very good. They make also a great deal of hard soap which is pretty good & cheap. They keep about six galleys here; on board of which are a great many unhappy and miserable wretches [who] have committed some offence against the laws. Some are there for life, others for a certain number of years. Amongst these unhappy creatures I met with an English man who was there for life. He told me, there was another English man on board of another galley who was also condemned there for life. He told me himself was sent there for his deserting from an Irish regiment in the French service. I gave the poor creature some money to buy tobacco & a bottle of wine, the other I think I did not see.

The 8th of the month call'd February 1748/9 we sailed from Merseilles for the island of Sardinia. The night we left the bay, came on a hard gale of wind at N.N.W to N.W which lasted us about 20 hours, & blew so excessively for some part of the time that we could *not* steer the ship before the wind, the sea run so high, but was obliged to try to under a balanced mizen.[148] The 10th about 6 in the evening we made sail the weather growing moderate, & the 11th saw the west end of the island Sardinia & the 16th in the afternoon, after encountering [*f. 45r*] with contrary winds and cabins, we doubled Cape Saroe, which is nearly opposite to Cape Carbonnera. Betwixt these two capes lays the great bay of Cailary.[149]

148 A mizen or mizzen was a sail on the third or after mast: *IMD*.

149 Cagliari in Sardinia.

The 17th about 4 in the morning came to an anchor in 9 fathoms water, the citadell NNW. about 3 miles distant from the mole or harbour. Arrived also a brigantine[150] from Curraco but last from Gibralter who had a Turk merchant on board passenger, who they took on board at Gibralter to carry to Leghorn. But finding they put into Cailary where they are at continual war with the Turks, this merchant fearing the captain might sell him, or betray him to the inhabitants took possession of the cabin, & would not let the captain enter but handed out such things as he asked for. But this not being satisfactory they endeavour'd to enter by force, but he resolutely stood upon his defence & repulsed their attemp[t]s. They fired through the bulkhead with intent to kill him, but he by shifting avoided them. The poor Turk expecting he must dye cutt all the best of his things to pieces & toss them out of the cabin windows. Also endeavoured to set the cabin on fire & burn the vessel with himself. But the people prevented him by heaving water & putting the fire out as fast as he could kindle it. They also got some soldiers from the shore to help them to overcome him. One of which the Turk wounded in the leg with his scimeter, and sent him packing ashore again. But the captain & boat's crew coming on board in the evening from the shore, and being as it was said all in liquor, were resolved to storm the castle & kill the poor Turk. In order for which they took an old broken topmast, which they made use off as a batering ram to force the bulkhead and make a breach to enter. But the poor Turk being now grown quite desperate play'd so valiantly in the mouth of each breach as they made it, with his well temper'd scimeter, that none had courage enough to enter when they had made a breach. They next betook themselves to handspikes,[151] renewing the fight again with fresh vigour, till by their irregularity in their pushes & sweeps one of them (an Irish man) either designed to or accidentaly stroke the captain over the head with his handspike of which he dyed, which put an end to this heroick affair, and I believe saved the life of the unfortunate Turke gentleman though it was the loss of the poor unhappy captain's who died of the wound received [*f. 45v*] from the handspike, the 18th, about 9 in the forenoon and was brought on shore & buried the 20th in the afternoon. Some of the people were confined in prison for a while but afterwards set at liberty, not being able to prove that it was done designedly.

We arrived here the 17th and did not sail from hence until the 28th of the 3d month call'd March viz 39 days, meeting with many interruptions while loading. It being the custom for such captains as come here to load with salt, to go ashore to the salt works and chuse such a heap of salt as they chuse to load off and the heap being once chosen, they are to take their cargo off that

[150] A brigantine was a two-masted square-rigged vessel, like a brig but without a square mainsail: *IMD*.

[151] A wooden bar, used as a lever or crow, chiefly on shipboard artillery service, rounded at the end by which it is held, and square at the other end and shod with iron: *OED*.

heap only. Accordingly our captain chose a heap off which after having received about 100 sumes, they began to stop hand and refused to let him have any more of that heap but would have forced him to have taken an ordinary sort not fit for his market. He complained to the English consul but got little but promises. Our captain bringing money with him to pay for his cargo himself, without paying for commission to either the English or Swedish consells, which is generaly the custome, and they look upon themselves to have a right to such perquisites.

At this time the Swedish consul bore a great sway here, many large Swedish ships coming here to load salt. But our captain not valuing himself upon either (as they call it,) they both endeavour'd to cross and disappoint him what they could. On the 18th of 3d month call'd March, the captain & myself going ashore to our salt heap to seek for salt according to custom but finding he was not lik[e]ly to get any to day, & seeing some Sweeds about his heap and preparations making for them to load off it, fell into a violent passion & drew his sword in order to drive the Sweeds away from his heap. Upon which the clerks, the guards of soldiers & carters surrounded him, & fell upon him, and would certainly have kill'd him if he had not directly have drop'd his sword, which they took up & carried to town. After this disappointment we went on board our ship not knowing how to help ourselves.

The 14th being a fast day, stood on board. [*f. 46r*] The 15th myself and the captain's son went ashore to our salt heap to see if we could get any salt, but when we came there the chief scriven or clerk told us, he would not let us have any, and called the captain bad names. Upon which we return'd to the town, where we met the captain come on shore, to whom we told our bad success. I also with much ado persuaded the captain to get a petition wrote in Italian, & to present it at court for address of the flagrant violation of our right. The captain through much persuasion agreed to it, and we apply'd to a person call'd Little John to be our interpreter who spoke good English. After we had got one drawn up we carried it to the secretary. From him we went to the palace with it, and from thence to the Intendant General & administrator of justice who sent us to the English consul, who was in a great passion, thoug*h* the captain had complained to him several times before with out effect. In his passion he threatened to put Little John our interpreter in prison for three months, but I think he did not. This petition had the desir'd effect, for now the director promised us salt from our own heap; but before insisted upon his taking salt not fit for his market. They were all grieved, that they were oblig'd to act contrary to their avaricious wills. We having obtained a promise to have salt the next day, went on board in the evening after much fatigue & refresh'd ourselves over a bottle of wine, which the captain produced on account of our good success.

The 16th & 17th; being bad weather we staid on board. The 18th, I went on shore to seek after salt, & when I came at our own heap, found all things chang'd for the better. Now no objection was made against our loading off our own heap; but all the carts order'd to load for us, and the same dayly when the weather would permit until we had as much as completed our loading. The 25th, we took in the last of our cargo of salt, making 613 sumes which cost 5515 reals of their money. The 28th sail'd from Calary Bay in the island of Sardina for Cadiz in Spain in company with several vessels bound to different ports. Next day saw the island of Gallicia[152] on the coast of Barbara & the 16th of the month call'd Aprill [*f. 46v*] were off the port of Malaga about 7 or 8 leagues from land. The 19th we arrived in the Bay of Gibralter after a long tedious passage from the island of Sardina from encountering with contrary winds, we anchored in ¼ less 9 fathoms water. Here I found the variation of the compass by an indifferent good amplitude 15° 25 west. While I lay here did not go ashore. The 20th the wind coming fair we left the Bay of Gibralter. And the next day the 21st anchor'd in the Bay of Cadiz in five fathoms sand & ouze. We were oblig'd to lay eight days quarantining because we came from the straits. Here I found the varia. 16° 9 W. We remained till the 7th of the month called May without any thing very remarkable, except that the 29th past the second mate went ashore very bad of the French disease to be salivated.

The 7th of this month the captain & I having had a falling out, I demanded my discharge, offering him a month's pay if he would give it me, which he consented to & I went ashore with my chest & beding, & he paid me the remaining part of my wages. Here I staid without doing any thing except spending money until the 15th of the month called June when I got to be master of a small sloop call'd the Lovely Peggy in order to go in search of the Galleons, which we did, but mist of them, so return'd from an unsuccessful voyage, having cruized between Cape St Vincent & Cape St Mary on the coast of Portugal. The 29th of the month call'd July the vessel was sold, & I again out of employ; remaining so until the month call'd December, being often put to straits for want of money, and was oblig'd to apply to the English consul several times.[153] But this month ship'd myself in a Spanish South Sea man, refusing to go master of a brigg,[154] which I had then the offer of.

The name of the Spanish ship I had engaged to go to the South Seas in was, the St Juan Babtista St Antonio de Padoua, Y de Las Animas de Purgatorio alias Grand Tuscany, commanded by Don Santo Mathias, a native of

[152] This is the island of La Galite, about 25 miles off the north coast of Tunisia.

[153] At this time Cadiz was the main Spanish port frequented by English ships, and was used by many as 'an information centre for Mediterranean shipping': Davis, *The Rise of the English Shipping Industry*, pp. 230–2.

[154] A brig was a two-masted, multi-purpose, square-rigged vessel, and was among the typical ships of the middle decades of the eighteenth century: *IMD*; Davis, *The Rise of the English Shipping Industry*, p. 77.

Corsica, & navigated by Monsieur Louis Louison a French man, the second pilot Gilles Swillevant an Irish man, the third pilot a Spaniard, the 4th pilot a French man, brother to the first pilot. The 7th of the month wrote home. [*f. 47r*] The number of hands or men on board were about one hundred & sixty besides passengers, a gathering almost out of all nations, being at least fifteen different tongues or languages spoken on board. On the 29th of the month called December we sailed from Cales or Cadiz (being call'd by both names) with a fresh breeze easterly. From this day till the 9th of the month call January <nothing> we happened with nothing remarkable, when putting the ship's company to three pints of water a day, giving them the same quantity of wine, but the quantity of water not being thought sufficient, caused a general murmuring amongst the ship's crew. One of them, a Greek, for speaking too freely was put in irons. This occasioned our touching at Tenerif one of the Canary Islands to take in a larger stock of fresh water.

On the 11th, of the month call'd January 1749/50 anchor'd in the road of Santo Cruz at the island of Tenerif one of the Canary Islands belonging to the Spaniards. Here we took on board about 48 pipes of water & 4 pipes of wine with greens, pumkins &c for the ship's use. Here the Greek was sent ashore to prison, with two more that had abused the master of plate when ashore & one man was run away; we ship'd another in his room. We were upon our passage from Cales to St Cruz fourteen days, found here three English vessels at an anchor in the road, besides some Dutch vessels. The town of Santo Cruz is situated by the sea side, & not very large, the houses of a middling height & tolerable well built. A small distance from the water side is a large fountain built up with stone, & seems to be a piece of antiquity. From this the town & shiping are supply'd with water. At the back of the town is a large space of level land which carrys a gradual ascent towards the foot of the mountains, which appearing green & pleasant affords an agreeable landskip. As we lay in the road we can see when clear of clouds the Pie cover'd with snow. This Pie of Tenerif[155] was once accounte[d] the highest land in the world, but more modern discoveries have altered that opinion. Yet we reckon the Pie of Tenerif when clear may be seen above 40 leagues. [*f. 47v*] We found in with the island about 11°, or a point west variation this island is reckoned to lye in latt 28° 23 N & longitude from London 16° 28 W.

When we sailed from Cales there was another young man an Irish man who was a navigator besides myself. After we got out of the harbour, the chief pilot gave us both liberty to take an observation by the sun yet with a seeming reluctance. But after a few days he forbid us observing any more;

155 Mount Teide, Tenerife, height 3718 metres. In 1668 the mariner Edward Barlow considered this mountain to be 'one of the highest hills of land in the world'. He claimed it could be seen 60 leagues away and thought its summit was 27 miles above sea level: Barlow, *Barlow's Journal*, i, pp. 143–4, 282.

under the colour of some false pretentions, though doubtless he had his particular reasons for so doing. This was a hindrance to me from keeping a regular journal of the whole passage from Cales to Lima as I desired. The 13th of the month call'd January having got all on board, at night got under sail, though not without some damage, occasioned, by our shipping a horser [hawser] a litle too soon. We falling on board a Dutch ship carried away the stanchion[156] of our ensign staff,[157] the people jumping on board the Du[t]ch ship cast his cable & stroke some of his hands. This brought the Dutch consul on board to demand demage. There was a long dispute betwixt them but how it ended I know not, but we soon after got under sail & left them.

After we left the island we fell in with a fresh trades wind accompanied with serene pleasant weather, steering SSW & I was finding the variation of the compass to decrease as we approach'd the Tropick the wind holding much the same. The 16th crossed the Tropick & last night saw the stars call'd the crossiers.[158] Continue to have our water at full allowance & wine as before. We steering SBW & SSW making about 54 leagues distant in 24 hours or 162 miles. The 18th after I came from the helm the chief pilot told me I might observe again. Soon after we came out they chose eight helmsmen [*f. 48r*] to steer the ship, 4 in each watch most English and Dutch & I was one of the number, which post I continued all the voyage. These helmsmen they call Timoniers, & generaly pick them out amongst those they account the ablest seamen whether of their own country or strangers. Their chief business is to steer the ship & to asist each other when there may be occasion in bad weather.

Having now got liberty to observe, took an observation to day found we were in latt 18° 8 North. The 19th about 9 in the morning saw a sail upon our starboard quarter. Standing to the SE till she got into our wake then bore away after us, hoisting an English ensign & seem'd very desirous to speak with us. Some on board pretend they saw black colours hoist, but whether it was so or no I will not pretend to say, but we fearing they might be pirates, clear'd our guns and all hands to quarters. At noon she coming but slowly up with us, gave over chase, haul'd up her coarses,[159] lowered her topsails[160] upon the cap & haul'd the wind. This strengthen'd our suspicion that she was a cruizer, being between the Cape de Vord Islands[161] & the main of Africa, a proper station to catch outward bound Guinea men. Saw a tropick bird to day & a great many flying fish. Judge we are about

[156] A stanchion was a rough log, used as a pillar in the ship's hold: *IMD*.

[157] The ensign was a flag carried by a ship as insignia of her nationality, hoisted on a pole or staff over the upper part of the ship's stern: *IMD*.

[158] The crosiers were the four stars that comprised the constellation of the Southern Cross, a navigational aid for sailors in the southern hemisphere: *OED*.

[159] Courses were the sails attached to the lower yards of a ship: *OED*.

[160] In a square rigged vessel, the topsail was the single square sail set above the lower sail or yard, the uppermost sail: *OED*.

[161] The Cape Verde Islands.

16° North lattitude. Nothing very remarkable until the 26th, we having been in what the sailors call the trolly lollies for several days, which are the variable winds between the NE & SE trade winds often attended with thunder and lightening & very heavy rain. This day catch'd a shark, in hauling which along the deck with the hook, prick'd the chief pilot's ancle, in so much that he is oblig'd to keep his cabin. In lattitude 3° 19 North. The 28th as a French sailor named Peter Anglois, was standing upon the boomes[162] he was knocked off by the flapping of the main sail & striking his head against one of the guns, hurt himself very much but did not fracture his scull. About 7 in the evening the priest gave him the sacrament. In lattd 2° 40 N° varia: 3° west the 29th saw some dolphins being the first time we have also catched several sharks within these few days past and encounter'd with variable winds & squalls.[163]

Nothing very remarkable till the 1st of the month call'd February, when two of the Spaniards quareling one of them cut a large piece [*f. 48v*] of flesh out of his arm, near from the bent of his arm down to his wrist. The wound was sewed up & drest & the man that did it put in irons to terrify others from fighting. 2d, towards the evening of this day the priest gave a general exhortation to the people to stir them up to confess and receive the sacrament, demonstrating to them the necessity thereof. And this morning the captain, doctor & some others receiv'd it. It was also administered to the sick. In the aftertoon catch'd two sharks.

NB. Having no liberty when I left Tenerif to keep a journal, this day got liberty from the chief pilot being in lattitude 2° 1 N & longitude from London 28° 29 west. From this kept a regular journal the remaining part of our passage to Lima. From which journal I have taken the following remarks. The 7th, crossed the line having met with nothing very re*markable* since the 2d instant except variable winds & heavy rains. 8th, this being the first day of the week, we having now got hold of the SE trade in the afternoon, the following odd ceremony was performed according to the Spanish custom, to make the passengers pay for crossing the Equinoctial line as well as such sailors as had not cross'd it before. And was performed in the following manner. Two of the sailors strip'd themselves naked to the waist and had their bodies painted with divers colours, & also their faces one carrying a fishgigg[164] in his hand, the other the cook's large chopping knife, having their heads drest up in a strange manner, endeavouring to imitate sea gods, but look'd more like some of the enfernal crew. These two had to

[162] A general name given to a pole that provides an outreach for extending the foot of a sail, mooring boats, handling cargo, or bearing a ship away from a quay wall: *IMD*.

[163] A squall was a sudden and violent gust of wind, or succession of gusts. Often accompanied by rain, snow or sleet it was frequently associated with a temporary shift of wind: *IMD*.

[164] A fish-gig was an instrument for striking fish with several barbed points fixed on a pole, about six feet long, loaded on the end with lead: *OED*.

accompany them the judge, father confessor & Jack Catch, with the scrivener or clerk to take down confessions, with attendance of officers & soldiers, who bring each one before the judge to be examined whether ever he cross'd the line before. If he have or have not, he is obliged to go to the father confessor, with whom if he have not cross'd the line before he is oblig'd to compound with him upon as good terms as he can for so much money & so much liquor. Jack Catch standing by with a rope reeved through a block at the main yard arm, ready to sling him for ducking if he refuse, often putting it over his head to terrify him the more when he is hard of coming to the confessor's proposals.[165] When all was over, the judge, confessor, scrivener & hangman were duck'd for diversion. The liquor is for the people, but the money for the church to pray for the souls in [*f. 49r*] purgatory; which shows the priest draw utility from every thing whether evil or good.

To day in latt^{d} 2° south & long^{d} 25° 42 W^{t}. 2nd month 9th we being now gotten in a settled SE trade with a fresh gale & fair weather accompanied with flying clouds, which greatly blunts the sun's scorching rays & makes the weather much more temperate than otherwise it would be so near the sun. For were it always serene it would be almost intolerable to bear the heat. We keep the ship about one point from the wind to make faster way through water & less leeway. This I approve of. 14th this day cross'd the sun's zenith *that is* past under the sun, being lattitude 13° 15 South & long^{d} 33. 42 from London. We had not the weather so hot as might be expected under the sun, though we have dry weather & the sun clear by intivals. The nights are cool & pleasant & the sea smooth. Nothing further remarkable till 17th. This day saw the island of Abrolho[166] on the coast of Brazil which lies about 20 leagues from the mainland, & is situated in the lattitude of 17° 40 south, and by our English charts & books lyes in 40° west longitude from London. From this island I took a regular departure. N.B: since we left Tenerif our journals generaly agreed within 30 or 40 miles excepting that allowance I made for a currant near the line on both sides of it; which I believe none allow'd for besides myself. Nor did we try the currant once in our passage, which was a great neglect & might have proved of fatal consequence had we fel in with the island in the night i[n]stead of the day; for we had no look out or expectation of seeing land reckoning our selves above one hundred leagues from land when we saw the island right ahead at about 5 leagues distance we steering right for it. We found it much to the northward of what it is laid down in our charts. From the island to seaward & a considerable

[165] A variant of this custom of 'crossing the line' was also common to English merchant vessels. Sailors who had not crossed the equator before either paid a fine (usually a bottle of spirits) or be ducked three times from the yard arm: Earle, *Sailors*, p. 96; Rediker, *Between the Devil and the Deep Blue Sea*, pp. 186–8.

[166] The Arquipélago dos Abrolhos is about 450 miles northeast of Rio de Janeiro.

way to the south & south west lays a large bank on which is shoal water where the Porteguese catch a fish much like our rock cod. There is not above 14 or 15 fathoms water 5 or 6 leagues from the island to the NE and the soundings seems to run out a great way farther.

Soon after we made the island we saw two fishing boats, at one of which we fir'd a gun & caused to come on board. She belonged to Port Segura. Our captain bought some fish of the Porteguese. They told us we were about 18 or 20 leagues from the mainland. There was one or two white men in the boat, the rest negroes. They told us there was a strong currant selleng [*sic*] to the south west. [*f. 49v*] 2^d^ mo[n]th, 18th the same evening after we spoke [to] the boat [we] saw the main land very plain. It appearing very high & mountainous we kept standing to the southwards making about SSW course one time with another: our run about 37 or 38 leagues in 24 hours. Meeting with squally weather some times, other times fair. When the squalls were heavy we clewed up[167] our mainsail, lower'd & clued up our topsails, seldom taking in reefs according to the English custom, which gave us a great deal trouble & labour that might have been saved by reefing[168] the sails in squally weather.

The 20th of 2^d^ month being in lattitude about 23° south, we put all our guns down into the hold excepting the two after ones upon the quarter deck, keeping up all hand on this occasion, which is the first time since we left Cadiz. Our daily employment when weather permit is mending sails, knotting rope yarns for spun yarn, spinning spun yarn, with other necessaries for the preservation of the masts & rigging. In running to the southward generaly found ourselves by observation to the southward of account, which we imputed to a currant seting to the southward; which I believe generaly do, except when retarded by strong southerly winds, & runs nearly parallel with the shor[e] or as the coast lay. The 28th being in about 32° 30 latt^d^, we saw abundance of fish called bonetas[169] about the ship, our people catched about 40 before the sun rose, after which they did not bite. The 29th three Spaniards were putt in irons, two of them for fighting with each other, the third for filling the irons on his legs.

3^d^ month the 9th we saw several large fowls called albertrosses as we have now & then for these two weeks past, but are not so large as those about the Cape of Good Hope, being most of them grey though to day saw one with the back & belly milk white in latt'd about 39° south. We also daily see a great many of those inamicable birds called sharewaters & pitterens,

[167] Clewing up was to draw the lower ends or clews of sails up to the upper yard of the mast in preparation for furling: *OED*.

[168] Reefing was to reduce the extent of a sail by taking in or rolling up a part and securing it: *OED*.

[169] The 'boneatas' fish caught en route were also an important supplement to the sailor's diet on Barlow's voyage to Rio de Janeiro in 1663: Barlow, *Barlow's Journal*, i, p. 82.

esteemed by the sailors the harbingers of bad weather. The 12th, being in lattd 41° 39 south we had close weather & cold sharp air, sounded but no ground at 60 fathoms though the water appear colour'd like sounding. The 17th being in lattitude 45° 30 about half an hour [*f. 50r*] after midnight, having a moderate gale at ESE with close dark weather, the wind shifted suddenly to *the* southward & blew very strong, giving us no warning, split our foresail[170] & fore staysail,[171] the latter blowing all to pieces. At last got our sails handed with much ado, called up all hands, which is the first time on such an occasion since we left Cadiz. Reckon this but a tast[e] of what we may expect to meet with before we double Cape Horn being so late in the season.

3d month, 19th being in lattitude 46° 11 so[uth], it being what they call St Joseph's day, many of the people confess'd & receiv'd the sacrement. We had also mass. The 20th being in about 46° 30 & calm took our topmasts down from the booms & laid them snug upon the main deck. 21st saw three whales to day. 22d saw 2 divers birds seldom or ever seen out of sounding. Also sounded & got *ground* in about 67 fathoms fine red & black sand. Reckon ourselves about 40 leagues from land, the computation being here 80 fathoms. At about 50 leagues distant from the shore saw a great variety of sea fowls to day while becalmed. The 27th being in lattitude 50° 43 south we had a serene temperate air & delightfull pleasant weather, the sea smooth like a river. This day being the day called Good Friday, a day held for the passion of our Blessed Saviour, kept with great reverence by the Roman Catholicks. The people being set to work as usual, caused many high words between the captain & priest. The captain carried the day, a thing not customary that priest should be foiled by a layman.

The 28th in lattd 51° 9 so[uth], this day saw several land birds and in particular a white sort, about the bigness of a large pigeon & resemble them much in flying. About a doz[e]n of them perked upon our main top gallant[172] yard one of which was shot but fell over board. The 29th catched one of these white birds, which differs nothing from a pigeon but the bill which is thicker at the head & sharper at the point than our pigeons. We judge they come from the Sybold de Ward islands,[173] we not being far from them, though not in sight. [*f. 50v*] 3d month 30th this day saw the land bearing from us about SW distant 15 or 16 leagues. To day also saw a great many whales some of which were gendring. The land we saw was about Cape Virgin Mary the northern most cape entering the straits of Magelan. The land below appears like white cliffs. This cape by one lys in lattd 52° 20

[170] The foresail was a triangular sail bent to the foreyard in a square-rigged vessel: *IMD*.

[171] The fore staysail was a jib-shaped sail set from the forestay: *IMD*.

[172] The top gallant was the mast, sail or yard above the topmast and topsail, a top at the head of the top mast, and so in a loftier position than the original top castle or top: *OED*.

[173] The Falkland Islands.

south and longitude from *London* 68° 10 west. Steer'd along shore one time with another SSE.

The 31st had fresh variable gales with serene sharp air. To day had a fair prospect of the land of del Fuego, a place so much spoken of by those that have been this way; but appears no way so frightfull as it have been represented by many. The land in the lattitude of 54° 00 south, as far as we could see to the southward & also to the northward, appear near the waterside not much unlike the Yorkshire coast from Flamborough Head to the Tees. We saw also a great many trees upon the land, but further in land are many ragged piked hills which seems to be of a considerable height & far inland. Upon the tops of several of them we saw snow. But there also appears to be a great deal of level land which possible might be fertil[e] if cultivated. In sailing along the coast of del Fuego I took several sketches of the land & of Staten Island, for which I refer to my journal.

As doubling Cape Horn, though in the most proper season of the year, has generaly prov'd a troublesome navigation from strong westerly winds, so subject to that part of the world, and high mountainous seas. So that we, who had to pass round it, when the season was so far advanc'd towards winter could expect nothing less than a rough & uncomfortable passage round, if able to accomplish our diseres. Therefore intend to give a short daily narrative of the most remarkable incidents, from our passing through the straits of Le Maire till we got round the Cape. [*f. 51r*]

4th Month 1st being in lattitude 54° 24 S we had close cloudy weather with little wind inclining to a calm. From this day until the 4th stood sometimes to the northward and some time to the southward waiting for a suitable opportunity to pass the straits of Le Maire.

4th this day having a fresh gale of WNW about 2 a clock in the afternoon entered the straits of Le Maire, & about four might call our selves through, having the southe*r*most point of Staten Island called Cape Batholomy NE & E distant about 7 leagues. From whence I took a new departure and reckon it to lay in lattitude 54° 43 SO & longitude from London 65° 34 W. At 6 in the evening were abreast about 4 miles distant from a bluff point called Cape Gonzalas. Saw an island bearing southwest from us about 6 leagues distant. Of this cape we were becalmed till about about [*sic*] midnight. Bent a cable & got an anchor clear but did not let it go. The wind freshening up at SSWt & steered SE.

5th these 24 hours had variable winds, with a large swell for the most part from the SE which caused us to rowl pretty much having the wind aft. This morning had 3 white cape pigeons flying about us. Two of them were seen to light in the sea & continue sometime. Catched one of them alive upon one of our topsail yards. It is a very tame bird & will sca[r]se shun being taken hold of. It greatly resemble[s] a pigeon [and] is not web footed, but the bill shap'd much like a sparrow being sharp at the point & thick at the head.

6th these 24 hours some part squally with hail, at other times serene cheerfull weather, with wind in the SW^{t} quarter and cold sharp air; the swell running from every part of compass counter one against another makes the sea very irregular. To day saw a cape pidgeon & several grey albertrosses of a smaller kind than those we saw to the northward of the straith [*sic*] of Magelan. In $latt^{d}$ 56° 41 so[uth].

7th these 24 hours had for the most part a fair wind at NE and the air soft & moderate steer'd SSW & SW & S to day saw a cape pidgeon seting in the sea with checquer'd wings and spotted very beautifully. In lattitude to day 57° 38 S.

[*f. 51v*]

4th month 8th these 24 hourse [*sic*] unsettl'd weather with variable winds with cold sharp air & a large counter sea, which caused us to rowl pretty much. To day saw another sort of cape pigeon of a blueish colour with black strakes round the wings and the bill different from the former having a small nobble at the point. In lattitude 58° 12 south.

9th, these 24 hours variable breezes & calms with changeable weather. Some times fair other times foggy with mizley rain. The whole accompanied with a cold sharp air. Att 8 pm our tiller rope[174] broke, reev'd another of tar'd rope, saw a great number of sea fowl about us, different from what we have seen before. They are of a small size about the bigness of a pigeon, their bodies & wings straked with black & white much resembling checkerwork, & very beautifull to behold. Our often changing sea fowl shews the alwise Providence hath allotted to each species of kinds their different stations. There is no numbering the great variety in the wonderful works of creation! In $latt^{d}$ per estimation 58° 45 south.

10th, these 24 hours for the most part close foggy weather with variable winds & a long western swell. The air mild considering the lattitude & season. $Latt^{d}$ per obser[vation] 59° 5 south.

11th, these 24 hours variable winds & close foggy wea[the]r for the most part. The middle part a strong gale at NNW. Air the air [*sic*] mild considering the season. In latt'd to day per estim[ation] 59° 15 south.

---

[174] A tiller rope or wheel rope was the line that connected the barrel of the steering wheel with the tiller that turned the vessel's rudder: *IMD*

12th these 24 hours variable winds & very uncertain weather some times moderate, at other times strong gales & squalls ac*c*ompanied with rain & hail. To day saw several sorts of sea fowl flying about us, different from what I have seen before. To day by observation in latt 59° 45 south.

13th these 24 hours fresh gales & varieable with a cold sharp air. To day a Suede & an Italian having some words went went [*sic*] into the steerage to fight, after a litle strugle the Suede being too strong, the Italian drew his knife & lifted up his arm to stab him, the other's head being turn'd away. Which I seeing ran & stop'd his hand, which he endeavouring to clear, drew the knife through my hand & cutt my middle finger; which ended the fray. Latt 59° 57.
[*f. 52r*]
4th month 14th these 24 hours the first & middle part hard gales and variable; the latter part little wind & calm with a large NW sea which cause us to rowl much, but as yet have receiv'd no damage thereby. Our ship rowling very easy & is an extraordin*ary* good sea boat, yet find it very uncomfortable in this high lattitude by reason of the rain we have had for these 3 days past. Lattitude per estimat[ion]: 60° 28 & longitude from London 75° 43 W.

15th the first & middle part strong gales & variable; the latter more moderate, at 10 past m[idday] being almost calm. The sky though mizled with thin clouds, appeared very red & firery and shot up & down like our northern lights, or as they are vulgarly called by seamen merry dancers. About half an hour after the wind, came on like a clap of thunder at SSE without farther warning. So that it was with great difficulty we got our foresail & mainsail handed, being all the sail we had set. It blew very hard for about 2 hours and was extreamly cold. Lattitude per observ[ation]: 59° 59 south.

16th fresh gales & variable with squally unsettled weather and a cold sharp air, intermix'd at times with hail & snow. In the evening handed mainsail & lay too under bare poles lest lest [*sic*] we should be catch'd as last night. But this proved more moderate, being for the most part little wind & rain. Our hopes of doubling Cape Horn this season seems to flatten, depending chiefly upon the next full moon for a shift of wind. Being now in a very uncomfortable latitude, the sun now riseing 20 degrees above the horizon at noon. Lattitude by obser[vation]: 60° 13, longitude 75° 24 west.

17th squally the first part, the middle & latter calm for the most part, excepting some squalls, the whole attended with a cold sharp air & a large swell from the western board. As yet we continue a heathfull ship's company never having above two or three sick at a time since we left Cales, excepting those infected with the French disease. There being a pretty many of them, but most of them able to do their duty, which may be attributed to way of living. The scurvy being a stranger amongst us. Latt^{d} per estimation 60° 12 south.

[*f. 52v*]

4th month 18th these 24 hours hard gales & variable all round the compass. The first part, accompanied with snow & rain, the middle part little wind & calm, the latter part a hard gale at SWbS with heavy squalls of hail and snow. Accompanied with a very great sea & cold sharp air. Have a great many sea fowl about the ship which keep hovering under our lee quarter to catch what may be hove out of the ship. To day by obser: we were in latt^{d} 59° 38, long^{d} 75° 40 W.

19th, hard gales & squally the first & middle part with snow & hail & a large sea. The latter moderate & fair with a cold frosty air per obser: in latt^{d} 58° 37 S.

20th, fresh gales intermix'd at times with heavy squalls and a cold piercing air. At 6 in the morning lay too under a reef'd mainsail. The sky appearing with such a dismal winterly aspect, as [s]trikes a damp upon all our spirits, and our hopes of seeing the South Sea inhabitants are almost lost, though our pilot encourage us what he can. Latt^{d} per obs: 58° 37 S.

21st, variable winds & squally unsettled weather accompanied with hail & snow, and a cold freezing air. Lye too with her head to the south ward till 11 pm at which time being calm a fresh wind sprung up at south, wore & made sail letting out reefs making another push for doubling the Cape. Latt^{d} per obser[vation]: 57° 46 S, long'd from London 75° 25 W.

22^{d} fresh gales & squally accompanied at times with snow & hail, the air very sharp & cold. The middle & latter milder, inclining to rain. Betwixt 10 & 12 pm split our main topsail, and though bad weather & night unbent it & bent another, which took us about six hours before all was finished about 5 am. Wore & stood to the southward, the wind coming so far to the west we afraid of coming too near the land of Del Fuego. Lattitude per obser: 57° 16, long^{d} from London 75° 46 W.

[*f. 53r*]

4th month 23^{d} these 24 hours fresh gales & squally for the most part intermixt at times with shows of rain, the first & middle part a pretty large sea. The latter part the sea much fallen the air softer which gives us hopes of a northerly wind shortly. At noon in lattitude by obser: 57° 53 S, long 75° 18 W.

24th fresh gales & variable accompanied with close hazey weat[her] and drizly rain, the air indifferent soft, the wind NW & W no obser[vation].

25th fresh gales & variable as per log with thick hazey weather accompanied for the most part with drizly rain with a large sea setting from the WNW^{t}. Lattitude by estimation 59° 41 S.

26th variable winds & uncertain changeable weather the first part drizly rain & a softish air. The latter squally with snow & a cold piercing air, which makes it very uncomfortable in so high a lattitude and so late a season. The sun's altitude to day at noon was but 16° 51 above the horizon. Latt^{d} per obser[vation]: 59° 32 S.

27th squally uncertain weather for the most part with variable winds some times blowing fresh, at other times little wind, with a cold sharp air. Have constantly a great many sea fowls hovering about the ship night & day. Especially one sort about the bigness of a pidgeon, beautifully spotted with white & has a web foot like a duck & seems very tame. Today saw a large albetross not having seen any for a long time per obser: to day in latt^{d} 58° 58, long^{d} 79° 28 W.

28th fresh variable winds the first middle part with very unsettl'd weather the latter a fresh gale at SSE^{t} which we wish to continue. Steered away NW to day in latt^{d} per obser[vation]: 58° 46 South.

29th fresh variable winds accompanied some times with rain at other times with snow. Yesterday our hopes were greatly elevated by having a fair wind, but today the wind shifted again to the westward, so uncertain are fair winds to go to the westward, in this part of the world at this time of the year that generaly for one hour's fair wind we have a dozen contrary, it blowing almost always betwixt the SW & NW^{t}. To day by observ[ation]: in latt^{d} 57° 48 long:^{d} from London 80° 20 W^{t}.
[*f. 53v*]
4th month 30th these 24 hours variable winds & squally uncertain weather accompanied with snow & hail, with some intervals of fair weather, the whole attended with a cold sharp uncomfortable air. To day saw several albartrosses of a grey colour, and some other sea fowl like grey gulls. Which I take to be harbingers of bad weather. Latt^{d} per obser: 56° 10 S, long^{d} from London 81° 20 W^{t}.

5th month; 1st hard gales & variable attended with heavy squalls of hail and snow & a large mountainous sea, though not without some intervals of moderate weather; especially the first part betwixt 10 & 11. In the evening the sky clearing up in the southern quarter appeared of a firery red fierce colour with a brightness like a pale flame shooting or darting up a cross it; resembling our Northern Lights but of a more terrible aspect. At the same time we saw three or four corpusants.[175] One on the main topmast spindle, two at the cross jack yard arms,[176] and one at the fore topsails yard arm. A corpusant as the sailors call it, is a light often seen on board ships at sea in a hard gale of wind and generaly in the fore part of the gale is seen on the deck, gunnel, or lower part of the rigging or lower yards; and afterwards rises higher. And when it is seen hanging to the vane spindle at the main of fore topmast head, the sailors reckon the gale nearly at an end. Its appearance at a distance is like a pale flame about the size generaly of the flame of a middle siz'd candle but appear globulor, & not much unlike the twinkling of a star in the firmament. But when close at it, appears only a brightness without any visible material substance. Sometimes several are seen at one time fix'd on different parts of the yards or rigging. The name seem deriv'd from the Porteguese or Spaniard having a near affinity to corpusants or saint's body or holy [*f. 54r*] body in those languages which through superstition might be given to this light or vapour & indeed there seems something wonderfull in it, if seriously considered.

About half past 11 in the evening ship'd a very heavy sea, which carried away the quarter deck rail to windward, stove a large hencoop which stood upon the quarter deck grattings[177] all to pieces, broke two large water jarrs, & some of *the* longboat's lashings, & did some other damage, but through the mercy of providence had none washed over board, though washed down to the lee side of the ship; & the people wet in their hammock*s* and *in* the quarter deck. Latt: per obser[vation]. 55° 05 S, long^{d} from London 81° 11 W^{t}. We reckonned our selves in the lattitude of Cape Horn when we ship'd this large sea, which frightened some *of* the Spanish sailors so much that they threatened never to return back that way which proved true to some who died in the country & others run away.

2^{d} the first part a fresh gale with a large mountainous sea accompany*ed* with squalls & snow. The middle & latter more moderate & the sea much fallen, which gave us an opportunity to put our launch and boats to rights, displaced by the great sea we ship'd yesterday. To day in lattitude per estimation 54° 3 & longitude 81° 48 west.

3rd moderate breezes & fair weather, inclining to be calm with indifferent smooth water, the first part, the middle & latter light variable breezes inclining to rain & a soft air. Have had several of our people fall sick since the last gale of wind, which I make no wonder at, as the greatest part of them lay

[175] Corpusants were the ball of light sometimes seen on a ship, especially on the masts and yard arms during a storm, also called St Elmo's Fire: *OED*.

[176] Cross jack yard arms were the lower yard arms on the mizzenmast: *IMD*.

[177] A grating was an open lattice work of wood or metal so arranged to form a flush surface admitting light and air: *IMD*.

upon *the* deck without hammocks or beding except a sheep skin or trum'd [sic] matt, & but badly provided with cloaths for cold weather. Lattitude per estimation 53° 52 S, long: 82° 27 Wt.

4th fresh variable gales for the most part attended with showers during the night kept a good look out for fear we should be to the eastward of reckoning, but I saw no signs of being near the land, neither by fowls or any other token. At noon by observation found our selves to the northward of Cape Victory, so altered our course & steered more northerly. In latt'd per obser[vation]: 52° 28 & longd , 83° 8 Wt.

5th fresh gales for the most part accompanied with squalls & showers, our spirits much elevated at present, with the hopes of shortly arriving at a place of refreshment. Latt'd p[e]r obser[vation]: 50° * S. Longd from Lond[on]: 83° 00 west.

6th fresh gales & squally intermixt with fair weather, the sea very smooth carried a stiff sail all this 24 hours runing per log 174 miles lattd per obs: 47° 20 S. [*f. 54v*]
5th month 7th fresh variable gales, the first & middle part attended with squalls & showers, the latter fair pleasant weather, & smooth water the air temperate. Got up our top gallant masts[178] and rigg'd our spritsail yard, we approaching apace the peaceable ocean or as it is generaly call'd Mar Pacificam. To day by observation in latt'd 45° 17 S longd 80° 25 west.

8th fresh gales for the most part with fine settl'd weather, smooth water & a temperate airr [*sic*]. Carry'd our lower steering sails all night. In the forenoon got our main & fore top gallant masts & yards up. To day I had some words with a sort of Mastee Indian. He accuse[d] me with spilling oyl upon his bed & also wiping my hands upon it. Which being false put me in a great passion. Insomuch that having a piece of bisket in my hand I hove it at him & hit him in the face, which he resented so much that he went directly & fetch'd a billet of wood & hit me over the shoulders. This made a great noise and the captain coming to us, stroke me twice, the Indian telling him a false story & the Spaniards that were present siding with the Indian. A while after, the Indian watching when I went down the fore hatchway to fetch my allowance of wine, stroke me twice over the head as I came up again. We were immediately parted & so the affair ended. I mention this to shew the vindictive nature of the Indians when they suppose themselves to have receiv'd an injury, true or false. To day by observ[ation]: in lattd 43° 32 S, longd: from London 79° 32 west.

[178] The top gallant mast was the mast next above a topmast. It might consist of a separate spar or a single stick with the topmast: *IMD.*

9th these 24 hours a fresh gale & squally the air mild & temperate and sea indifferent smooth. Carry a stiff sail & have made a fine run having 170 miles on our log. To day the chief pilot call'd me into his cabin & desir'd me to keep what he told as a secret, which was our not touching at the La Conception in Chile as was generaly expected, which is a great disappointment to the people who expected we should put in there for refreshment. Lattd per obs[ervation]: 40° 55, Longd 78° 00.

10th variable winds the first part, with a strong gale & large sea the middle & latter moderate with serene pleasant & temperate air. To day at noon several albatrosses [*f. 55r*] with two or three spotted birds formerly mentioned, also two seals which by their gestures seem'd to be engendering. To day one of our mocas or lads washing in the fore chains fell over board, but catching hold of a rope hanging out of the main chains & so was help'd on board again. As yet thanks be to god we have not lost one man neither by sickness or miscassualty. Latt per obs[ervation]: 39° 22 S, longd 77° 38 Wt.

11th, fresh variable winds the first & middle part, the latter squally with showers. To day the people began to penetrate into our new design of going directly for Lima without touching at any place in Chili. Lattd 37° 10 S, long:d 77° 08 Wt.

12th moderate gales & variable for the most part, with serene temperate air & smooth water: the agreeable production of a temperate climate. To day hoisted the guns up out of the hold & mounted them in their proper places, being 30 in number. To day one of the after guard named Juan de Bria, having a quarrell with the captain of the after guard stroke him upon the quarter deck. But being parted by the boatswain, the said John de Bria took the opportun*ity* in the evening & stroke the other over the forehead with a billet of wood & cut him pretty much for which he was immediately put in irons on the forecastle.[179] He is a hot cholerick person & evily inclin'd. Latt'd 35° 31, longd 75° 53 Wt.

13th serene pleasant weather & smooth water with fresh variable winds about 8 this morning saw the island of Juan Fernando[180] bearing from us NbWt about 10 leagues distant. This being the first land we made after we left the straits Le Maire. I have been the more particular in putting down a little of our daily occurrences & notwithstanding the many different courses occasioned by contrary winds, boisterous seas & winds, often trying too,

[179] The forecastle was a short superstructure situated over the bows: *IMD*.

[180] The Islas Juan Fernandez off the coast of Chile are named Robinson Crusoe and Alejandro Selkirk.

sometimes under bare poles, other times with some sail out, often waring ship as the wind shifted, besides the drift the ship made when trying too; as well as when under [*f. 55v*] sail from mountainous seas some times on the bow, other times on the beam, & other times on the quarter, sometimes right a head to some times right a stern, which hitches the ship from her true course steer'd & also augments or retards her way or distance, in the same nature as a current do. These according to my judgment I allow'd for in my reckoning which I believe no other who keep a journal did. I told them the day before we saw the island Juan Fernando that if my journal was right, & we continued the same course we should see the island. But was not then believed as our chief pilote reckoned himself many leagues to the eastward of it, think he said eighty. Yet this morning about eight a clock when we made thc island it was almost right a head of us. And my journal agreed to the greatest exactny*ss* N:B. since I took my departure from Cape Virgin Mary the east entrance of the straits of Magellan to the island Jual Fernado I made out 6° 26 west longitude & the English chart by Sir John Narborough[181] who went through the straits lays down from the said Cape Virgin Mary to the island Fernando 6° 28 which answers to my account to the greatest exactness. Whilst a French chart we have on board which begins at straits Le Maire & lays down the coast in the South Sea makes us at least 90 leagues further to the eastward. And another chart on board, I think by Monsieur Frasser,[182] which shew the coast of Brazil & runs to Cape Horn, which also lays the land near the straits of Magellan 70 or 80 leagues too far to the eastward. Our chief pilot who is a French man, says he has found the same error on both sides the Cape two voyages running. [14th] At 4 this afternoon the island Fernando bore from us WbS, distance about 7 leagues. From whence I take a new departure and allow it to lay in 33° 40 S by three diff[erent] observations and in longitude from London by my est*i*mation 74° 35 west and from Paris 2° 15 east of London 76° 50 west.
[*f. 56r*]

[181] Sir John Narbrough was captain of the *Sweepstakes* on a voyage to promote English trade with the Pacific coast of south America from 1669–1671. He was the first Englishman to navigate the Straits of Magellan both ways and his journal of the voyage was published in 1694, as well as a map of the straits which 'long remained a standard authority'. Like Secker, Narborough expressed sympathy for the natives suffering under Spanish rule: G. Williams, *Buccaneers, Explorers and Settlers: British Enterprise and Encounters in the Pacific, 1670–1800* (2005), I, p. 28; J. D. Davies, 'Sir John Narborough (1640–1688)', *Oxford DNB*; P. J. Marshall and G. Williams, *The Great Map of Mankind: British Perceptions of the World in the Age of Enlightenment* (1982), p. 38.

[182] Amédeé-François Frézier (1682–1773) was ordered by Louis XIV to chart the Pacific coast of South America in 1711. He did so onboard a merchant vessel from 1712 to 1714, charting the Straits of Magellan and sketching the coast, harbours and fortifications. His work was recommended in the official publication of Anson's circumnavigation: E. Taillemite, *Dictionnaire des Marins Français* (1982), p. 127; Williams, *Buccaneers, Explorers and Settlers*, I, p. 35; Walter and Robins, *A Voyage round the World*, pp. 15, 90.

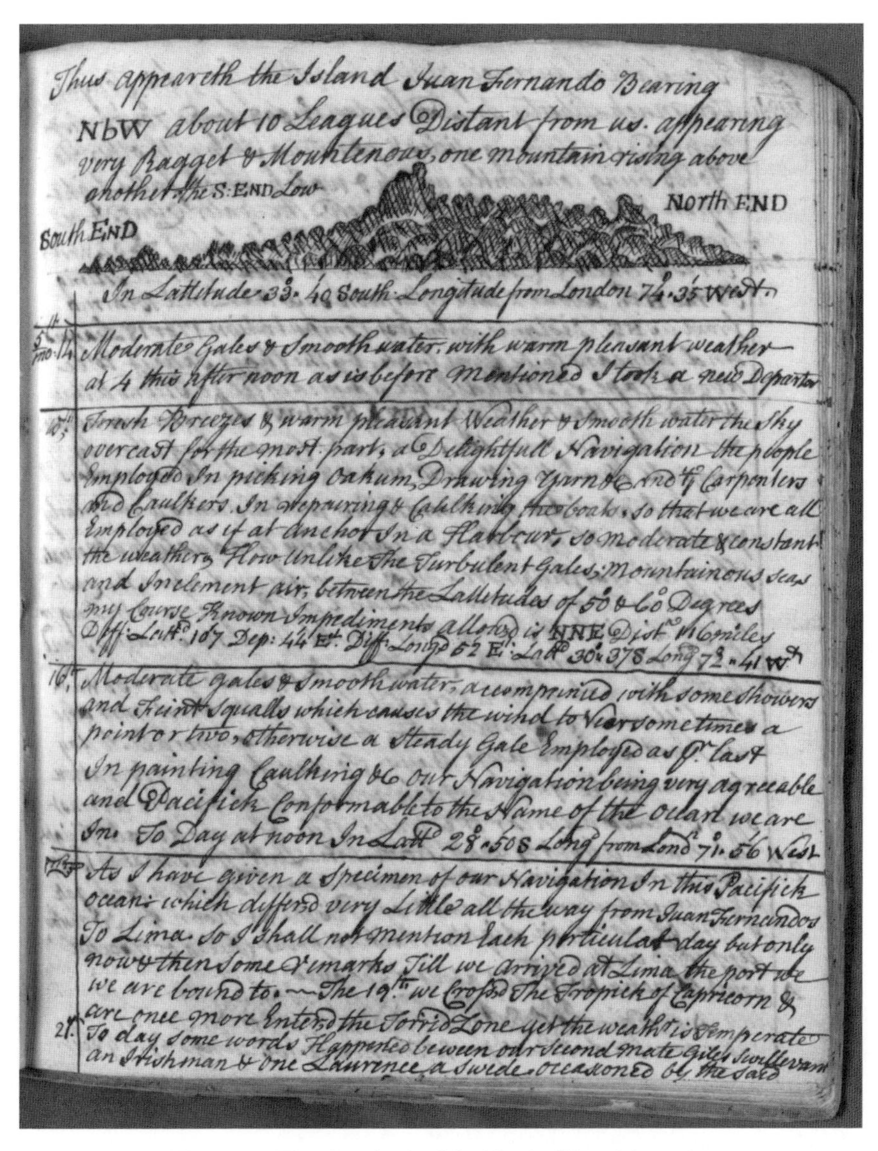

Thus appeareth the Island Juan Fernando Bearing
NbW about 10 Leagues Distant from us. appearing
very Ragget & Mountenous, one mountain rising above
another the S: END Low

North END

South END

In Lattitude 33° 40 South Longitude from London 74° 35 West.

5 mo. 14 Moderate Gales & Smooth water, with warm pleasant weather
at 4 this after noon as is before mentioned I took a new Departur

15 Fresh Breezes & warm pleasant Weather & Smooth water the Sky
overcast for the most part, a Delightfull Navigation the people
Employed In picking Oakum, Drawing Yarn &c And ye Carpenters
and Caulkers In Repairing & Caulking the boats. so that we are all
Employed as if at Anchor In a Harbour, so moderate & constant
the weather How Unlike the Turbulent Gales, Mountainous Seas
and Inclement air, between the Lattitudes of 50° & 60° Degrees
my Course Known Impediments allowed is NNE Dist 116 miles
Diff Latt 107 Dep: 44 Et Diff Long 52 E: Latt 30° 378 Long 73° 41 Wt

16 Moderate gales & Smooth water, accompanied with some showers
and faint Squalls which causes the wind to Vear sometimes a
point or two, otherwise a Steady Gale Employed as Pr last
In painting Caulking &c our Navigation being very agreeable
and Pacifick Conformable to the Name of the ocean we are
In. To Day at noon In Latt 28° 50 S Long from Lond 71° 56 West

17 &c As I have given a Specimen of our Navigation In this Pacifick
ocean which differed very Little all the way from Juan Fernandos
To Lima. So I shall not mention each particular day but only
now & then some Remarks Till we arrived at Lima the port we
we are bound to. — The 19th we Crossed The Tropick of Capricorn &
are once more Entered the Torrid Zone yet the weather is Temperate

21 To day some words Happened between our Second mate Giles Swillevan
an Irishman & one Lawrence a Swede. Occasioned by the said

Figure 1 *Elevation sketch of the island of Juan Fernandez*

Thus appeareth the island Juan Fernando bearing NbW about 10 leagues distant from us, appearing very ragget & mountenous, one mountain rising above another: the S: END Low

In lattitude 33rd 40 south. Longitude from London 74° 35 west.

5th month 14th moderate gales & smooth water with warm pleasant weather at 4 this afternoon as is before mentioned I took a new departure.

15th, fresh breezes & warm pleasant weather & smooth water, the sky overcast for the most part. A delightfull navigation, the people employed in picking oakum, drawing yarn &c and the carpenters and caulkers in repairing & caulking the boats, so that we are all employed as if at anchor in a harbour, so moderate & constant the weather. How unlike the turbulent gales, mountainous seas and inclement air, between the lattitudes of 50° & 60° degrees. My course known impediments allow'd is NNE distance 116 miles, diff: latt:^{d} 107 dep: 44 E^{t} diff: long^{d} 52 E: latt^{d} 30° 37 S, long^{d} 72° 41 W^{t}.

16th, moderate gales & smooth water, accompanied with some showers and feint squalls which causes the wind to veer sometimes a point or two, otherwise a steady gale employed as p[e]r last, in painting, caulking &c. Our navigation being very agreeable and pacifick, conformable to the name of the ocean we are in. To day at noon in latt^{d} 28° 50S, long^{d} from London 71° 56 west.

[Symbol drawn in shape of a hand pointing] As I have given a specimen of our navigation in this Pacifick ocean: which differ'd very little all the way from Juan Fernandos to Lima so I shall not mention each particular day but only now & then some remarks till we arrived at Lima the port we we [*sic*] are bound to. The 19th we cross'd the Tropick of Capricorn & are once more enter'd the torrid zone yet the weather is temperate. 21st to day some words happened between our second mate Giles Swillevant, an Irishman, & one Laurence, a Swede, occasioned by [*f. 56v*] the said Laurence giving him the lye & his tongue too much liberty. In latt^{d} to day 18° 39 S, long'd 70° 50 west. Employ'd in tarring sides & painting ship with other odd jobbs being constantly watch & watch which falls light upon the people. The 23^{d} perceiv'd the water colour'd & we had a large ground swell. In latt'd 16° 05 long^{d} 70° 04 west. 24th fresh gales & cloudy with a large ground swell setting to the NE^{t}. About 2 this afternoon saw the land bearing from us NE^{t} distance from by computation 17 or 18 leagues and appears to be very high. By the chart take it to be about Cape St Michael. We immediately *altered our Course* & steer'd to the west[w]ard of the north viz NW & NWbW^{t}. At noon was about 8 or 10 leagues from the shore. The course along shore by compass seems to be nearest NWbN & SEbS. In land appears a very high ridge of mountains which seems to run nearly parallel with the shore, descending gradualy to a moderate height near the shore.

We *are* now arrived upon the coast of Peru, having past the land of Petagonia & the Kingdom of Chili without seeing other land then the small island of Juan Fernando. In latt'd 15° 18 S: Long^{d} 70° 33 west. 25th a fresh gale with a close set sky for the most part and indifferent smooth water. The air temperate to day, we past several deep bays. To day had no observation so cannot be quite certain what land we are abreast off. The land near the water side of a moderate height at noon about 4 leagues from land, latt.^{d} per estimation 13° 57. 26th temperate close weather accompanied with a fresh gale at sun set were a breast of Pisco. At noon the norther[n]mo*st* point of land in sight, which is point Chilia or Chincha appear'd as under

A point Chincha N ½ E^{t} dist[ance] about 7 Leagues

At noon in lattitude per estimation 12° 16 S: Long'd 72° 09 west.
[*f. 57r*]

5th month 27th. These 24 hours light breezes & calms for the most part accompanied with close weather. Have taken several sketches of the land at noon. Had a tolerable good observation by which I correct from the 24th instant, the last day of observat:*n* until to day, according to the best of my judgment, & believe the error betwixt the observ'd latt'd & that by estimation is occasione*d* by a current setting a long shore to the southward about SEbS nearly the run of the shore. My true course known impediments allow'd since the 24th instant is N32°W dist. 220m: × latt'd 184m. Dep: 118 W^{t} × long'd 122m W^{t}. Latt'd per obser: 12° 16 S, long^{d} 72° 35 W^{t}. Long'd from Juan Fernando 2° 01 E^{t}.

From Abrolho on the coast of Brazil 32° 35 west.

From Cape Virgin Mary 04° 25 west.

From Paris 2° 15 east of London 74° 50 west.

At noon the island St Laurence bore N ½ W dist 10 miles. Round this island lay the Bay of Caloa[183] which is the port for the city of Lima & the largest & most frequent*ed* in these seas where ships ride very safely, no tide. Anchor'd in the Bay of Caloa, after a passage from Cadiz in old Spain of five compleat calendar months. [The pointing hand symbol] The increase & decrease of the variation of the compass from the island Albroho on the coast of Brazil in lattitude 17° 40 south & longitude 40° 00 west from London from where I took a regular departure untill we arriv'd in the Bay of Caloa so noted here under viz: from latt'd 17° 40 S & long'd 40° W^{t} to straits Le Maire in latt'd 54° 34 S and long'd 66° 04 W our easterly variation encreas'd from half a point to 2 points. From Straits Le Maire to the latt'd of 60° 13 south and long'd from London 75° 24 W our variation encreas'd from 2 points to 24 east. From thence to the island Fernando it decreased from 11° degrees to 7° degrees. Which variations were rectified by good amplitudes taken at the rising & setting of the sun seldom missing an opportunity when the sun rose & set clear. [*f. 57v*]

Being arrived & moor'd in the Bay of Cal*l*oa the 28th of 5th month May in the year 1750, I shall before I proceed farther in my narrative give some

[183] Callao in Peru.

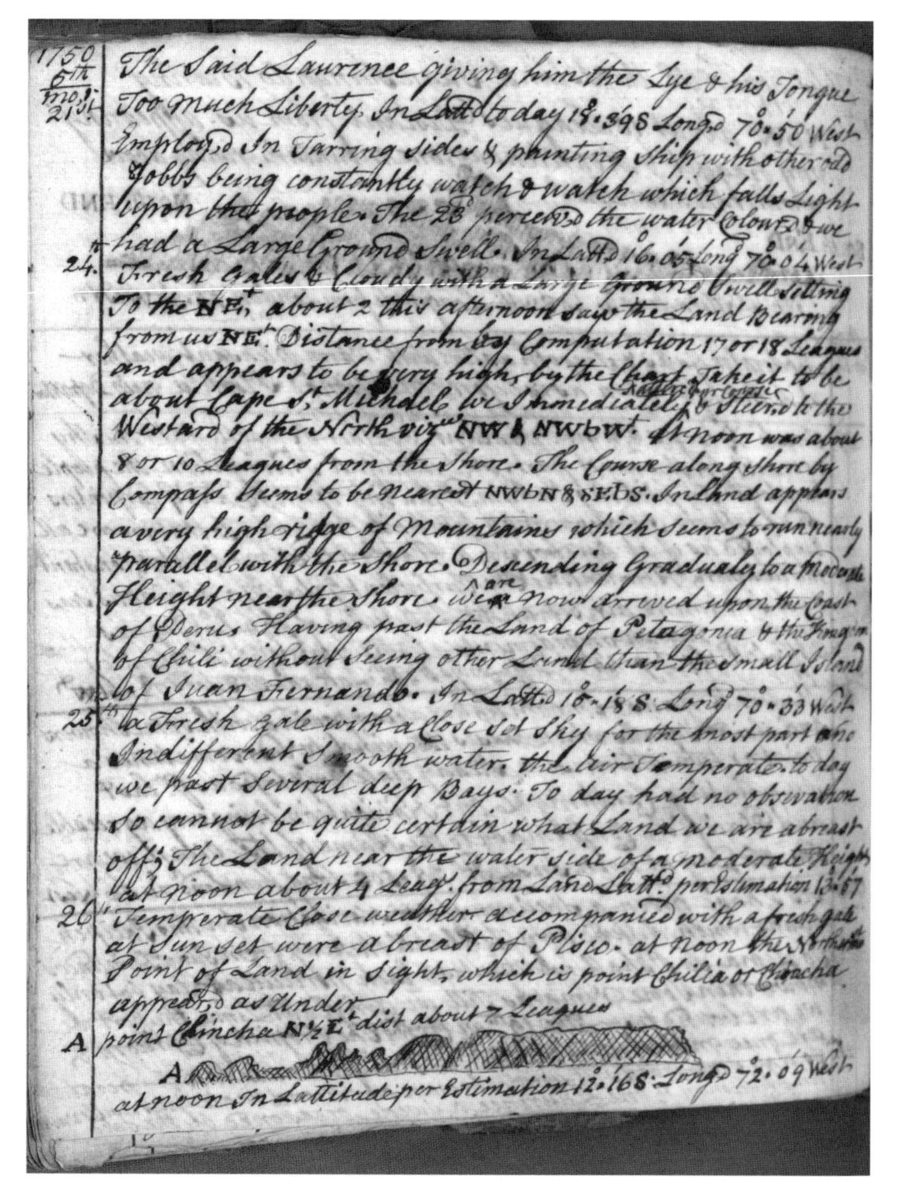

1750 5th mo. 21st The Said Laurence giving him the Lye & his Tongue
Too much Liberty. In Latt.d to day 18.39 S Long.d 70.50 West
Employ.d In Tarring sides & painting Ship with other odd
Jobbs being constantly watch & watch which falls Light
upon the people. The 23d perceiv.d the water Colour.d & we
had a Large Ground Swell. In Latt.d 16.05 Long.d 70.04 West
24th Fresh gales & Cloudy with a Large Ground Swell setting
To the NE, about 2 this afternoon saw the Land Bearing
from us NE.t Distance from by Computation 17 or 18 Leagues
and appears to be very high, by the Chart Take it to be
about Cape St Michael we Immediately Hauled our Wind & Steer.d to the
Westard of the North viz.t NW & NWbW. At noon was about
8 or 10 Leagues from the Shore. The Course along Shore by
Compass Seems to be nearest NWbN & SEbS. In Land appears
a very high ridge of Mountains which Seems to run nearly
parallel with the Shore Descending Gradualy to a Moderate
Height near the Shore. We are now arrived upon the Coast
of Peru Having past the Land of Petagonia & the Kingdom
of Chili without Seeing other Land than the Small Island
of Juan Fernando. In Latt.d 18.18 S. Long.d 70.33 West
25th a Fresh gale with a Close Set Sky for the most part and
Indifferent Smooth water. the Air Temperate. to day
we past Several deep Bays. To day had no observation
So cannot be quite certain what Land we are abreast
off; The Land near the water side of a moderate Height
at noon about 4 Leag.s from Land Latt.d per Estimation 13.57
26th Temperate Close weather accompanied with a fresh gale
at Sun set were abreast of Pisco. at noon the Northern
Point of Land in Sight, which is point Chilia or Chincha
appear.d as Under
A point Chincha N½E dist about 7 Leagues
A
at noon In Lattitude per Estimation 12.16 S. Long.d 72.09 West

Figure 2 *Elevation sketch of Point Chilia or Chincha*

sketches of the land taken as is before mentioned as it appear'd in different positions & distances. Thus appears the island St Laurance & the high mountains in land which are seen over the Island when NWbN dist: 6 or 7 leagues

Being Arrived & moor'd In the Bay of Caloa the 28th of 5th mo may
In the Year 1750 I Shall before I proceed Farther In my
Narative Give Some Sketches of the Land Taken as is before
Mentioned as it appeard In different Positions & distances
Thus appears the Island St Laurance & the High mountains
In Land which are seen over the Island, when NWbN dist: 6 or 7 Leagues

E E E ENE Inland

A B C

A·B Isle St Laurence, C Island Caloa

As Under appears the Island St Laurence NNW dist: about 5 Leagues. Isle Caloa at B. N½W about 4 Leagues

A B

As Under appear'd the Island St Laurence at Noon being in
Latd by observation 12°·16 South the point at A: N½W 10 miles
The point M: North about 9 miles. The Small Island Calao at C
NbE½E dist about 9 miles

Island Saint Laurance M Island Calao C

A

The Island Saint Laurance by my Estimation Lay in Lattitude
12°·8 South & 2°·35 Wt Longitude from the Island of Juan Fernandez
and In 72°·35 Wt Longitude from London. and In 74·60 Wt Long
from Paris. within this Island lay the port of Calao. which is the
port for Lima; and the Largest & Safest In these Seas 7 miles from the City of Lima

Figure 3 *Elevation sketches of the islands of St Laurence and Callao*

A.B Isle St Laurence, C Island Caloa

As under appears the island of St Lawrence NNW dist: about 5 Leagues. Isle Caloa at B. N ½ W about 4 leagues

As under appear'd the island St Laurence at noon being in latt'd by observation 12° 16 south the point at A: N ½ W^{t} 10 miles. The point M: north about 9 miles. The small island Calao at C NBE ½ E^{t} distance about 9 miles.

The island Saint Laurance by my estimation lay in lattitude 12° 8 south & 2° 35 W^{t} longitude from the island of Juan Fernando and in 72° 35 W^{t} longitude from London, and in 74° 50 W^{t} long^{d} from Paris. Within this island lay the port of Calao whis [*sic*] is the port for Lima; and the largest & safest in these seas 7 miles from *the city of Lima* [*f. 58r*]. The following sketches or appearances of land I have have [*sic*] drawn as under, to show the ragged & mountanous forms of land in these remote parts of the world. The first is the appearance of Staten Island which bounds one side of the straits of Le Maire or the sea straits. The land of Del Fuego bound the other side of the straits. Staten Island EbS distant about 5 leagues appear'd as under: this island appears to be nothing but mountainous inaccessible rocks.

As under appear'd Staten Island bearing EbN distant about 5 leagues, being then about the narrowest part of the straits of Le Maire which to my judgment did not exceed 5 or 6 leagues in breadth from the E^{t} end of del Fuego, named point Diego or James to Cape Batholomy the W^{t}, end of Staten or States islands. C: Cape Batholomy the W^{t} end of Staten Island. A the E^{t} end of Staten Island.

As under appeared the land of Terra del Fuego from Los Fres Harmanos (or the Three Brothers) mark'd HHH to point Diego (or James) at A entring the straits of Le Maire. Bearing from us south distant about 8 or 9 leagues. N:B. The Three Brothers are the remarkable mountains nearly resembling one another.[184] B northernmost land in sight.

Nearly thus appear'd the island Juan Fernandez bearing from us NbE^{t} about 10 leagues S the south end & Nth end.
[*f. 58v*]

The under imperfect draught taken by the eye from Monsieur Frazier chart though imperfect shew somewhat of the form of *the* coast from the straits of Magelan to the straits of Le Maire & from thence to C: H: Cape Horn. We found here in the year 1750 two point east variation.

As I took my departure from the island Abrolho on the coast of Brazil in lattitude 17° 40 S, and longitude as laid down by Sir Edmund Halley,[185]

[184] These hills were also mentioned in Anson's account: Walter and Robins, *A Voyage round the World*, p. 82.

[185] Secker was at pains to demonstrate he was well acquainted with the work of Edmond

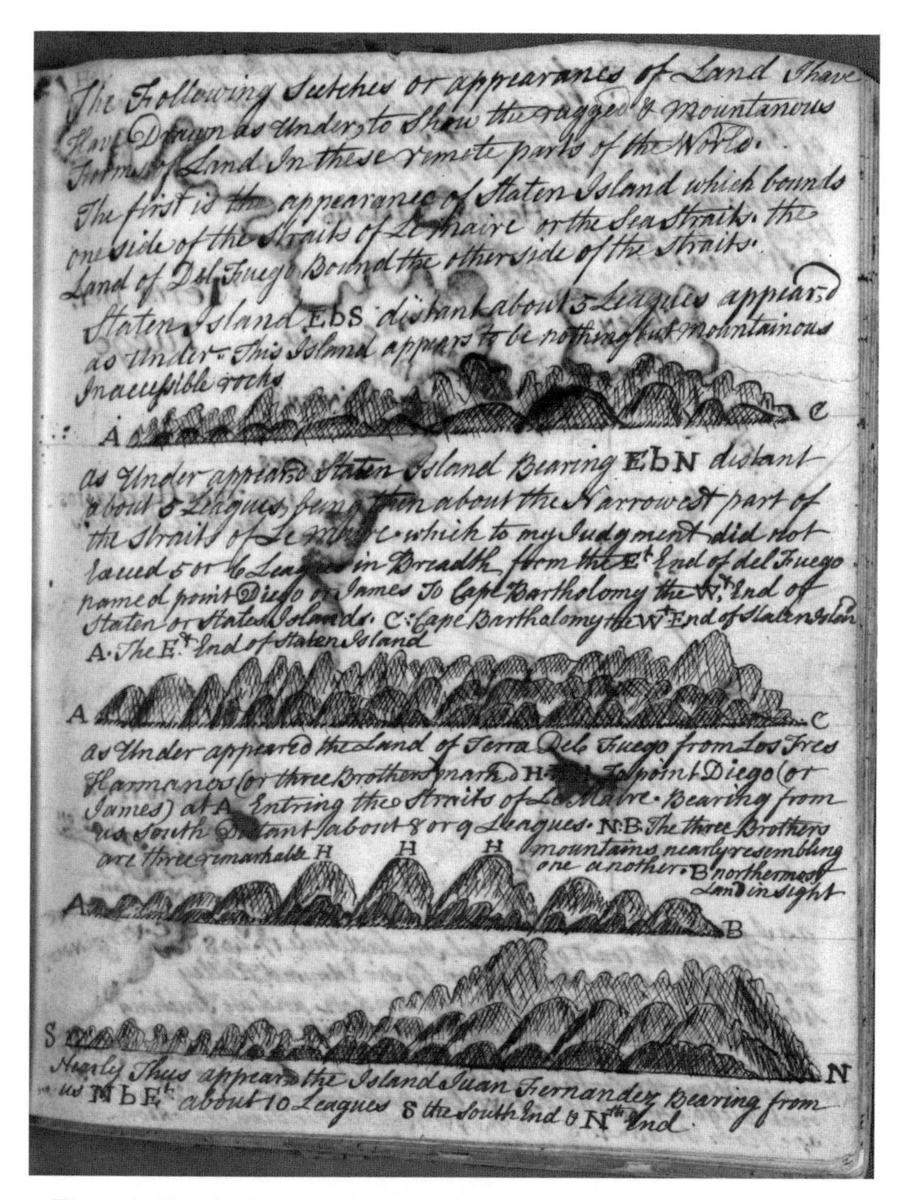

Figure 4 *Elevation sketches of Staten Island and view of the land of Terra del Fuego and island of Juan Fernandez*

Halley, astronomer royal, who had sailed to the South Atlantic on board the Paramore in 1698–1701 in order to develop new navigational methods: Williams, *Buccaneers, Explorers and Settlers*, II, 120; A. Cook, 'Edmond Halley (1656–1742)', *Oxford DNB* .

40° 00 W^{t} from the meridian of London, and we touching no where, but runing directly for the straits of Le Maire, I have reason to believe the latitudes & longitudes of the following are very near the truth. Cape Virgin Mary, in latt^{d} 52° 20 S long^{d} 68° 10 W^{t} London. Point Diego: 54° 34 S & 65° 58 W^{t}. Cape Bartholomew 54° 48 S & 65° 29 W^{t} from London. Cape Horn in 55° 40 S & 68° 59 W^{t} from the meridian of London.

[*f. 59r*]

Being arrived & moored in the Bay of Cal*l*oa after a passage of five compleat calender months as is mentioned before, and also given several sketches of the appearance of land, shall now reassume my narrative, though I cannot be punctual as to times. Yet shall mention such particulars as shall seem most worthy of notice as far as I can now recollect from memory & such memorandums as I have yet preserv'd by me. Here under is a plan of the port of Callao & the adjacent country.

The above plan though not correct shew the port for Lima with the road from Callao to Lima about 7 English miles. The city of Lima with the gardens, plantations, sugar works laid out in squarish plots with the whole plain of Lima to the foot of the mountains. The city of Lima is reckoned to *be* two miles in length & about one mile and a half broad, its circumference round the wall six or seven miles. The city is divided by the river, but much the greatest part on the south side. [*f. 59v*] Having given a plan of the port of Callao, the island San Lorenzo, or by the French St Laurence; with the island Callao, with some of the ajacent rocks & the <Coast> *coast* to the southward as far as the head land call'd Morro Solo, and to the northward as far as the northern extreamity of the great Bay of Callao, which is reckoned the largest and safest port in these seas. The trade wind constantly blowing betwixt the south & east & for the most part moderate. The point of Callao & the island St Laurence break of the run of the sea, so that the ships lay always in smooth water. Here is no flood nor ebb. The sea only rising 4 or 5 inches some times through the force of wind. In this bay are seldom less than 8, 12, 16 & sometimes twenty country ships, from two to five hundred tuns burden, besides small craft, which chiefly trade to Pisco & other ajacent places where they load with brandy, wine & other comodities for the place. The large vessels' trade is divided, the greatest part of them to Valparaiso, La Conception, Baldivia & Chiloe.[186] At the two first mention'd places they load wheat, lard & jerk'd beef. At Baldivia & Chiloe, timber & boards for building, cabinnet ware, punchos [*ponchos*], hams &c. Their other trade to leeward is not so large: that is to Paita, Guiyaquile, Sansonat, Penama &c.[187] The trade to Guiyaquil is chiefly for timber, cocoa & drugs. That to Penama small since the Spanish ships have found the way round Cape Horn, the treasure from thes[e] parts being now carried to Spain in those European ships.

[186] Valparaiso, La Concepcion, Valdivia and the Isle of Chiloe, are all in modern Chile.

[187] Paita is in Peru, Guayaquil in Ecuador, Sonsonate in El Salvador and Panama in Panama.

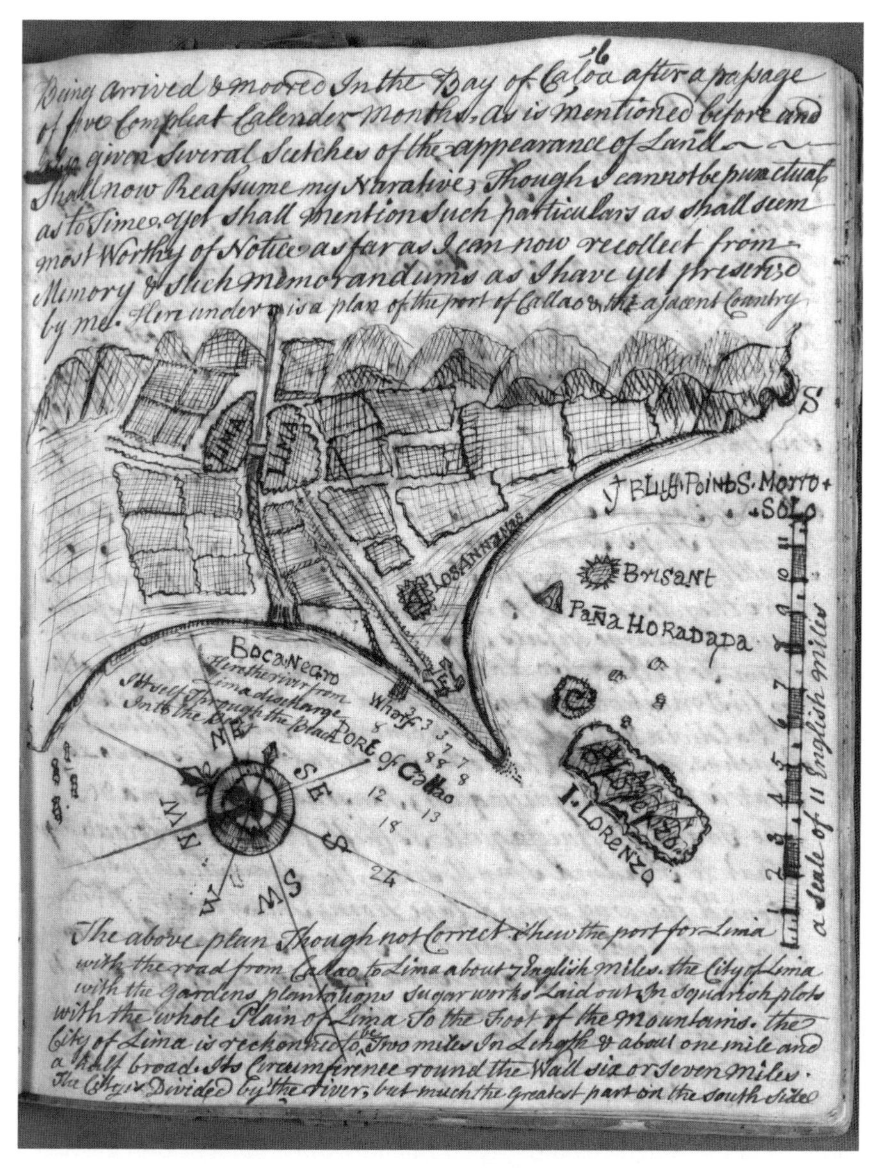

16

Being arrived & moored In the Bay of Caloa after a passage of five Compleat Calender Months, as is mentioned before and given several Scetches of the appearance of Land
Shall now Reassume my Narative, Though I cannot be punctual as to Time, yet shall mention such particulars as shall seem most Worthy of Notice as far as I can now recollect from Memory & such memorandums as I have yet preserved by me. Here under is a plan of the port of Callao & the ajacent Country

The above plan though not Correct shew the port for Lima with the road from Callao to Lima about 7 English miles. the City of Lima with the Gardens plantations sugar works Laid out In squarish plots with the whole Plain of Lima To the Foot of the Mountains. the City of Lima is reckoned to be Two miles In Length & about one mile and a half broad. Its Circumference round the Wall six or seven miles. The City is Divided by the river, but much the greatest part on the south side

Figure 5 *Sketch plan of port of Callao and city of Lima*

But now to give some discription of Callao & its destruction. Callao was situated upon the neck of land where the fort now stands, was very compact, wall'd round and strongly fortified for the defence of its self & the port and also accounted a bulwark for the security of [*f.60r*] Lima. Its destruction happened on the 28th, of the month called October in the year 1746, by a dreadfull earthquake and innundation of the sea. This city was said to *be* very populous being pleasantly situated upon a neck of land betwixt the sea & bay, so no doubt a healthfuller air than Lima. Besides I was told here was many foreigners married & settled here, one of them a Scotch man who had been a gunner in the place and was saved. I often convers'd with another that was saved, being one of the country, I sailed with afterwards in *a* voyage to Chiloé. From these & others I have had the following relation of the progress of the earthquake until that fatal night when the city of Calao was swallow'd up or destroy'd by the earthqua*ke* and innundation of the sea, which is nearly after the following manner.

For about two or 3 months before the shocks of the *earth* were more frequent than usual & more violent, and as the fatal period approch'd, they grew more so, that for 2 or 3 week[s] before its destruction; the earth kept almost continual tremor or shaking: so that many of the inhabitants began to be greatly alarm'd, fearing what they call a general earthquake which they say commonly happen every 30 years. So that many of them remov'd to other places, but the greater part stay'd, destined as it seems for destruction. The fatal night, though the air was calm & serene, there came on such a tremendous earthquake, which shoke the earth in such a terrible manner that the people could neither stand nor sit, without great difficulty, the earth rising & falling like the waves of the sea. This threw down the houses both at Callao & Lima, but at Callao the sea rose to such a prodigious height that it darkened the horizon. & by three successive mighty waves; three from the sea & 3 out of the bay meeting each other over the city and in retiring off again carried all before them so that in about two hours, there sca[r]se appeared any signs that a city had formerly stood there. About 40 I think I was told were taken up next day found upon pieces of timber & other [*f. 60v*] floatible things. And amongst the small number that was taken up next day floating upon the wreck of the city, I think I was told were some women & children, which shews the Almighty is able to preserve whom he is pleased to preserve. One king's ship & all the merchants ships in the bay were lost being some carried over the walls & house far upon the land and there left dry when the sea return'd. Part of 2 or 3 of them were still remaining when *we* arriv'd in the year 1750. These tremendous waves carried up with them thousands of tuns of chingly stones to the distance of half a furlong or more from the waterside, too great a quantity to be thought of removing.

To mention an instance of the irresistible force of those waves, I was told that a large brass cannon, I think a 32 pounder, which was known by its marks to have been planted on a battery next to the bay, was carried by the violence of the water over where the city stood & left near half a mile from thence upon the marshes. Before I proceed farther to give description of this place, [I] shall mention a relation of one I afterwards sail'd with in a voyage to the island of Chiloé. He said before he was carried of[f] into the bay, he heard the lamentable cryes & shrieks of people under timber & other heavy things which the sea had floated upon them, & in running off left upon them which at its return again, floated them all, & carried them off together, both those which were crush'd to death and those that were only maimed. He say he was carried quite out into the bay & seeing a truss[188] of tobacco, swiming he got to it & rested upon it, and *was* carried out by the sea toward the island St Laurence, where seeing a small vessel driving backwards & forwards; he quited his truss & swum to her finding only a woman [*f. 61r*] on board. I think this was almost the only vessel saved, and the same I afterwards made a voyage to Chiloé in.

When we arrived at Callao in 1750 Callao remained an intire desolation; no remains of the city to be seen, but a few pieces of broken walls standing on the land side. For a considerable time people were forbidden to look amongst the ruins; until they had made a strict search for what they call the church plate. But long before we arriv'd the prohibition was taken off so that many of our people as well as myself, often took the pains *to* search amongst the ruins. Some of them found some dollars; but I never had the luck to find any thing of value. Yet I observ'd we generaly had a foot or more of earth to remove before we could come at the pavement either of houses or streets. The violence of the water forced great quantities of bones out of the graves or other repositories where they lay their dead. For I saw in the way to Los Animas near the road side large heaps of human bones piled up with little wooden crosses placed a top of them, by some superstitiously pious people, who no doubt judg'd it a meritories act. At present besides the ships' tents, where they lay their commodities till disposed of, there are but few houses which are chiefly Indian huts built with canes, excepting 3 or 4 shops or eating houses, where they also sell wine & brandy. These are also built with canes & clay'd over.

Since the ruin of Callao, they are building a town about a mile from Callao by the road to Lima where they say the sea stop'd. This town is called Los Animas (or the souls). The houses also in this village are many of them built with canes, one end stuck in the ground standing right up & cross'd with others, wrought something after the manner of hurdles. A top they lay pieces of cane a cross and cover them with bulrushes. The better sort of houses are built with bricks dry'd in the sun & slightly cover'd as they have little rain or high winds here, the climate agreeing with the tittle given the ocean, Pacifick or peaceable. Before I proceed to give some discription of Lima, I shall just mention the prodigious height the sea rose when Callao was destroyed [*f. 61v*] as I was told. The high mountainous island called by the French St Laurence which *is* at the mouth of the bay had only the tops of the mountains above water.

[188] A truss was a bundle or collection of objects bound together: *OED*.

I shall now endeavour to give some discription of the great & rich city of Lima, the metropolis or capital of Peru.[189] Lima is about two Spanish leagues or seven English miles from Callao & bears from each nearly due east & west so that if lattitude may be reckoned the same, so that by my estimation the city of Lima is situated in 12° 8 south lattitude and in 72° 28 west longitude from the meridian of London and from the meridian of Paris 74° 43 west. Its bearing and and [*sic*] distance in a direct line from London is nearly southwest 5400 miles. But round by Cape Horn the nearest distance is 9931 miles, though a ship must sail several hundred leagues more to double the Cape. The city of Lima being the capital of Peru the vice roy resides here. It is also the seat of an archbishop, the secretary of a new one we carried over in our ship from Spain. But his grace, did not chuse to venture his person with us, though we brought his secretary & baggage, himself going round by the West Indies as the safer way. This great city is regular built, the streets broad & spacious. It is compos'd of many little squares, besides the great square or placa before the vice king's palace, where the largest & principal market is kept, and is well furnish'd according to the country: with beef though ordinary, mutton, cabereta or goats' flesh, fowls &c and with plenty of many sorts of greens, and a great variety of fruits as oranges sour & sweet lemons, pineapple, guavas & many other lushious fruits suitable to the climate. Also European fruit as apples, pears, peaches &c; though the European fruit which grow in Peru are nothing near so good as those which grow in Chili where they far exceed in quality those which grow in the northern countrys of Europe. This city is by some reckoned two miles in length, one mile & a half broad & [*f. 62r*] six miles round by the walls; by some much more. It is divided into two parts by a river or fresh, over which is built a strong stone bridge with many arches. This river is supposed, a great part of it, to proceed from snow melted from the high mountains in the hottest seasons, the tops of which are never free from snow, though the sun passes & repasses over them and are seen from the shiping in the bay, when the tops of the mountains are clear of clouds. This river is showl and rapid, divides it self into many branches, one of which run down to Callao. But the largest branch discharge[s] itself into the bay through the beach at Bocca Negro about two miles to the eastward of Callao. Besides this river, there is in the great square or market place, a very fine fountain with a large image of brass erected in the middle which continually keep spouting out water through sever*al* branches and fall down into a large stone bason. From this fountain many of the inhabitants fetch their water, and no dought but there is many more fountains for conveniency in the city. So that the city of Lima is well supply'd with water, a gratefull blessing in a

[189] Henry Hutchinson, a former factor of the South Sea Company was one of the very few Englishmen to have visited Lima before Secker, probably doing so in 1736 or 1737: Williams, *Buccaneers, Explorers and Settlers*, I, p. 46.

hot country. That part of the city to the eastward of the river is small compared with the west side. The houses in Lima are built low, on account of the frequent earthquakes. The vice roy have a stately palace on the east side of the great square with a prison adjoining. I have seen it related by an author in his discription of Lima that there are in this city 8 parishes, 3 colleges, 28 monastries of friars, and 13 of nuns, and 2 hospitals for the sick, poor & disabled. Though I know there are many of each sort & have been with the Spaniards in several of those of the men, yet had no opportunity to ascertain the exact number of either. Their churches are very rich & costly within, and have a hansome appearance without. The better sort of houses though low; were pretty regularly [*f. 62v*] built before the great earthquake in 1746.

But in the year 1750 when we arriv'd the city appear'd like one that had suffered a long siege and from bombardment & cannonading had most of the houses damaged & partly knock'd down. The streets were so full of rubbish from the fallen houses & other edifices. Their churches had many of their steeples thrown down, or rent from top to bottom & their bells some down and some hanging by the way upon the ruins of the walls. Some of those spires & turrets which did not fall directly down, leaning so frightfully as if just going to fall. Many of these were taken down, and great repairs made both of their churches & houses while we remain'd in those seas. The earthquake having made sad havock in this city as well as other parts of the plain lying betwixt Callao & Lima.

One day being at Lima, I took a walk over the bridge into the east part of the city, where coming to a convent pleasantly situated at the foot of the mountains, belonging to the Franciscans, and meeting with one of that order who seem'd very courteous in his behaviour, with whom falling into discourse he told me their convent received no hurt from the earthquake. And asking him what number of people they judg'd might be lost by the earthquake, he told me that by their registers they computed that at Lima, Callao & ajacent places, to be about seventeen thousand. But as there were a great many foreigners not register'd, he thought the number must be greater. Though the deluge of the sea did not reach Lima by about six miles, yet great numbers of people lost their lives, by the fall of houses & other edifices. There is one thing very troublesome here, especially to a protestant; the great number of begging friars, who are to *be* met with almost in every place. They go generaly two & two but some times but one. These carry an image inclosed in some thing like the head case of a clock, with a glass door before it, which they open for people to kiss this saint, in whose name they beg theirs [*f. 63r*] alms, & it is accounted an affront neither to kiss it or give something.

A trial of this kind I was once put to at Callao. A great number of our ship's company of different nations with myself, standing in a row handing water from one to the other in buckets, to fill some casks in the boat for our ship's use. One of these begging friars came with his saint, and began to present at one end of the rank to each as he came along, who all of them took it and kiss'd it and so return'd it to him again. When coming to me, who stood about the middle of the rank and offering it to me, as he had done to the others, I told him in Spanish I did not chuse to kiss it. He look'd sternly at me but said nothing, but offer'd it to the next and so from one to the other, until he had offer'd it to all, none refusing but myself.

Now it had been a common practice with me, both at Lima & els[e]w[h]ere when I saw any of *them* coming towards me, to turn off some other way on purpose to shun them that I might not give offence, but being at this time hemmed in by the rest & upon duty I could not step out of the rank without the rest taking notice of it. Howsoever after we had done handing water, I walked away by myself very serious, and pondering in my self what might be the consequence of my refusal; having been told there was at Lima an Inquisition. And walking some stones t[h]row from the place where we handed water, I heard by the ratling of the stones some one coming after me, and turning to look, saw the same friar with his saint coming after me who had watch'd to catch me alone, that he might have an opportunity to speak to me. I stopt till he came up; when he accosted me in Spanish, nearly in the following manner. 'Sir', said he, 'I perceive you are neither of our country nor religion'. I told him I was an English man & a protestant, & that it was not the custom in my country to kiss such things. He said, he commended me for not denying my principles, [*f. 63v*] and said to me if you should come into any trouble while in this country on account of your religion, do but let me know it, and I'll do you all the service I can. I return'd him thanks. He also invited me to go with him to one of the Pulperias or eating house to drink a glass of wine, but I refused & thank'd him. The friar seemed to be greatly affected at my constancy to my principles, singly alone amongst such a great number of different nations for *we* might be about 30 of us in all natives of several countreys. Howsoever this proved of great service to me afterwards as I often went to Lima, this friar shew me to others of his begging brethren, telling them the story, and that I would neither kiss it or give any thing. They soon knew me so well that they would pass by me without offering their image or wooden saint to me to kiss and if another was in company they would offer it to him without taken notice of me, which freed me from the from the [*sic*] fatigue of shunning them by walking out of their way.

Having given some discription of Lima & Callao, & of that dreadfull calamity which befell them from that most tremendous earthquake & innundation of the sea, shall before I proceed to mention our own affairs, shall give some account of the inhabitants. Here are to be seen, I think almost all the colours that are to be found amongst the human species; as while black mustees, malatoes,[190] & tawny Indians, besides a mixture of all these. The white people are in general pretty civil & courteous to strangers, and seems better affect'd towards the English than the French, though we have been so lately at war with them. Most of them speak respectfully of Commodore Anson, & say he was a man of his word, & that he used his prisoners well. And indeed the character they give the English in in [*sic*] general, is that they are people of their word. This I presume from a people tinctur'd with prejudice against such as are of different principles in religion, is no small character, more especialy in these remote parts of [*f. 64r*] the world, where they have but little opportunity to be aquainted with foreigners, nor of their principles or morals. These people as I said, behave behave [*sic*] civily, excepting that impertinence which is too common in most Roman Catholick countreys. That is, to ask a stranger whether he be a Christian that is a Roman Catholick, all other Christians under what ever denomination they esteem as hereticks. If one answere Catholick, they will make much of him; if otherwise some will dispise, others seem to pity.

Such as one a particular instance of this I had some few days after we arrived in the Bay of Calao. Myself with some others accompanied with some Spaniards, went to see the city of Lima; & being in the placa or market place, a gentleman & his wife being in their coach about to leave the city, but seeing many people flock about us, asking questions and observing us different in dress to the Spaniards with us, ask some of them of what nation we were, who told them we were English. He said to his wife, 'my dear these are the people we have been so long at war with; they look to be cleaver men, what a pity it is, they are not Christians'. Which shews how people of noble & generous minds are biased in their judgments through a blind & superstitious zeal and wrong notion of Christianity. Whereas true Christianity enrich the mind with charitable sentiments for their fellow creatures making allowance for the disadvantages they may lay under from example & precept, well knowing that true religion consist not in nation & form, but in nature & practice. For certainly justice & charity, proceeding from an upright heart, are works of Christianity and when shown by such as do not go under that name, yet at the last will have a Christian reward. They proceeding from the same divine principle or seed of grace in the heart, which the good works of Christians are acted from, and doubtless will have the same if not a higher reward, considering the superior advantage one have over the other.

But now after this long digression, I shall endeavou*r* to give some account of our own transactions. Sometime after our cargo was discharg'd & carried up to Lima, many of our people fell sick of what they call the

[190] A mustee was the offspring of a white and a quadroon. A malatoe or mulatto was an individual with one black and one white parent. More generally, both terms were applied to people of mixed race: *OED*.

countrey disorder which is a fever inte*r*mixt with aguerish symtoms which [*f. 64v*] most strangers are subject to till season'd to the climate. Of this disorder I believe we had five or six died; & I myself seemed at one time to appearance likely to add one to that number. At first our sick were sent up to one of the city hospitals at Lima. But some Protestants falling sick and being sent to that hospital; the friars who look after the sick there, used such importunity to make *them* turn Christians as they call it when they get a Protestant to change his religion. This usage was so perplexing to the sick Protestants and one Laurance a Sweede dying there, who we were told by his country men who visited him there had been sorely perplex'd by those superstitious friars, they useing both promises and also threatenings to make him *turn* but without effect. From several other circumstances which came to our knowledge we had great reason to believe he was not fairly dealt by at last. I believe our captain though a Roman Catholick thought the same. For after the death of Laurance the Swede our captain sent no more Protestants to the city hospitals, but made one of an up[p]er room at the factory where our own doctor look'd after our sick, & I think we had no more Protestants died of the country disorder after Laurance.

Whilst poor Laurance was sick at the city hospital, I being at Lima had a great desire to see him, but having one of our ship's company with me who would go with me who was an Irish Roman Catholick so that when I got to him I could ask him but few questions of his usage, but just how he did & whether they gave him any physick, & biding take such things as he found did him good, & such as he found made him worse to empty into his chamber pot. Which put the Irishman in such a rage, that it was long before I could pacify him. What did I think he said the fathers would give him any thing to do him harm. Yet we Protestants firmly believ'd he had not fair play for his life. But as they had used him badly, according to what he told his country men, & he continuing stedfast, they [*f. 65r*] resolved he should not come on board to tell of his usage. This was our belief, but whether true must be left to him, to whom no secret is hide.

After many of my shipmates had been taken ill of the fever, & sent to our new hospital at the factory, it also fell to my lot. Where after staying some considerable time and getting a little better, myself with several more, return'd to the ship, hoping the fresh air in the bay would conduce to our quicker recovery. After being on board some time I had a great desire to have my head shaved, which I got one of our people to do for me; and going on the fore castle of the ship to have it done in the fresh air, & sitting a considerable time bare headed, the pores of which being much open by a great deal of sweating, the cool air struck directly through my head into my stomack, so that my breath was in an instant stopt, that I could not fetch my wind. I run down directly unto the main deck, making a frightfull noise, I striving to get my wind. The boatswain, a French man, walking the main deck, hearing me, run directly & got hold of one of my arms calling another man, who took hold of the other arm; and kept me from falling down, or I must have expired directly. They led me about the deck, and ordering some fresh broth, which was boiling for the sick people on board to be brought, I got with much difficulty some of it down; which made way for the wind to come up and I to breath again. This boatswain who was thus instrumental in saving my life said in a voyage before at this place they lost a man in the same manner I was taken, by suffication. This disaster t[h]rew me back again brought, brought [*sic*] on the yellow jaundice & bloody flux so that I was oblig'd to go to our hospital at Lima again.

But before I proceed to relate my journey to Lima I shall just mention what I saw the night before I was taken with the suffication. Some time in the night I having occasion to go upon deck to make water, going into the starboard gangway & looking forwards, saw a shade come off the starboard side of the fore castle, moving directly towards me, (to my great [*f. 65v*] surprise), when it got about the middle of the main deck, then turn'd under the booms which lay over the main deck and went forewards again where *I* lost sight of it. This frightened me much and was a fore token of what happened next day. For it came off the same side of the fore castle & took the same turn upon the main deck as I did the day following when taken with a suffication. After waiting some days & not getting better, I concluded to go to our hospital again and was order'd to be put on shore. I walked to Los Animas intending to hire a mule there to carry me the other six miles to Lima, but at that time there was not one to be got so was obliged to walk all the way, setting often down upon one thing or other to rest myself being very weak & disheartened, looking upon myself as past recovery. Yet it pleased kind providence to enable me to get up to Lima though I was a a [*sic*] long time in doing it: and indeed if I had got a mule to ride on, the [a]lighting so often as my distemper would have occasion'd would have been very troublesome to me. The next day after I got to Lima I went into the market and *bought* some sower oranges & radishes. These I sliced & put in a dish covering them with lump sugar, & set them out all night in the dew which disolved the sugar & made a syrup, which I was to take in the morning fasting. This cure for the jaundice I had from a Spanish boatswain of one of the country ships. I not only drunk the syrup according to his advice, but eat oranges, radishes & all, which after repeating it a few times cured me of the jaundice. Having a dry'd briony root[191] by me, which I got at Tenby in Wales when master of a vessel by direction of my mate a West Countrey man, who cured a countrey man of his who was mate *of* a sloop which came from Jamaica and put in there by contrary winds, who was so reduc'd by the flux that he was carried a shore like a dead corps[e], be*i*ng

[191] Briony root was the English name for the plant genus Bryonia, especially in its common wild species: *OED*.

wasted so much, that he appear'd nothing but skin & bones. My mate gave him of this root powder'd about as much as would lay upon a sixpence, twice a day, which cured [*f. 66r*] him of his flux, so that in about two weeks he was able to go on board his vessel again to do his duty. Of this root I also took in broth twice a day about the same quantity which soon chang'd the bloody flux into a white one, and in a short time quite cured me. So that in about two weeks from the time I left the ship I return'd again on board the ship in a good state of health without taking any of our doctor's physick, to the great amazement of the people on board. This was another great deliverance from the merciless jaws of death and which I ascribe to the tender mercys of of [*sic*] a gracious Creator who was pleased to give a blessing to the remedies I took. And from that time forward, all the time I remained in these seas was favour'd with a good state of health.

Yet before I leave this subject, shall give a short account of the process our doctor took with his patien[t]s, when they came up sick with a fever to the hospital. First a vomit, next a glister, to cool & prepare the body for the bark, which he prepared in the following manner. He took such a quantity of the bark powder'd, as is sufficient for the number he has at that time to prepare for, put it in a bowl, to which he squeeses in as many sower oranges as will make it of a proper consistancy, sweetening the whole with lump sugar, & then gives to each patient, in quantity according to his judgment, which generaly carried off the fever; though in some few instances failed. As we had several died at our own hospital, one of which a Spaniard, who died while I was there, when jus*t* expiring and even until he was quite dead, two of his countrey men got their mouths close to his ears crying Jesus Maria, Jesus, Maria till quite dead, which seemed to be intended by his zealous comrades to stir up the dying man's dependance for mercy on Jesus & his Mother.

The next thing in order which I shall relate and what befell me in consequence thereof, is my voyage in a snow belonging *to* Lima, called the San Pablo or (Saint Paul), to the island of Chiloé and Baldivia. But first as a necessary introduction, our sick people being all recover'd who did not dye and [*f. 66v*] having liberty both Spaniards & foreigners to work on board the countrey ships or on shore, or go where we lik'd, so we were but forth coming when wanted. The captain desiring to have no more on board than to keep the ship sweet & clean, which was a great saving to him as all sorts of provisions are very dear here, and the ship likely to lay a long time here before the cargo could be dispos'd of. So that we often wrought on board the countrey ships where we got a dollar a day & our victuals & when we had no work went on board our own ship, until we we [*sic*] met with another jobb.

But I having a mind to see what I could of the countrey ship'd myself in the snow before mention'd called the San Pablo or Saint Paul commanded by one Captain Colee, an ancient Frenchman who had been many years a pilot in these seas, & now had got the command of this vessel, in which myself & a comrade of mine, a Londoner named Isaac Sequin, born in London but of French discent, his parent fleeing from France in the time of the persecution settled in London. This man with several others who came out with the ship from London to Cadiz, shiped themselves for the South Sea in her. This ship was built in London for the South Sea Company who expected to have got liberty at the conclusion of the peace in 1748 to have traded to Spanish America; but being disappoin*ted* sent her to Spain to be sold. She was about 1000 or 1200 tun burden, & was called the Grand Tuscany, and bought by the Spanish merchants for a South Sea man.

But to return to my own affairs, we two having ship'd ourselves with the captain for the island of Chiloé, sailed from the Bay of Calao the 20th of the 11th month (Nov.) 1750. I think we were to have 12 dollars per month. Nothing worth remarking happened in our passage there but what is customary in such voyages to the southward, we having the south east trade wind against us, streck'd off between the south & west as the wind would admit, until we got into the lattitude of about 30 degrees south, where meeting with variable winds we stood to the eastward, directing [*f. 67r*] our course for our intended port. The direct course from the Bay of Calao to the island being south 4 degrees 42 east, distance 1794 miles. But we being oblig'd to run off between the south & west on account of the SE trade make the distance make the distance [*sic*] much greater. The 24th of 12th month (December) we arriv'd in English Bay, anchor'd in 9 fathoms. English point bearing from us NW to N distance about one mile which point be a good observation lays in 41° 48 south and in longitude by my estimation from London 72° 58 west. We were 34 days on our passage to this bay.

The 25th we weigh'd & run up to the town of Chockow, about 30 miles from from [*sic*] this bay call'd English Bay. I suppose it had this name from the English buccanneers & privateers, formerly visiting this place for provisions. Their town of Chockow is the principal town in the *island*. Here the governor resides, and it has a fort for its defence against an enemy. This town is not compact, but stands strag[g]ling and is not very large. Each house for the most part have a yard & garden adjoining to it. The Indian farms are scatter'd all over the island. Some of these Indian farms I have been at. Both Spaniards & Indians are civil to strangers, not subject to that bigotry as at Lima & other more populous places, being freer from priest craft, the bane to civility, spoiling the peoples & principles & makes them worse than they would *be* by nature. The Indians though under the denomination of Christians and under subjection to the Spaniards, yet they do not like them in their hearts, but keep up by tradition from age to age a revival of that barbarous usage & massacre their forefathers suffered from the Spaniards. And to a stranger they are very free in expressing that loyal regard they have still for their former Incas or emperours, and by their words seems to live in hope that some time or other they shall be freed from the Spanish yoke & this being a poorish place & not so much gold & silver storring [*sic*], so they have but few priests, & those of the simpler sort sent out by their superiors, sent from Lima & other great places. And I have observ'd where the people are freest from the superstitious doctrine of their priest & left more to simple nature, their [*f. 67v*] prejudice to strangers is less, & civility more. It is a custom here when a stranger go into their houses, after setting down a while, to present him with a roasted potatoe, which grow in plenty here. The chief manufactory amongst them is making what they call puncios which are worn by most of the Spaniards. These are of different prices, according to their different qualities, some are white & some blue. They are of an oblong form something like a blanket, with a slit near the middle for the man to put his head through, falling down behind & before & also over the shoulders. They are all wrought round the sides & the slit with divers colours & devices. While I was in these seas I was vain enough to buy one of these puncios, a white one which are the cheapest & I think six or seven dollars. This was to put on when I went ashore that I might appear some thing Spanish Don like. Besides puncios, they manufacture cabinet ware, which they carve very ingeniously with their knives, which are carried to Lima and other parts. I brought 2 boxes of their making to England with me. They also make a great quantity of hams & export cedar planks, cypress & other boards for building.

Having given some discription of this island & its inhabitants, [I] shall proceed to give some account of our own affairs. After discharging such things as we brought from Lima, before the vessel was fitt to take in her cargo of boards we had occasion for a carpenter to do some jobbs on board. And there being a French carpenter settled in this place, the captain hired him to do what was wanting. And I having a pretty deal of discourse with him while he wrought on board on various subjects, some of them being on navigation. He reported that there was two English men navigators on board, though my comrade Isaac Sequin did not understand navigation. This coming to the governour's knowledge he sent for us on shore and when we came to him he told us *the* reason of his sending for us was that we being navigators he wanted one of us to pilot a ship he was building for the governor of Baldivia[192] to that place. But understanding my comrade was no navigator his application was wholy to me, telling me if I would pilot his vessel to Baldivia, he shortly *should* put another vessel upon the stocks & I should go captain of her. I [*f. 68r*] told him that I was an English man & a Protestant, and that I came from Spain by the King of Spain's licence in our ship now laying at Calao and intended to return to Spain again in her.

[192] Now Valdivia in Chile.

He said he did not care what religion I was of, it was a pilot he wanted, and that he would make the captain pay me my wages. But after many great promises & much intreaty & finding he could not prevail, he let us go on board our vessel again.

After we had taken on board our cargo, chiefly of boards, we expected we should have gone directly for Lima but instead of that our captain was bound to Baldivia which he kept a secret from us, until out at sea. The 21st of month, 1st (Jan:) 1751 we sailed from Chockow, leaving behind us a small snow called the Brilliante belonging to Lima. Taking in a cargo for Baldivia, we had a pettiago to asist us t*h*rough the narrows, in case of being becalmed which is very dangerous if a vessel have not a commanding wind, by reason of the rapid tide & strong eddys & *a* rock which lay near the middle of the channel, called the stones. We being becalm'd under the high land & casting off our pettiago too soon, a small breeze springing up and afte*r*wards proving calm again, we had like to have been drawn ashore by the eddy upon two points, one called Mapapinda & the other point Gallan, & was so near the shore as to touch the ground twice or thrice. But the pettiago coming to our asistance again and a breeze springing up we got clear & into the broad channel, but being again becalm'd we drove out to sea with the tyde between English rocks & point Calinmapo. The tyde run so rapid here as to make a great sea, & the channel to look like the breach upon a shoal. A small breeze we stood out to sea all right steerings NWt to clear the norther[n]most point of land.

Next day the wind backing to the out ward, we bore away for English Bay & anchor'd there. He*re* we shifted our botegars, or water jars, from forewards aft, to put the vessel in a better trim, she being too much by the head. After several fruitless attemp[t]s to get to sea on the 5th, we left the bay & proceeded on our voyage for Baldivia. Whilst we lay in English Bay I was once ashore, & saw the form of the land, & that there *was* several families of Spaniards live upon the point who have plantatio*n*s. [*f. 68v*] Before I proceed to give an account of our voyage to Baldivia and what occurred in consequence of that voyage I shall endeavour to give a draft of the harbour channel & the appearance of land on both sides the channel & though not perfect, yet the best I had the opportunity to take in my situation being amongst a people always jealous of strangers.

This vulcano cast out fire to be seen in the night which seems to *fly* above the top of the *vulcano* a very great height. The top appears black, but below cover'd with snow, and where clear may be seen at least 40 leagues.

NB: in the *above* sketch of the entrance of the channel of Chiloé, the land of the island of Chiloé is not rounded enough to the northward for the distance from English point to point Coulin by my computation is 8 leagues ENE ½ Et. From thence to point Gallan Et. 2 miles. From pt Gallan to point

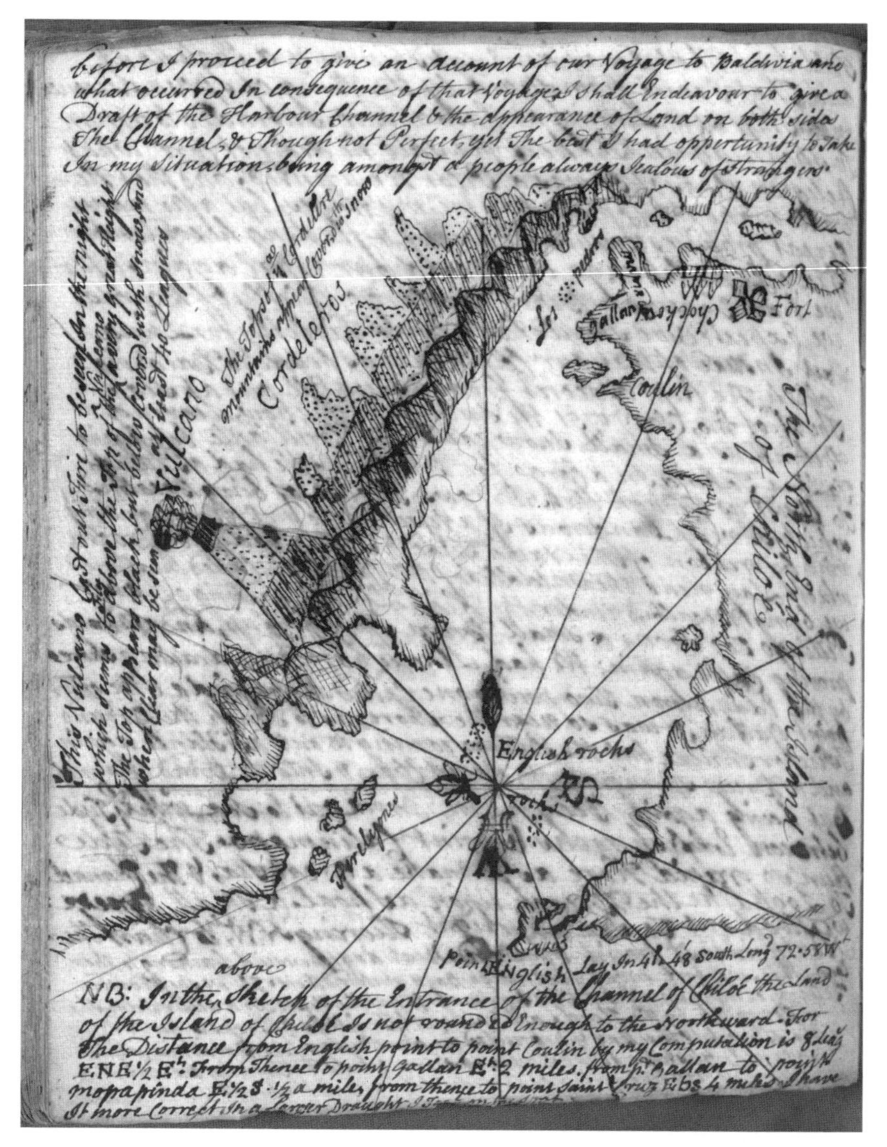

Figure 6 *Sketch map of the north end of the Island of Chiloé*

Mopapinda E ½ S ½ mile from thence to point Saint Cruz EbS 4 miles. I have it more correct in a larger draught I took on the spot. [*f.* 69*r*]

Having left English Bay on the 5th of 2d month (Feb) 1751 as is before mentioned we proceeded on our voyage for Baldavia, and the 8th arrived of the mouth of the harbour of Baldivia. But the Captain possest himself with a notion it was not the harbour, but that it was a place inhabited by Indians at war with the Spaniards, who would murther us if we fell into their hands. I had a very good observation off the port, & found by the chart of the South Sea that we were in the lattitude, being in 40° 00 S, but the captain could not be perswaded it was so, stood off to sea again. But while we stood in yesterday we got embay'd and it proving calm we were in great danger of being hove ashore by the swell of the sea. In so much as the captain was so terrified, that he kneeled upon the quarter deck and fervently prayed to the Virgin Mary for deliverance, the tears running down his cheeks, which I observ'd, and He who judges from the uprightness of the heart & not from the outward appearance of address I believe heard his prayer with acceptance. For almost immediatly & quite unexpected a breeze sprang up which set us free from the danger we then seem'd to be in and we clear'd the land & stood out to sea again.

The next day the 9th to day as we stood off about 4 in the afternoon we saw a sail, which we judge to be the snow named the Brilliante which *we* left at Chockow. She strech'd a head of us until she could fetch the harbour & then tack'd & stood in. We told the captain she would stand directly into the harbour. But he <no> said no, she would tack & stand off again. Night coming on lost sight of her, and she run directly into the harbour in the night, but as she approach'd one of the forts she was fir'd at & oblig'd to send her boat on shore. After being satisfied who they were, they demanded what vessel that was in the offing, that had been standing in & off the harbours for two or 3 days and did *not* come in. They said it was Captain Colee, a man well known there. The governour *asked* what is the reason he don't come in. They answer'd they *did not know* for he had two English pilots on board. O, said the governour, then they *are* sounding the coast.

We being at sea knew nothing of this till after we got in next day. About 5 in the morning we tack'd & stood in for the shore & not seeing the Brilliante we concluded she was gone into the harbour, so stood close in & the captain knew the land. So we stood in. But as we approach'd one of the forts they fir'd at us which surprised us but lowering our topsails & running in under an easy sail they let us pass, and we stood in & came to an anchor. But while I was pulling service upon the cable, I saw a la[u]nch coming from the fort of Mancero full of soldiers with the governour rowing directly for our vessel, who soon [*f. 69v*] [came] on board. The governour first set upon the captain in a very rough manner, asking him the reason why he had stood off & on for 2 or 3 days & did not come in, which frightened the captain so much that he could sca[r]se make him any answer. Next he asked where the two English pilots he had on board were. I being being [*sic*] still bussy in putting service upon the cable and hearing the governour ask for us, as the saying is, began to shake in my harness.

I went down upon the main deck off the forecastle and the soldiers were order'd to search my pockets. In which they found a piece of paper on which I had made a memorandum scroll of the bearing of the forts one from the other with my computed distances, but in such a manner none could make any thing of it but myself as the 3 forts one in front on the island Constantine called Mancero which signifies tame. The other two one on each side going in, called one Neblar, in English cloud, the other fort Coral which I named in the sketch I took child's play thing. These precautions I had taken for fear of surprise, seting it down after the following from child's play thing to tame, such bearings & distance setting them by compass. The governour order'd all my things to be brought out, not suffering me to go for them myself. Now I had only with *me* my hammock, in which I stow'd my things, having left my chest on board the ship I came in from Spain. The things I brought with me were a Hadleys Quadrant,[193] a chart of the South Sea, some books of navigation and a French Bible I bought in Holland. All these the governour took from me. But luckily the Indian sailors on board, hearing the rough language of the governour and having often seen me drawing sketches of the land went to the head of *my* hammock before it was brought out to be search'd & took out all the loose paper they could find, & hide them up, amongst which was a draught of the channel of Chiloé from whence we came so that he had only [*f. 70r*] the scroll of bearings & distances of the forts in fictitious names, my Hadleys Quadrant, a chart of the South Sea, some books of navigation & a French Bible. These the governour made prisoners, with myself & comrade Isaac Sequin.[194]

There was in the harbour a ship from Lima, called the Christo, or in English Christ. This ship was bound to Valparaiso. In this ship the governour intended to send us to the President of all Chili who live[s] at a city called Saint Iago[195] which lays some considerable distance in land from Valparaiso. While the governour was searching my hammock & taking away what is before mention'd, the captain & boatswain of the Christo came on board, and finding how severely the govern[ou]r intended to use us, pleaded hard for us; so that instead of being sent a short [*shore*] to one of the forts & kept in irons until the Christo sailed, by their intercession, who pass'd their words that we would not offer to escape, we were sent prisoners directly on *board* the ship. The same evening after it was dark I got the boatswain of the Christo, to let

[193] A quadrant was an instrument, shaped as a graduated quarter-circle, used to make angular measurements to calculate altitudes in astronomy and navigation, here named after its inventor, Edmond Halley: *OED*.

[194] Four of Sir John Narbrough's crew had been detained by the governor of Valdivia in 1670 for having inspected the harbour and fortifications there. Further English ships were prevented from trading there in 1684 and 1689/90, while Spanish authorities righty feared that this small garrison town had been singled out for projected British colonisation as early as the 1690s: Williams, *Buccaneers, Explorers and Settlers*, I, pp. 29–33, 38, 44.

[195] Santiago in Chile.

their boat put me on board the vessel we were taken out to get some of *my* things left behind which he kindly comply'd with. By which means I recover'd the papers the Indian sailors had hid, with some other trifles, but they had made free with some of my wearing apparel. I afterwards was twice at this place, in our own ship, & the governour took no notice of us.

After the ship was ready we sailed for Valparaiso, the governour sending the things he took from me with a letter of accusation to the president of St Iago. When we arrived at Valparaiso, we were order'd before the governour of that place where a council being held to consult whether we should be sent to the President of St Iago, or remain in irons in the fort until they had receiv'd his answer to the governour of Baldivia's letter. But here again our good friends the captain & boatswain of the Christo pleaded for us so we were sent prisoners on board the ship. The captain & boatswain accompann[y]ing the messengers sent by the governour to St Iago, a council was held & it was concluded as the ship we came out of Spain lay at Lima to send us to the Vice Roy of Lima with the letter [*f. 70v*] received from the governour of Baldivia & the things taken from me. The boatswain & captain having aquaint'd the president with the liberty our captain gave us to to [*sic*] go where *we* lik'd till he wanted us.

After our officers return'd from St Iago, our restraint was taken off, and we had liberty to go ashore & walk about, the same as if we had not been prisoners. After *our* ship was loaden with wheat the principal with some jerk'd beef & lard we sailed from thence for Lima, the captain giving us what they call a whole place. This is the same wages their best seamen had. We left Valparaiso the 3^{d} of 4th month, (Aprill) 1751 and arrived in the Bay of Calao the 22^{d} being 19 days on our passage. The governour of Baldivia's letter & the things taken from me being sent up to Lima to the vice roy, the next day he sent soldiers to conduct us to Lima. These, taking us ashore with them, put us in the stocks at the fort till they had provided a mule for us to ride on, which they mounted us on tying our legs together. And I being the oldest had the honour to ride before. After we were mounted on the mule, for our greater mortification they conducted us down towards the waterside amongst the Spanish sailors, giving us a bad name, telling the people we were English spies; so that some were for having us hang'd, some burnt, but none durst lay hands on us because of the soldiers.

After they <had> they had exposed us thus to the unthinking populous till the dusk of the evening, they set out for Lima, one part of them going before, & the other behind us. After we got to Lima they put us into a prison next the placa or market place. But we [*f. 71r*] were but just lock'd in, when orders came from the palace to remove us to the palace prison. In which we remained until released which was about 2 weeks, during which time we were several times brought into court & examined by the chief oyedor or judge. They being prepossest from the false account the governour of

Baldivia gave of us in his letter to the President of Chili that we were sent out by the government of England as spies to make observations in that countrey, though the English government knew nothing of our going, it being an act of our own. He first began to ask our parents' names, also what occupation they were of, with abundance of other frivolous questions. The oyedor could speak French so that in my examination (I being the principal offender) because I unde*r*stood navigation I was oblig'd to speak such words as I could to recollect in answer to his questions some times in Spanish, other times in French. But the oyedor not satisfy'd with this hoge poge[196] language, hearing of a Spaniard who lived some distance from Lima in the countrey, sent for him that he might examine us in English, it being reported he unde*r*stood that language. He being come we were order'd into court to *be* examined.

After we came into court the oyedor addrest himself to us in the following manner: 'I suppose' says he 'I can shew you a man who knew you in your own country, should you be glad to see him'? The oyedor thinking that if we were spies sent out by the English government, as he judg'd us to be, we should be stroke with fear. I saw thro the drift of the oyedor & directly answer'd that I should be very glad to see any one that knew me in [*f. 71v*] England. Then the oyedor orders the elderly man to ask us such questions as he should propose to him. This elderly Spaniard then stood *up* & said he lived in the country some distance from Lima, and that he was sent for to be interpreter for the oyedor. Then the oyedor desired him *to* ask us such & such questions which I answer'd, telling him that we came out in our ship with licence from the King of Spain. The captain having liberty to carry out so many foreigners, I think if I remember right fifty, because of his going round Cape Horn so late in the season. After I had told him what I thought most material, the oyerdor desir'd him to repeat what I had said to him but he told him quite different from what I had said to him so that I was obliged to call out that I said no such thing but so & so. Then the old Spaniard reply'd I thought you had said so. I told him no. He did not understand English. He said 'about 30 years ago I lived in London & could speak the language but I have forgot *it* after that'.

In the remaining part of our examination we proceeded as at first, sometimes in French other times in Spanish as I could recollect. After several examinations, and *not* being able to make out the governour of Baldivia's charge against us, we were sent for to the court & set at liberty. The oyedor behaved himself with great civilty, telling me to come to his house & he would deliver the things taken from me. Which accordingly he did in a very courteous manner and was very free in talking with me on various subjects. I shall now mention what I was told by the Spaniards of the reason of that rigourous behaviour of the governour of Baldivia towards us. It seems that

[196] Hodge podge was a disordered mess or clumsy mixture: *OED*.

the governour in his passage to the West Indies when he came from old Spain was taken by an English privateer, by which he was plunder'd & otherwa[y]s [*f. 72r*] used ill. For which loss & bad usage, he had threatened to be revenged on the first English that fell into his hands which happen'd to be the lot of myself & comrade.

I shall next mention a particular dream I had before I left the channel of Chiloé. I dreamt I saw a great number of very fine feather'd fowls pass by me, & afterwards in my dream I thought I was accused of something that I was wholly innocent of, but nothing would serve them but they would crucify me. *I* thought though I was innocent of what they charg'd me with; yet I was not worthy of such a manner of death. Being fixed on the cross I awoke, but at that time could not comprehend the meaning of my dream. Though afterwards I had reason to understand the meaning when I came to be brought before so many great men & afterwards suspected for a spy & tried for my life; which charge I was innocent of, & what observations I made in those *seas* was only out of curiosity, not having ill design against the Spaniards.

After we were thus set at liberty from our imprisonment, and also freed from the danger we seemed to be in of being put to death for spies, we went on board our own ship Tuscany, still riding at anchor in the Bay of Callao, having been absent from her about five months and 16 days. The vice roy soon after hired our ship to carry stores & provisions to Baldivia and the island Juan Fernand*ez*. The 7th of 8th month (August) 1751, began to rigg our ship for the intended voyage. 9th month 26th having taken on board a cargo for the above mentioned places, we were paid 25 dollars advance and 30th sailed from the Bay of Callao. And on our passage the 16th of 10th month spoke [to] a ship call'd the Trinidado, or Trinity bound from Callao to the island of Chiloé. She had been out 24 or 25 days. The 29th of same month we arrived at Baldivia, after a passage of 30 days. Having discharg'd the cargo we brought here, the 6th of 11th month we sailed from this place for Valparaiso to take in [*f. 72v*] provision for this place. Were 6 days on our passage from Baldivia to Valparaiso, arriving there the 12th when we took in a cargo of provisions and sailed again for Baldivia, and arrived there the 19th of 12th month 1751. The 10th of 1st month 1752 sailed from Baldivia for the Bay of La Conception, & the 11th in the evening arrived in the bay. Here we remained till the 31st, taking provision for the island Juan Fernandez.

But before I proceed any farther in the progress of our voyage [I] shall endeavour to give some account of Baldivia and the city of Pinco in the Bay of La Conception. But first of Baldivia, the place where the governour took myself & comrade out of the San Pablo snow as is before related. But now there was no notice taken of us. But the third & last time I was there got liberty to accompany some Spaniards in our boat to the city of Baldivia which lay up a branch of the river about 8 or 9 miles from where the ships anchor to unload. The city of Baldivia by my computation is situated nearly in the lattitude of 39° 56 south and in longitude 68° 48 west from the meridian of London. It stands upon a level neck of land; & seems to be laid out in quadra's or squares, according to the general custom of all citys in Chili & Peru. The houses, a few excepted, are but indifferently built, & those mostly of wood. Being thin of people the quadras are *not* filled up with houses, but instead of houses they are filled up with orchards & gardens, in which they have plenty of apples, strawberries & other fruit & garden stuff. Here the governour chiefly keep[s] except when there are ships in the harbour, then he goes down to Fort Mancera on the island Constantine where he remain[s] till the ships sail.

The land in general both up the river & along the coast is very mountainous & full of wood, excepting some savannas [*f. 73r*] or meadows near the water side and places cleared by cutting timber for building and exportation to Valparaiso and Lima. Some of the mountains are said to be very *rich* in gold from which doubtless the governour reap[s] great benefit, for it is reckoned a very profitable office to be governour of Baldivia. The forts are extreamly well situated for defending the port and *would* be very difficult to take were it defended by a sufficient number of resolute men and the gun carriages kept in good repair, but the case is quite otherwise. They have but few capeable men, which are most of them officers. The common people being most of them what they call forces or transports from Peru, & other parts of Chili for crimes commited, *&* would certainly revolt if they met with encouragement from an enemy of getting their freedom, for they *are* little better than galley slaves for the time they are transported and when their time is out many times under one pretence or other, are detain'd & cannot get away. The rich people at Lima sometimes send their sons here for 2 or 3 years to break them of those common vices of galantry & gaming. The Spaniard in general are free from drunkeness, but the afore mentioned vices are very prevalent amongst them.

The Indians betwixt Baldivia and La Conception are generaly in truce with the Spaniards but those to the southward between Baldivia & the island Chiloé are implacable in their hatred toward them, seldom sparing any that fall into their hands. Even those that venture to trade with them are often cutt of[f]. Many dismal storys of their barbarity have been told me by the Spaniards of Baldivia. [I] shall just mention the strength of the forts built to defend the harbour. First on the starboard side going in is Fort Amargo mounts eight 9 pounders. Next Fort Corral mounts six 9 pounder[s]. Next Fort Mancera on the island Constantine where the governour resides mounts twenty guns, 24, 18, & 9 pounders. On the larboard or northside going in is Fort Niebla, mounts twenty one 24 & 9 pounders. NB two of the forts I was not in I had the number of guns from the Spaniard.

[*f. 73v*]

Figure 7 *Sketch plan of the harbour of the city of Valdivia, including a scale of 21 English miles*

V. a volcano or burning mountain the same seen at Chiloua. Estim[ation] 30 leagues from Baldivia. The upper part, the top excepted is cover'd with snow. I have seen the same volcano at Chiloé by day sometimes clear of clouds by day cover'd with snow & by night casting fire a prodigious height above its top. But most in rainy weather or against raine & storms. A north & south moon nearly make high water at full & change.

A. The city of Baldivia in 39° 56 S & 68° 48 W.

B. Island Marequisa

C.C. Two small rivers running out of the [?larg]

E:E: The ship channel.

F. The Fort Mancera where ye governour resides when shipping in the harbour called the Island Constantine, 20 guns.

H. Rio Claro, or the clear rivier.

I. Fort Corral, 6 guns.

M. Fort Niebla, 20 guns.

l. Fort Amargo, 8 guns.

O. Morro Bonifacia in 39° 53 S, 68° 58 W.

P. Morro Gonzalos in 40° 00 S & 69° 13 W.

S. Island Le Muerte.

D. Island Del Ré.

R. Point Galera in 40° 10 S, 69° 13 W.

N. Boat channel.

N:B. In the year 1751 we found on the coast of Badivia 12 degrees E variation which is allow'd for in the draught & though not exactly true so near enough for a ruff scetch.

NB The figures show the depth of water.

[*f.* 74*r*]

Having given a sketch of the harbour of Baldivia *or* Valdivia, for more exactness I refer to my large draught. From this place in the year 1751 in the 2^{d} month called February myself & comrade Isaac Sequin were taken out of the San: Pablo as is before related, and sent prisoners to Valparaiso 421 miles, & from thence carried to Lima 1285, so that we were *carried* prisoners seve*n*teen hundred & 6 miles. Considering which, few besides myself would have run the risk of making so many observations and sketches of their ports.

I shall now proceed to the Bay of La Conception. First from the port of Baldivia 34 leagues and lyes in lattitude about 38° 30 south. About 16 leagues to the westward of La Macho lays another large island pretty high land & appears to be but little less than the island Juan Fernandez. The Spaniards say there is Indians live upon it, & a great many wild horses, but no port except for boats or launches. It lyes about 10 or 12 leagues from the main land. From the port of Baldivia to the [*sic*] island Quiriquina. Entring the Bay of La Conception is large & runs up some leagues betwixt the island Quiriquina & the main land, towards the head of the bay on the NE^{t} side stood the city of Pinko or Pinco.

This was a pretty large city situated in a fine climate lying nearly in lattitude 26° 43: & longitude 68° 19 W^{t} from London a place where provisions, wine & fruit were very plentifull so that it was reckoned an excellent place for ships coming into these seas to to [*sic*] touch at for refreshment. This city was destroy'd some months before we arrived there by a violent earth quake & innundation of the sea. Yet their loss of lives was not so great as might have been expected, they not loossing by their account not above 32 or 33. The earthquake coming violently on before the innundation, they had time to flee to the neighbouring hills where they were safe, but saw their property carried off by the sea. I think it was but the day after this great earth quake & over flowing of the sea [*f. 74v*] that the surge of the sea reach'd us in the Bay of Callao, which put the people in a great fright. Our ship swinging with her head to the sea the water run past her like a strong tide, till the water & land seem'd upon a level, then run off again towards the sea with the same velocity. This though repeated several times grew less & less till it remained still as before. The reason of this we knew not until about two or three weeks after when a ship which had touched at the Bay of La Conception brought word of the general earthquake upon the coast of Chili, and of the destruction of the city of Pinco.

But to return to La Conception, at this place I met with an ancient English man, who told me he was born at North [*i.e. Great*] Yarmouth, & had lived in that countrey about 36 years. He with several more being taken prisoners, they belonging to an English privateer who sent them ashore in the boat to seek water or other necessaries, the Spaniards laid in ambush for them & made them prisoners. But afterwards changing their religion they were set at liberty, married & settled in the countrey. I think he told me there was one or two besides himself at that time living but at some distance from thence in the countrey. This man had a wife living whose hair with age was white like wool, & also sons and daughters grown up to men *&* women. The inhabitants of this place are very affable & kind to strangers.

After we had remained here about 20 days, and taken in provisions for the island of Juan Fernandez, on the 31st of 1st month call'd January 1752 we sail'd for the island of Juan Fernandez. But before I quite leave this place I shall just mention that before *we* left as they were going to remove the guns of the fort built here for the defence of this place to another place beyond the head of the bay where they intend building a new city, out of reach of the flowing in of the sea. In a great earthquake this city having been distroy'd about 30 years before, by an earthquake & innundation of the sea. To prevent [*f. 75r*] which for the future, they now intended to build a new city in a place of less danger, & the sea not known to reach. But to return after we left the Bay of La Conception, we kept along shore till we past the rocks called Rappel which lays about 18 leagues to the southward of Valparaiso, and run off from the shore 2 or 3 leagues. Taking our departure from the main land, we stood off for the island Juan Fernandez & arrived there the 3^{d} of 2^{d} month (Feb:y) 1752. We staid here till the 10th, putting ashore such stores & provisions as we had brought for them.

This island Juan Fernandez, at which in the year 1741 Commodore Anson touched to refresh & recover his people, those who still remained alive being most of them very bad with scurvy, was at that time uninhabited.[197] But the Spaniards considering that this island had always been a rendezvous for their enemies[198] to refresh themselves and recover their sick after a tedious passage round Cape Horn, in order to cruize upon their coasts & plunder them, have since Anson was there settl'd it, built a small town, in a valley to the southward of the rising ground where Commodore Anson pitch'd his tent.[199] I saw some of the Pavement, as the Spaniards who dwelt there told me, also upon the shore some small remains of the Annpink.[200] But some months before we arrived at this island, at the time when the great earthquake happened upon the coast of Chili which destroy'd the city of Pinko in the Bay of Conception, this island though it lay so far from the main land, yet the sea rose such a height here & flow'd over the land that it destroy'd their new town and drownded about thirty of the inhabitants with their governour. Which caused a Spanish woman who lived in a house standing on the further *part* of the plain where Com: Anson's tent stood say to me as I was walking, by her house, understanding I was an English man, 'sure no people are such fools [*f. 75v*] as we Spaniards. Commodore Anson came here only to stay a little while, yet he had his tent erected upon this high ground. But we foolish Spaniards built our town down in a valley almost even with the sea, which flow'd in upon us and drownded us'. She farther told me that there was such a number of rats that destroy'd almost every thing they sew [*sic*].

I went also with some others to see some Indian chiefs who lived at a plantation to the eastward of the above mentioned lawn or plain. These Indians were transported here from Lima being taken prisonners by the Spaniards in the war betwixt them & the Indians. They had several cows; gave us some milk & behave very civily, & understanding that myself & another were English, they knowing the English had been not long before at war with the Spaniards, took an opportunity when the Spaniards that came with us were walking about their plantation to let us know how desirous they were that the English would come & take them away from that place; and what gold mines

[197] For the official account of Anson's time on Juan Fernandez see Walter and B. Robins, *A Voyage round the World*, pp. 111–61.

[198] The island had been recommended as a port of call to refresh English ships as early as 1682: Williams, *Buccaneers, Explorers and Settlers*, I, p. 32.

[199] A view of Anson's tent on Juan Fernandez was one of the illustrations that accompanied the 1748 edition of Anson's *Voyage*: Walter and Robins, *A Voyage round the World*, pp. 84–5.

[200] The Anna Pink was one of Anson's storeships that had been too badly damaged to continue the voyage and was broken up on Juan Fernandez in September 1741: Walter and Robins, *A Voyage round the World*, pp. 30, 64, 129, 135–41, 152–3.

they could discover to them if they attact the Spaniards ashore. These Indian chiefs spoke good Spanish and seem to be more industr[i]ous, & live in more plenty upon the island than the Spanish inhabitants who seem to be quite sick of the place since the deluge of the sea which drownded so many of them. They have erected a battery fronting the bay by Anson called Cumberland Bay, I suppose in honour of the Duke of Cumberland then living.[201]

I shall now mention the situation of this island. It lays in a very temperate climate being by a good observation in latt'd 33° 40 south and longitude by my estimation 74° 35 west from the meridian of London & 76° 50 from the meridian of Paris, which lays 2° 15 to the eastward of London [*f. 76r*] and lays distant from the follow[i]n[g] places on the main land as under specified vizce:

From the island Juan Fernandez to Valapariaso E[t] 5° 36 N 360m or 120 leagues.

From [Juan Fernandez] to Baldivia S 36° 50 E[t] 470 miles.

From [Juan Fernandez] to the Bay of La Conception S 59° 6 E[t] 356 miles.

From [Juan Fernandez] to the entrance of Chiloé - - S 7° E[t] 492 miles.

From [Juan Fernandez], to Lima the course is N 4° 53 E[t] 1300 miles.

From [Juan Fernandez] to the island Masa Fuera or the Lesser Island Fernandez WSW[t] about 60 miles or 20 leagues.

Thus this small island, which according to Commodore Anson's survey is not above 4 or 5 leagues in length and not quite 2 leagues in breadth, very mountainous and irregular in appearance at a few leagues distant is situated at the above noted distances from the principal Spanish ports on the continent of Chili & Peru. There is plenty of fish to be catch'd in the bay and also large cra[y]fish or lobsters, but we not being in want of provisions took but little pains to catch them. But before I quite leave this island, I shall just mention that walking & looking amongst the ruins of the houses destroy'd by the earthquake & innundation of the sea, I found a Spanish lancet[202] such as is used in bleeding which as a relick of curiosity I brought away with me having layn here about 7 days.

The 10th sailed from it for Valparaiso, & the 16th arrived there. Here we staid from the 16th of the 2[d] month to the 29th of 4th month, taking a cargoe of wheat, jerk'd beef & lard. The lard is used in this part of the world instead of butter, there being but *little* butter made here. This lard is taken from the cattle they kill for jerk'd beef, fry'd up as we do pork suet and then put into sheep skins with *the* wooly side outward, the sheep being flea'd [*flayed*] as we do rabits. It is surprising the quantity that is carried from this

[201] This comment shows that Secker was writing at least this part of the autobiography in 1765 or thereafter: W. A. Speck, 'Prince William Augustus, Duke of Cumberland (1721–1765)', *Oxford DNB*.

[202] A lancet was a surgical instrument, usually with two edges and a point like a lance: *OED*.

place & La Conception to Lima, w[h]ere the cattle they have are lean & yield but little fat. [*f. 76v*]

I shall next endeavour to give some discription of the port or road; as also the town of Valparaiso in the kingdom of Chili in the South Sea. Having been there three times, the town of Valparaiso, or in English the valley of paradise, lays by my estimation in the lattitude of 33° 5 South, and in longitude from the meridian of London, 67° 39 west. The port is a sort of bite or bay shelter'd by the land from the SE: S & SW^{t}, winds & also the west, NW^{t}, & northerly winds seldom if ever blow there, especially in the summer months when the shipping come shore to land. The town or city is situate by the bay side running back in a valley and spreading it self upon the descent of some neighbouring hills. To the eastward of the town & contiguous lay a fruitfull plain diversified with houses & gardens, wherin most sorts of European fruits as well as those of hotter countreys grew in great plenty. Here the apple & orange tree both thrive a like in the same garden. The beautifull quince tree bowing down with its large golden fruit, hath some times brought before the view of my mind the garden of paradice. These quinces are not only large & beautifull to look on, but when ripe both palatable & pleasant eating. Here the productions of nature shew themselves in their greatest perfection. Those sweet herbs, such as time, winter savory &c, which in England we nourish up with care in our gardens, grow here spontaneous without sowing as their natural soil producing an agreeable fragrancy as we walk upon them and on the hills sage grow in great plenty as fern or brakes do on our hills in England. Though the countrey is hilly, yet the valleys & those parts that will admit of cultivation are rich and produce plenty of wheat, large quantities of which are exported to Lima & other places. They have also a great many horses as well as other cattle of the neat kind which at a certain season are *fat* when they kill them to jerk and for their lard which in general is used throughout this countrey in the room of butter to dress their vituals with, having but little butter. [*f. 77r*]

They have a fort faceing the road or bay to defend themselves and the shiping who anchor near the shore. This place is situated in a fine temperate climate, but as an alloy to earthly felicity they are often alarmed with earthquakes, which are very frequent here, so that the inhabitants always keep a light burning in the night that they may see to get their cloaths & children to flee to the adjacent hills or water side for saf*e*ty. Their convents always keep watch & give warning by ringing bells. The people in general are civil & courteous to strangers. I once in company with some Spaniards took a ride some miles into the countrey to one of their estancias or farms where the people behaved civilly to me though a stranger.

A sketch of the city & port of Valparaiso in the kingdom of Chili in the South Sea in lattitude 33° 05 south and by my estimation in longitude 67° 39 W^{t} from the meridian of London.

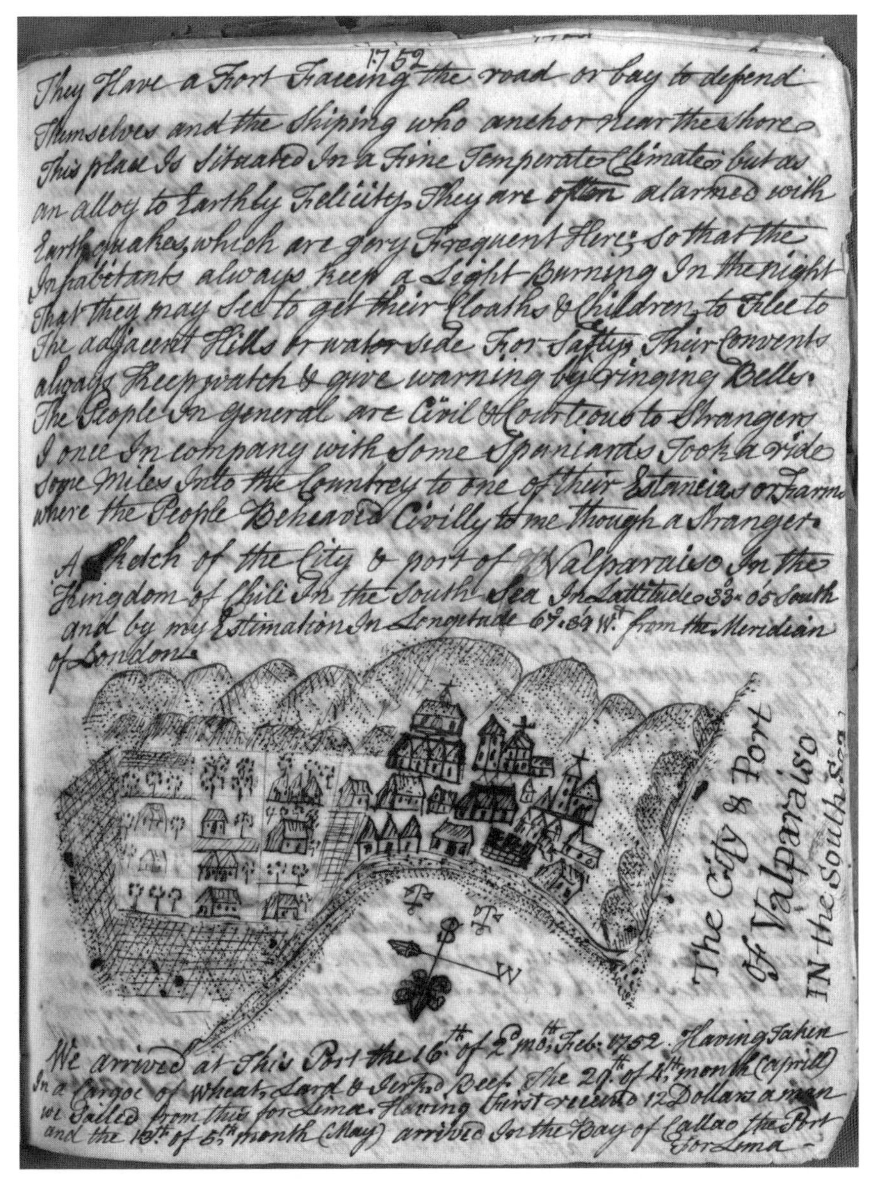
1752
They Have a Fort Facing the road or bay to defend
Themselves and the Shiping who anchor near the shore
This place Is Situated In a Fine Temperate Climate but as
an alloy to Earthly Felicity, They are often alarmed with
Earthquakes which are very Frequent Here, so that the
Inhabitants always keep a Light Burning In the night
That they may See to get their Cloaths & Children to Flee to
The adjacent Hills or water side For Saftey, Their Convents
always Keep watch & give warning by ringing Bells.
The People In general are Civil & Courteous to Strangers
I once In company with Some Spaniards Took a ride
Some Miles Into the Countrey to one of their Estancias or Farms
where the People Behaved Civilly to me though a Stranger.
A Sketch of the City & port of Valparaiso In the
Kingdom of Chili In the South Sea In Lattitude 33°.05' South
and by my Estimation In Longitude 67°.39' Wt from the Meridian
of London.

We arrived at This Port the 16th of 2d mo: Feb: 1752 Having Taken
In a Cargoe of Wheat, Lard & Jerk'd Beef The 29th of 4th month (Aprill)
we Sailed from this for Lima. Having First receiv'd 12 Dollars a man
and the 13th of 5th month (May) arrived In the Bay of Callao the Port
For Lima.

Figure 8 *Sketch plan of the city and port of Valparaiso*

We arrived at this port the 16th of 2nd month, Feb: 1752 having taken in a cargoe of wheat, lard & jerk'd beef. The 29th of 4th month (Aprill) we sailed from this for Lima, having first receiv[e]d 12 dollars a man and the 13th of 5th month (May) arrived in the Bay of Callao, the port for Lima. [*f. 77v*] But before I proceed farther in my nar*r*ative, shall just mention a facetious matter which happened in our passage in running down from Valparaiso to Callao. It being in Lent, the time when the priest confess the people, we had taken a priest of the countrey at Lima to go the voyage, a simple harmless *man* as he seemed to be. This man had bought at Valparaiso a pretty large quantity of apples for a venture which he put into a chest & was put betwixt decks. After we had been at sea some time, he had a mind to look at them to see if they did not begin to rott. He desiring an officer to go down with some help & bring his chest up, giving tokens by which he might know it, saying it was heavy. The officer after looking amongst the chests found one like what he discrib'd his to be, but seemed to *be* light and empty, and came up & told the *priest* of it. But he said it was none of his, for his was full & heavy & would have *him * go down again and & [*sic*] ransack. But coming up with the same story again the priest went down himself, & directly challeng'd his chest which openning he found empty & the apples stolen out. He came upon deck lifting up his hands, saying that one of the people confest to him he had stolen some apples, and he had absolved him and *could* not now tell who he was. The simplicity of the priest confession caused great laughter amongst the officers & others.

But to return from this digression to my narrative again. After our arrival at Callao in a short time we began to discharge our cargoe and the 5th of the month call'd June discharg'd the last of our wheat and the first of 7th month called July sailed from Callao for Guyaquill.[203] And the 11th arrived at the Punada, the norther[n]most end of the island Puna[204] where large ships lay to take in their loading, which is brought down in sloops from Guyaquile. Here is a town & governour. Here we lay until the 11th of the month called August taking in a cargoe of cocoa nutts, & some druggs, and the 11th of 8th month (August) sailed from the Punada for Lima. And the 9th of 10th, month (October) arrived at Callao, after a passage of 60 days. Having the [*f. 78r*] trade wind against us, we stretch'd off between the south and the west till we got into the way of variable winds & then run down our southing & easting which made the passage to[o] long.

I shall next give some discription of the Punada, the city & river of Guyaquile. At the Punada there is a small town, which may contain 20 or 30 houses, & a church of but a mean structure; also some scattering houses or farms here & there about the island. The houses have no ground floor, but are raised 10 or 12 feet from the ground by crotches of wood for fear of snakes, ants & other vermin & have a ladder to go up into their houses, which they can draw up. The city of Guiyaquil lys up a river about 7 or 8 leagues from the Punada on the island Puna, where the large ships lay to take in their cargoes which is brought down from that city in sloops. The

[203] Guayaquil now in Ecuador.

[204] The island of Puna in the Gulf of Guayaquil, off the coast of Ecuador.

city of Guiyaquil is about a mile or a little more in length & has one principal street, which run parallel with the river. Those which run backwards are but short & few of them. The town is situated for the most part upon a low, boggy ground which obliges them to have a wooden bridge over half a mile in length to pass from the lower to the upper part of the town. Otherways there would be no passing in the rainy seasons when the great freshes come down. The houses for the most part are built with wood & bamboes (a sort of hollow cane), not having much brickwork. Yet when consider'd what part of the world it is in is no despicable place as there are many rich shops & some of their *houses* have rich furniture. They have a pretty brisk trade with Panama, Peru & the ajacent countreys. & being the principal port in the South Sea for building large ships though small ones are built at several others. While I was there they were raising a large sh [*sic*] shed for building a sixty gun ship under it in the room of the Esperance an old fifty gun ship, broke up here, and was one of those which was sent out from Spain after Commodore Anson in the year 1740.

The produce of Guiyaquil is chiefly cocoa, timber for building, some balsams & drugs. The people seemed very civil to strangers. They *are* greatly pester'd with musketoes & ants, being caus'd to hang their vituals up in baskets to keep it from ants, [*f. 78v*] and to guard against the musketoes in the night to inclose their beds with thin linen or cotton, so that they can only buse about them. This place is very hot as it is situate but two degrees & 20 minutes to the southward of the line and their rainy seasons falls when the sun passes & repasses over them.

Having given some discription of Guiyaquil on the next leaf I have given a sketch of the land from Cape del Agujo & the island Lobos Marinos to Cape Blanco between which lay the town of Paita[205] *which* was taken by Commodore *Anson* plunder'd & burnt in the year 1741.[206] Also from Cape Blanco to the island Puna & up to the city of Guiyaquil & though not correct may show the form of the coast between those places. But for for [*sic*] more correctness & exactness of the form of the coast from Cape Blanco to Guiyaquil *I refer* to my large draught, which is drawn by a large scale the requisits for which I took in my voyage from Lima to Guiyaquill & is pretty correct. I shall next give some distances in the South Sea & then return again to my narrative just to shew the large tract of land the Spaniards inhabit in those seas from the island Chiloé.

From Cape Horn in lattitude 55° 40 to the north entrance of Chiloe 840 miles

From the island Chiloe in 41° 48 S & long^{d} 73° 20 to Baldivia in Chili 119–m

[205] Cape Aguja, Cape Blanco, the island of Lobos de Tierra, and Paita, are all now in Peru.

[206] For the official account of Anson's raid on Paita of 12 to 15 November 1741, see Walter and Robins, *A Voyage round the World*, pp. 178–92.

From Baldivia in 40° 00 & 72° 24 W to La Conception city Pinko- 200–m
From the Bay La Conception to Valparaiso harbour- 220–m
From the port of Valparaiso in 33° 5 & 67° 39 W^{t} to Lima- 285–m
From island Lobos in 5° 56 S & 76° 20 W^{t} to Paita- 60–m
From Paita in 5° 00 & 76° 00 W^{t} to to [*sic*] Cape Blanco- 51–m
From Cape Blanco in 4° 10 & 76[°] 8 to point Arena- 87–m
From point Arena on the island Puna to the Punada- 21–m
From the Punada in 2° 39 S & 75° 11 W^{t} to Guiyaquil- 25–m
From the island Juan Fernandez in 33° 40 & 74° 35 to Lima 1300–m
From Cape Horn to Aquapalco[207] in 17° N & 106° 8 W^{t} - 4773–m
From Aquapulco to Manila[208] W & S- 8883–m
From Aquapulco to Tenian[209] in 5° 8 N° & 219° [*sic*] 10 W^{t}.- 6811–m
[*f. 79r*]

Taken in the year 1752 in the 7 & 8 months called July & August.
[*f. 79v*]

Before I return to my narrative, to shew the vast extent of the coast the Spaniards inhabit in the South Sea [I] shall give the distance from the island Chiloé in the lattitude of 41° 48 south & longitude 70° 03 west from the meridian of London. Their southernmost inhabited part in the South Seas to Aquapulco in 17° 00 north and 106° 08 west longitude from London. Though by reason of the many deep gulphs & bays if measur'd by the coast would be a great deal more. From the island Chiloé to Aquapulco in a strait line the course is north 29° 41 west, distance 4861 miles. They inhabit also a long way further to the northward and west ward of Aquapulco, though but thinly in many places. I shall now reassume my narrative again.

We arrived in the Bay of Callao the 9th of 10th month, October, in the year 1752 in 60 days as is before related from the island Puna in Guiyaquil river. And now we began to prepare for our return to Spain, taking provisions & other necessaries for our homeward bound passage. Also amongst other preparations it was thought necessary to dry our gunpowder which was grown damp by being so long on board. Accordingly about the 18th, of *12th* month, December 14 barrels were sent to the island St Laurance about 4 miles from the ship accompanied by the gunner, Jacammo, his boy, Luisillo Perisano, & Furlong all of them Italians except the last. The 19th, the day after, about 2 in the afternoon the gunner & his boy being amongst the powder sprinkling strong Spanish brandy on it, to strengthen as they imagine, the sun shining out clear, which at that time was almost perpendicular, the fine effluviums of the spirits took fire by the heat of the sun & blew

[207] Acapulco, now in Mexico.

[208] Manila, now in the Philippines.

[209] Secker's 'Tenian' is Tinian in the Marinas Islands, where Anson refreshed his crew in August-September 1742: Walter and Robins, *A Voyage round the World*, pp. 276–310.

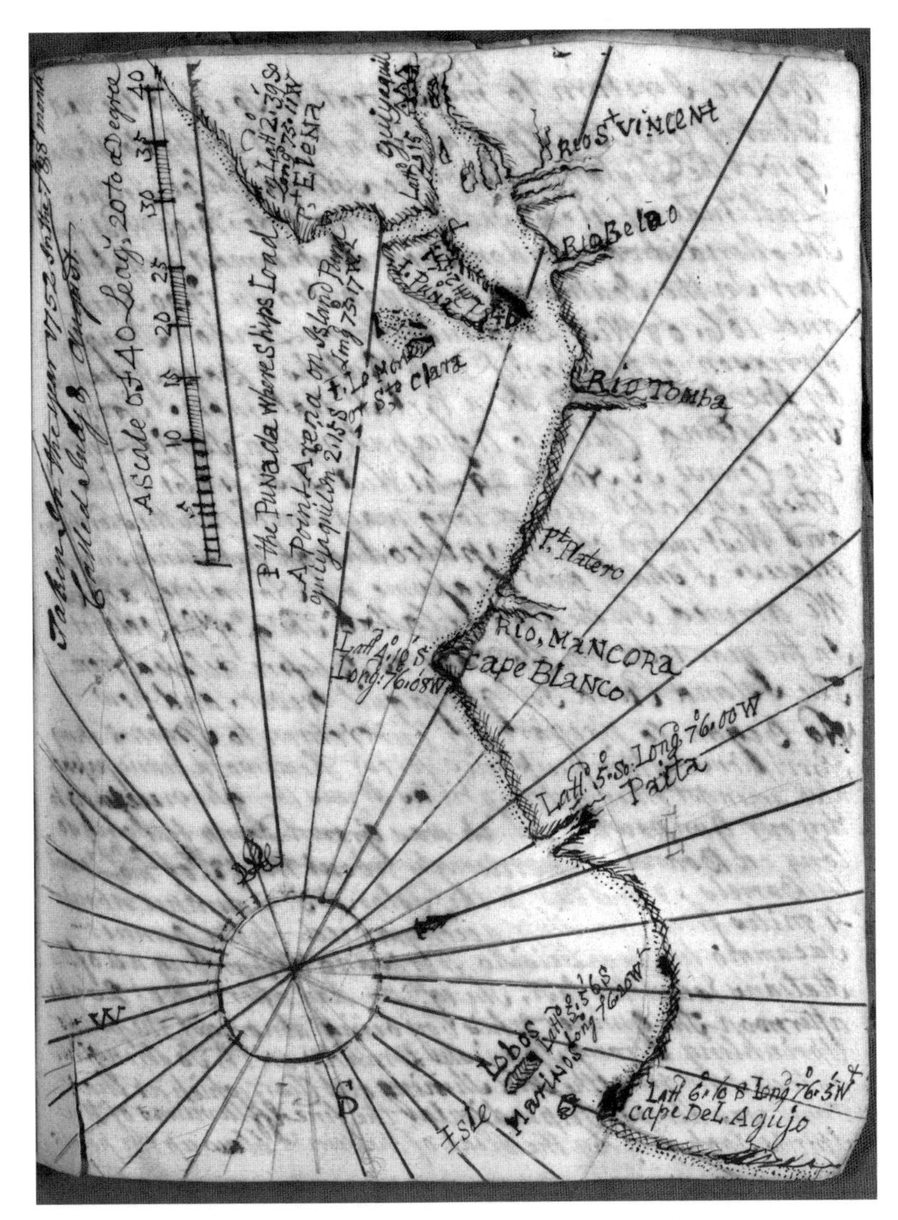

Figure 9 *Sketch of the coast from Cape Del Agujo to Guayaquil*

up the [*f. 80r*] powder. The gunner & his boy being amongst the powder were blown up in the air, & shatter'd to pieces. Perisano though lying along *in* the tent they had to sleep in had both his legs blown off. Furlong providentially saved his life by being sent to the water side at some considerable distance to get some crabs. He would have had Perisano to have gone with him but he said he was weary and refused going. Furlong had just got down to the waterside when the powder took fire; and being out of its reach saved his life. But the other three & a dog they had with them lost their lives. Our boat being sent to bring the powder on board, was gotten about half way between the ship and the island when the powder blew up. They proceeded to the island to see if any of them were left alive, where they found Furlong who gave us the above relation. Also that after he had got over his fright a little he went towa*r*ds the place where the powder took fire to see if any of the people were alive. The first he saw was the poor dog coming towards him dragging his body along with his fore feet with his guts trailing after him. When he came up to him he fell down & dyed. But turning him*self* towards the ship he saw the boat sent to fetch the powder on board drawing near the island, which in his surprize he had observ'd before. He went & joinned them; and they all went together in search of the dead bodies. Some of their remains they found a considerable way from where the powder blew up. Part of the gunner's body they found shatter'd in the following manner. His head smash'd all to pieces only the lower jaw & teeth being left. One of his feet was gone above the ancle & his other leg above the knee, his entrails blown away. His arms were fast to his body, but shatter'd to pieces. Luisillo was blown to pieces about the middle, having only the upper part of his body with his head & some part of his arms left, his others parts not being found. Perisano who lay in the tent had both his legs blown off.

Our boat in the evening return'd on board bringing them all the shatter'd parts of the bodies of those poor objects they could find. The same evening they were carried ashore, and so up to Las Animas, a town about a mile [*f. 80v*] from the landing place, and there laid before the church door. And the next day buried. The sail the powder was spread upon & the tent were burnt. At the time the accident happened I was upon the ship's quarter deck, the captain also. We heard the explosion & saw the smoke, the first sound was from the powder that took fire upon the sail. The other explosions were from the barrels that were fill'd & sounded like so many cannon fir'd one after another. The captain held up his *hands* with concern and we concluded they were all kill'd.

Before I leave this melancholy account I shall relate an accident of the same kind, that was told me about this time. That an English privateer at our island of Jamaica sent a large quantity of powder ashore to dry, with a number of men to guard it. At noon time when the boat brought dinner ashore, one of them being sprinkling spirits upon the the [*sic*] powder, the people setting by it to get their dinners, one man amongst them being more cleanly than the rest, went to some distance to wash his hands by which means saved his life. The powder in the mean while took fire from the heat of the sun kindling the spirits, & all lost their lives but that man.

Before I return to our farther proceedings, I shall mention a particular omited in its proper place. While we lay at the Punada in Guiyaquil river, one evening as I was walking the quarter *deck* by myself, casting my eyes upward I was greatly surpriz'd seeing a long row of lights seeming to move in the sky and calling some of our people up to look at it; & after viewing it some time, we concluded it was a proc[e]ssion at some city or or [*sic*] town, on the high mountains of Quito,[210] it appearing a great height in the sky. These mountains are for the [*f. 81r*] most hid by clouds, but when seen, appear of a prodigious height, and though near the equinoctial are said to be very fruitfull & the air temperate.

Having got provisions, water & other necessaries on board, 1753 1st month: January 11th we hoisted the flag of revisto or a flag for the people to come on board to be muster'd that the captain might know what number of people he had and who were missing, as several had died since we *came* into these *seas* & some had left us with intent to stay in the country. Month (Jan) 20th, we took 150 chests of money on board, & at sundry other times different q[u]antities of chests of gold, silver and wrought plate so that the whole quantity amounted to upward of six hundred chests for the king & merchants.

1st month (Jan:) 30th, 1753 sailed from Callao for old Spain having been in these seas since our first arrival at Callao in the year 1750 on the 28th of 5th month (May) about two years & 8 months. As I had sold my Hadleys Quadrant before we sailed to a Spanish pilot of one of the country ships, & shew him him [*sic*] how to use it for 50 Spanish dollars, I did not pretend to keep a journal homeward bound, but shall just mention some few particulars until our arrival at Cadiz in old Spain.

After we left Callao we stretch'd off between the south & west as near as the trade wind would admit till we came into the way of variable winds & then stood south eastward. And the 18th of 4th month (Aprill) being in about 38° 20 south and about 42° 00 to the eastward of Callao, we sprung our main yard about 3 feet without the parrel[211] on the larboard yard arm, and in lowering it down it brok[e] quite in pieces and not having a ship carpenter on board, could not fish it. But the mizen yard was taken & 2 fished we had for our lower masts if wanted. Hallowing them so that the mizen was about two thirds closed in the concave of the two fishes & the vacant spaces fill'd up with pieces of the old main yard the fishes[212] saw'd off. Then tapered it, shaped it a little in the form *of* yard nail'd & woolded[213] it well [*f. 81v*]

210 Quito, now in Ecuador.

211 A parrel was a rope, chain or iron collar by which a running yard or gaff was kept against the mast, but which allowed vertical motion: *IMD*.

212 Fishes were tapering battens of hard wood bound to a yard or other spar to strengthen it: *IMD*.

213 A woolding was a strong lashing tautened by the insertion of wedges: *IMD*.

and the 29th in the evening got him up, having been nine days in fitting it for want of a carpenter, our captain being master carpenter, & others asisting according to ability.

We stood to the southward to about sixty degrees of south lattitude & then *to the* eastward until we had doubled Cape Horn; and stood to the northward and cross'd the line coming into our northern hemisphere again. And the 5th of the 7th month (July) saw the island called Saint Marys[214] one of the Western Islands, having been five months & five days without seeing land. And the 6th, took our departure from the said island in lattd 37° N and longitude 22° 17 west from London for Cadiz in lattitude 36° 16 N & longitude 7° 00 Wt. Cadiz bearing from this island east 3 degrees south 245 leagues or 735 miles found 1 point variat[ion] to the west. N:B. a little to the west[w]ard of the island St Marys we were joined by 4 Spanish ships from the West Indies whose names were the Sainto Ann, Saint Reamondo, La Miserio, & La Carmelo. These being all large ships we kept company till we arrived at Cadiz for fear of meeting with any Barbary cruizers. We all arrived safe about the 19th of 7th month, (July) 1753, after a passage of five months & 20 days, having been on our voyage to the South Seas three years six months & 21 days.

After we had got the ship into safety & moor'd as many of the people as chose had liberty given to go on shore, which most of them did, especialy the foreigners, taking with them their chests beding & what else belong to them. A week or two after we went on shore, we were paid our wages in Spanish dollars. The number I receiv'd I have forgot. For part of them I got a bill from one Black a merchant who lived at Cales, on a coach maker in [*f. 82r*] London. The other part I carried with me & sold after I arriv'd in London. Being paid my wages, I met with a ship bound to London, the captain of which freely gave me my passage.

We left Cales some time in the 8th month, August and put into Faro in Portugal to take in some Faro figs, a pretty large number of baskets of which were put on board. I also bought some large clusters of red grapes to carry home for presents, these grapes they sell by weights. I had also an oppertunity of seeing how they cure their figs, which is by putting them into little baskets & hanging them to arms of trees in their Vin*e*yards, as they seldom have rain but at certain seasons. Some little time before we arrived at Faro, the Portuguese fishermen had brought into this harbour an English brigg they found driving about upon their coast not having any body on board, having been taken and plunder'd; and the people murder'd & thrown overboard by pirat[e]s, as there appear'd much blood sprinkled in several places upon deck. The chests broken open, papers & journals taken away so that

[214] The island of Santa Maria, in the Azores.

they could not at that time make out where she belong'd to. I went on board the vessel & saw the havock the vilains had made & saw the blood still visible in many places upon the decks. After my arrival in England I saw in the news papers the vessel belong'd to Dublin in Ireland and also that the villaines or some part of them were taken in attempting to cutt a vessel out of a creek on the coast of Portugal or Spain. The coast being alarm'd by the English consul writing to the other consuls in those parts, a watch was kept upon the coast so that when they went ashore in the night they were surpriz'd & taken. The pirate [*f. 82v*] vessel was a sattee[215] and the crew a gathering of several nations. They sailed from Lisbon, & whither the sattee with the remaining part of the crew were taken I forget.

Having taken a quantity of figs & some other articles, we left Faro, and arriv'd at London the 26th of the 9th mo (Septm) after an absence from my native country of near five years. The 27th wrote to my relations & friends in Norfolk. I staid at London until the bill I had from Black the merchant at Cadiz *was due* and receiv'd the money and those dollars I brought home with me I sold at London.

After which intending to get a passage by sea to Yarmouth went to the key where the Yarmouth vessels take in goods, where I saw some hogsheads of sugar mark'd Joseph Sparshall, Yarmouth, and was inform'd by the master that he was removed from Wells, to Yarmouth and also that he had been in town & went away that morning, and finding his name in the list concluded he was gone. But in the evening going to the Meeting in Grace Church Street, after meeting going out of the door, saw him amongst the croud. He would have me go with him to cousin Joseph Peckover's house, who I think departed this life that morning; which was the reason of his not going in the coach though enter'd to goe. This Joseph Peckover, was a son of our worthy friend Edmund Peckover of Wells in Norfolk and was educated to be a doctor.[216] It was supposed he catched cold in going [*f. 83r*] over the river in the evening to visit a patient.

He had also a little time before accompanied our friend Massa Bell,[217] who had a concern to preach the gospel in the in the [*sic*] streets & most of the publick places in London and was heard with sober & solid attention in

215 A decked vessel with a long, sharp prow with two or three masts, often used in the Mediterranean: *OED*.

216 An Edmund Peckover of Norwich, worsted weaver, was later among Secker's fellow trustees for the Quaker meeting house at Wells-next-the-Sea: NRO, MS 21393/51, 293 x 1, Indenture for Wells Meeting House 14 Nov 1767.

217 Anne Mercy Bell of York preached to large crowds at numerous locations throughout London between 5 August and 2 December 1753: Woodbrooke Library, Bevan Naish Collection, 5E3(v), J. Phipps, *A Summary Account of an Extraordinary Visit to this Metropolis in the Year 1753, by the Ministry of Ann Mercy Bell* (1754); M. Hope Bacon, ed., *Wilt Thou Go On My Errand? Three 18th Century Journals of Quaker Women Ministers* (Wallingford, Pennsylvania, 1994), pp. 96, 104.

most places where she made a stand. The people flocking about her in crouds, she meeting with little abuse from the populous many being greatly affected & tendered with her doctrine. It being a great work required of her and she being faithfully given up to perform it. Her divine master furnished her with wisdom, language & utterance, beyond all human ability, to preach such doctrine as was most suitable to the states of those her concern was to many of whom even of the most abandonned characters were greatly reach'd & tendered, so that it may be hoped it was of service to many who abode under the convictions they were brought under at that time. This faithfull woman closely attended our relation Joseph Peckover during his illness and was at his burial, where I heard her preach and thought she had the most harmonious voice & fluency of speech I had ever heard.

After his burial, I agreed with cousin Joseph Sparshall to send my things by sea, and accompany him by land to Yarmouth. Accordingly we hired post chaises from stage to stage & got there in saf[e]ty, though I think turn'd over twice by the way. I staid but a little while at Yarmouth before I went down into the country to visit my relations & friends. My dear mother being still alive & living with my brother William Secker at Swafield mill, the place where I was born, I took his house chiefly for my home while in the country.

Having staid in the country visiting relations and acquaintances until 6th month (June) 1754 I went to Yarmouth, and on the 22d of the same month was ship'd mate of a brigg called the Three Brothers by Charles Legris [*f. 83v*] one of the owners & Richard Smith the master, to have the same wages their former mate had, viz. fifty shillings per month. Three of the Gurneys having parts in this vessel she was named the Three Brothers.[218] I went mate of this vessel six voyages to Dublin,[219] and left her the 13th of 9th month (September) 1755 on account of the master fitting her out with guns, being now principled against fighting. I was greatly importuned by Charles Legrise one of the owners not to leave her, but in vain. I think it was taken in the Irish Channel by a small French privateer & ransomed. And when he return'd to Yarmouth *was* turned out of his employ, he not having fired one gun or made any defence to save the vessel after so great an expence in fortifying her.

When in Dublin, this last 6th voyage, on first day the 18th of 8th month (August)[220] being at Friends Meeting in Sygamore Alley, John Rumbelow[221]

[218] The 'Three Brothers' were John (1715–1770), Samuel and Joseph Gurney, the sons of Joseph Gurney of Keswick (1692–1750). John was a particularly prosperous merchant, boosting the family fortunes by introducing to Norwich new techniques in textile manufacture from southern Ireland: A. J. C. Hare, *The Gurneys of Earlham* (2 vols., 1897), i, pp. 13–14; J. B. Braithwaite, ed., *Memoirs of Joseph John Gurney* (2 vols., Norwich, 1854), i, pp. 4–6.

[219] Several of these voyages can be found in *Lloyd's Lists*, nos 1994, 2003, 2034, 2051.

[220] Secker may have been mistaken in this date as *Lloyd's List* records that the *Three Brothers*, with Smith as master, only arrived in Dublin from Yarmouth on 25 August: *Lloyd's List*, no. 2051.

[221] John Rumbelow embarked on a preaching tour in 1741 but was disowned by the Wells

& Benjamin Smith out of Norfolk were there. These men were gone into separation & left Friends. Benjamin Smith stood up & said a few words, by way of warning to repentance, but John said nothing. After meeting several elders went after them to enquire whether they had a certificate from Friends in England. But as I was told they did not answer them with that meekness which becomes ministers of Christ. Especially Benjamin who appear'd hot in his spirit, saying a certificate would not carry them to heaven or words of the like import. They taking up their quarters at a publick house upon the key, near where our vessel lay; I went in the evening & staid a while (being well acquainted with John Rumbelow) with them. And thought them the most forlorn of all men, bearing the scorn of being Quakers and yet not [*f. 84r*] accepted or owned by that people. John Rumbelow once lived at Fakenham in Norfolk, and it was believed by Friends in those parts that he came rightly forth in the ministry and had a large gift. But through some means or other, thinking himself slighted or not well used in some particular or other, let prejudice take root in his mind which as a canker worm soon eat out all good. So leaving Friends, ran into separation, joining some of the same stamp about Mattishall who had also let in that deadly poison of prejudice against Friends in those parts. These kept meetings by themselves and often traveled up & down the country where some joined them. I have been told by some I think of that people that John Rumbelow maried in the west of England, and that his wife behaved very unkindly to him, and in that part departed of life.

I shall after this long digression from my narrative give some account how I providencially escaped after empressed, being put on board a man of war. This happened in the night of the 6th of the 5th mo, (May) 1755.[222] We having begun to take in loading for our 5th voyage to Dublin. The sailors belonging to the ships in the port [*Yarmouth*] having been made to believe by the officers of the men of war, quarter'd in this town; that all such as kept on *board* their vessels & had a protection, were safe from being empress'd. This begot a careless security in the seamen and many lodg'd on board their vessels they belong to, who if they had thought themselves in danger of being prest would have lodg'd on shore. The 6th of 5th mo, in the night the press broke out. I boarding when at home at cousin Joseph Sparshall's, [*f. 84v*] I staid pretty late that evening after supper, so that my cousins would have persuaded me to stay & lodge at their house. But I chose rather to go on board, to look after the vessel I had charge of. There were also 3 lads

Monthly Meeting for insolvency on 1 September 1742. Warning of his disownment was sent to Quaker meetings outside Norfolk: S. Stevens, 'A Believing People in a Changing World: Quakers in Society in North-East Norfolk, 1690–1800' (University of Sunderland, D.Phil., 2005), pp. 152–3.

[222] In 1759 the Navy Office supplied figures to the House of Commons which stated that the navy had pressed 7843 men ashore in 1755 to serve as ratings: Rodger, *The Wooden World*, pp. 145–6.

apprentices who lodg'd on board besides myself, viz. Tho. Moise, Charles Sloeman. These two lads I think might be about 17 or 18 years of age. The other lad whose name I've forgot was small & too young to press. About the middle of the night the press broke out from protections. The men of war lying in the roads, having landed a sufficient number of men, who joining the constables were to board the vessels from the key. They also sent into the harbour a long boat, pinace[223] & yaul[224] to receive the men prest, and carry them on board the men of war lying in the roads.

Being thus provided they came up the harbour amongst the shi[p]ing in the dead of the night without much noise so that very little alarm was given. Boarding the vessels as they came along by land & from their boats took the hands out they found on board. We lay next the bridge or the next but one with our broadside pointing to the key, & a long plank from the gunnel to the shore for taking our loading in.[225] They came on board so softly into the steerage that I did not hear them till they had found the two lads they prest in their cabins, who calling out to me for help who was now in as bad a case as themselves. I directly slid back the door of my cabin & spoke to them, upon which they came directly to me & told me I must go with them. I told them I had charge of the vessel & argued with *them* a while but all in vain, for go I must. To pacify me they told me I should be cleared next day, but I had little faith [*f. 85r*] in their promises.[226]

Howsoever I immediatly put on a few things intending to get upon deck and make my escape while they were rumaging betwixt decks for more people; but when I would have gone up the companion scuttle I found a guard there who were for putting me into their boat directly. But excusing me to put on more cloaths went down again, and those below being gone forwards searching for more hands I took the opportunity of droping myself down in *to* the after hold out of the steerage where I had put a sail like a funnel to prevent the corn falling into it when shott down of the quarter deck. After I was down I could not get in amongst the malt in the middle room by reason of the bulkhead[227] but laid myself down by the kelsey[228] &

[223] A pinnace was a double banked boat, usually with eight oars and part of the equipment of a man of war, or a small, light vessel, usually two-masted and rigged as a schooner, often used in attendance upon a larger vessel as a scout: *OED*.

[224] A man of war's boat, resembling a pinnace but somewhat smaller, carvel-built and generally rowed with four or six oars: *IMD*.

[225] Defoe described the Yarmouth quayside in 1724 as packed with ships moored very closely together, 'with their bowsprits over the land', and 'their bows, or heads, touching the very wharf; so that one may walk from ship to ship as on a floating bridge, all along by the shoreside': D. Defoe, *A Tour Through the Whole Island of Great Britain*, ed. P. Rogers (Harmondsworth, 1971), 89.

[226] In theory, Parliament protected the masters and chief mates of all merchantmen of over 50 tons from the press: Rodger, *The Wooden World*, p. 177.

[227] A bulkhead was a vertical partition separating different compartments within a vessel: *IMD*.

[228] Secker probably refers to the kelson here, the line of timber inside a ship, along the floor timbers and parallel with the keel to which it is bolted: *OED*.

pull'd a matt over me where it easily *may* be believed I did not fall a sleep. But I was soon mist, & great blustering there was to find me. At last perceiving the sail that lead in *to* the after hold, put it by, and *one* of them dropping down & a lanthorn handed him, he soon saw a matt lye higher than the rest, he came and drew it off me, ironically crying out, here he is! I was hurried up & put into the boat alongside and carried to the pinnace where the lieutenant was & many prest men. I got into the stern part of the pinnace and sat near the lieutenant. I having in the hurry and fright forgot to take my watch and had besides only a white swanskin waistcoat, pair of trowsers, shoes & stockins on; and one of the yaul's crew that put me on board the pinnace bid them take care of the mate in the white waistcoat or he would get away from them all. But I sat silent & said nothing, intending if opportunity offer'd to jump overboard & swim for the shore, which if I could gain in a few strokes they dare not follow lest all the rest *should* escape. And several times when the boat sharing with the tide near the Golstone[229] side, was just about to make a spring [*f. 85v*] but the coxon[230] suddenly sharing her off again into the middle of the river, could get no fair opportunity. The other prest men in the pinnace were full of talk how they would get away at this and the other place, but I kept silent, well knowing if they had had courage enough to have rose all at once & unship'd the oars of them that rowed & seized on them, being so many more in number they might easily have freed themselves.

But to return, being disappointed of my first design of jumping over board to swim ashore, it came into my mind to ask the lieutenant to let the boat put me on *board* my vessel to get my watch & put some more things on. He at last consented so far as to say if the yaul or cutter came it might put me on board. Presently after this a boat came rowing up the river which being haled proved to be their cutter. She was order'd alongside the pinnace and by the lieutenant, who seemed much of a gentleman and very civil, to take me in & carry me on board my vessel to get my watch & such other things as I chose to get, but gave them a strict charge not to let me get away from them, which they as strictly promised him. So they carried me alongside my vessel, & some of them went up first to hinder my escape. I went directly down to my cabin & called some of them down to see my watch hanging there, that they might see I had not told them a lye. My thoughts were more upon making my escape than about my watch or any thing else at that time. I had some rum in flasks in my cabin I brought from Dublin. One of which flasks I took in my hand, they being in great hast to get me into the boat again. I made as if I would put it into my trowser pocket, which some of them seeing [*f. 86r*] said they would carry it for me. I said I

[229] Gorleston-on-Sea is now a southern suburb of Great Yarmouth.

[230] The coxon or coxswain was the person in charge of a boat and its crew in the absence of officers, often steering it with the rudder: *IMD*.

would carry it myself and immediately went to the rail, they surrounding me with pistols & cutlasse[s]. Took down a rope as if I would hitch it to the rail to go down into the boat by, upon which they took it out of my hand & made it fast themselves, they all came to the rail leanning over it. I then lifted up one leg as if going to straddle over the rail, turn'd round upon my heel, made a jump unto the main hatches & run for the plank & so on shore, jumping & skipping over the ship's ropes that were fast to the posts least I should be thrown down which I luckily, I may say mercifully, was preserved from as it was a very great risk in running over a long plank in the dark of falling onto the haven, & of going over so many ropes crossing one another without being thrown down. Their great surprise at this my sudden and unexpected escape from them, had such an effect upon them that they could only cry out shoot the dog! Kill the dog! The dog! The dog!

After *I* was clear of the ship's mooring ropes I ran directly for the opposite row;[231] but seeing *people* coming down it with a lanthern and my pursuers calling to them to stop me I thought it might be some constables with part of their gang, turn'd to take up another row. This gave them advantage to gain upon me, but I got into another before they could lay hold on me; fear giving me speed, I outstript them in running. But when near the up[p]er end of the row a piece of the pavement being broke, a stone taking my toe I fell down with my breast into a swash of water, it being showery weather. I was much bespatter'd [*f. 86v*] with water & dirt, my hat & wigg also flying off with the violence of the fall, but fear of my persuers raised me up. Catching my hat in one hand & my wigg in the other, took to my heels again; and cross'd the Middle Street, & turn'd up a row which led into the market place before they see which row I took. When they came into the Middle Street, I could hear them say one to the other 'he went up this way'. So they turn'd to the right and miss'd me, I having turnned to the left. After I had got clear of them, I went softly along into the market place, passing cousin Sparshall's house, but durst not call any of them up lest I should be heard, it being a very calm still night & about one or two in the morning. So went to the master's house towards the north end, where calling I was told by a person looking out of a window next door to his that he & his wife were gone down to the vessel to take care of her. The little boy they did not press, as I had order[ed] him had acquainted the master with what had happened. After I could get no shelter there, I walked out of the north gates, went into one of the gardens & walked about for some time. Then went to some cinder ovens belonging to Charles Legrise & dryed myself, and when the cinder burner came to the ovens who k*n*ew me I sent him to acquaint to acquaint [*sic*] my cousin Sparshall where I was & how I had escaped. He & Charles Legrise consulted together, & it was concluded to lend me a boat

[231] The Yarmouth Rows were the innumerable side-passages between the main streets.

& sails to go up the river to Dilham[232] & stay there till I might come with saf[e]ty to Yarmouth [*f. 87r*] again. Accordingly, Charles Legrise not only lent me a boat, but sent two men to row me up some miles & then leave the boat to me to proceed. Thus through the favour of Divine Providence I escaped from being put on board a man of war. Though not with*out* the hazard and peril of my life. Or if taken at that time grossly abused.

[Symbol of hand pointing] I staid in the country till the 24th of same month visiting my relations & then was sent for. I got to Yarmouth & the 25th got my things on board, the vessel being loaded up in my absence. The 26th we run down to the haven's mouth, came up again with the master who paid me my wages due after the rate of 3 pounds per month. We met with difficulty in getting hands for this voyage, so many having been pressed on board men of war. I went mate of her this voyage & another making six voyages in all to Dublin.

[Symbol of hand pointing] In preparing for the seventh voyage, the master persuaded Charles Legrise to fit her out with guns, which he through the persuation of the master consented to. Accordingly ports were cutt out and guns put on board and I being now principled against fighting left the vessel, though greatly solicited by Charles Legrise to have continued in her. I went mate of this brigg The Three Brothers, Richard Smith master, 6 voyages to Dublin & belong'd to her from the 22d of 6th month 1754 (June) until the 17th of 9th month, (Sept) 1755 being 15 months wanting 5 days. And should very likely have sailed in her much longer had not her being fitted for defence prevented me. The master & I parted in friendship, as far as I know, at least it was so on my part. I can safely say when we parted I felt a a [*sic*] tenderness in my heart towards him for his welfare. He is a man of a hasty passionate disposition & but little command over his tongue at such times, yet when his passion is over bears no malice. In his resolutions [*f. 87v*] wavering & timorous, in his friendship very inconstant yet through his whole character there is a promiscuous mixture of good nature.

[Symbol of hand pointing] I was very sensible he was not qualified in his disposition for a fighting man, not having that steadiness and calm resolution in time of danger which is requisit[e] both for their own & others' preservation. I had always found that in times of apparent danger he wanted presence of mind to *give* forth his orders with steadiness to extricate us out of them. And this my judgment was varified for the first or second voyage after I left him, falling in with a small French privateer in the Irish Channel he suffer'd himself to be taken without firing one gun, & so lost a good employ. The vessel & cargoe was ransomed, but at his return he was turned out of his employ.

I having now left of going to sea; [symbol of hand pointing] having fol-

[232] This route would have taken Secker up the River Bure and then the River Ant to Dilham.

lowed that occupation for about 25 years, viz from the year 1730 to 1755. I being now advanced to near 40 years of age, was very desirous to spend the remaining part of my days on shore. Accordingly after retiring into the country some time I made choice of a woman much about my own age for a wife. She was then newly got into a shop at a town named Ashill about 4 miles from Swaffham.[233] She had 4 brothers: John Ransome, shopkeeper at Walsingham, & Joshua a shopkeeper at the same place, also Richard Ransome who lived at Westacre Mill. She had a sister named Mary & a half sister, Elizabeth Kemp. [NRO, Y/D 41/105 ends].

[NRO, Rye MS 71]
Here the relators' travels ceased; yet he did not discontinue his Journal, but with like fidelity, & honest simplicity continued daily to record the occurences of a still retired life to the time of his decease. But these having little variety in them, it was not thought proper to transcribe the remainder. He continued at Ashill until the year 1760, when he removed himself and family to Holt in the county of Norfolk; having purchased a house in that town, and fitted it up as a shop. In which place he continued to the end of his days, having uniformly supported a very respectable character both as a tradesmen and as a member of the religious society to which he belong'd. He died the 23rd of 3 month March 1795 in the 79th year of his age, and is, we doubt not, safely moored in the haven of everlasting rest.

233 John Secker of North Walsham married Phebe Ransom of Ashill (1715–1783), at Swaffham on 10 March 1756: NRO, MF/RO 320/6, Registers of the Norfolk and Norwich Quarterly Meeting, SF 45 Supplement, Book 1575, pp. 326–30.

APPENDICES

Appendix 1: Vessels, voyages and cargoes

Name of Vessel	Dates	Secker's voyages on board	Secker's description of vessel and cargo
Unnamed	c.1729	From Yarmouth to Rotterdam to Yarmouth	Small vessel of 20–25 tons burden, William Jolley, master, cargo of malt. Secker's venture was two lbs of tea and three half stopes of brandy and cinnamon water.
Unnamed	Late summer 1730–1732	London and Holland trade	John Sparshall and Richard Wright of Buxton, owners, Thomas Parsons, master. Secker was cabin boy and cook.
The *Namur*	1732	None, he saw it anchored at St Catherine's, Wapping	A second rate or ninety-gun warship.
The *Royal Escape*	1732	From Wapping to the Nore	The tender on which James II made his escape when he 'abdicated' the crown.
The *Sunderland*	1732	The Nore, no voyage, only on board a few days	A sixty-gun warship.
The *Namur*	1732	From Black Stakes, Chatham river to Gillingham, 6 weeks on board	A second rate or ninety-gun warship. Secker was captain's servant, paid 5 s. 6 d.
The *Bonnetta*	1732	From Woolwich to Hellevoetsluis with the king's yachts under Lord Torington, to fetch George II on board the *Carolina Yacht* from Holland. Then from Hellevoetsluis to the Nore, to Sheerness to Plymouth to Sheerness	A snow commanded by Sir Roger Butler who had been second lieutenant on board the *Namur*. Secker was servant to Lieutenant Smith.
The *Tryal*	1732	None, he saw it at Plymouth	A new snow.
The *Bonnetta*	1732–late Sep 1733	From Sheerness to a new station on the Yorkshire coast between Flamborough and Shields, guarding against smugglers	A snow commanded by Sir Roger Butler. Secker was servant to Lieutenant Smith.

Name of Vessel	Dates	Secker's voyages on board	Secker's description of vessel and cargo
The *Old King George*	Nov 1733–Jan 1734	From Liverpool via Cork and the Canaries to Back River, Virginia	Captain Tarleton was commander. Cargo of rigging and stores for the *Two Traffords*, plus four Irish convicts.
The *Two Traffords*	Jan–Dec 1734	From Back river, Virginia, up the Potomac into the Wiccomaco river, Maryland, then returning to Liverpool	Captain Langton was commander. Cargo of tobacco, walnut tree and pipe staves.
The *Old King George*	Mar–May 1735	From Liverpool to capes of Virginia and then up Chester river to Newtown, Maryland	Cargo of wheat loaded at Newtown.
The *Old King George*	Oct 1735	From Maryland to Madeira	Cargo of wheat delivered and cargo of wine collected at Madeira for next voyage to Jamaica to be sold in order to take in a cargo of sugar and rum there. Secker deserted on Madeira.
The *John Snow*	Apr–May1736	From Madeira to London	A snow of Madeira formerly belonging to the west of England. Cargo of malmsey, verdona and sweetmeats. Secker was to be paid 40 s. for the voyage.
The *John Snow*	Jun 1736	From London via Le Havre to Vannes in Brittany. From there via Lisbon and Madeira to Terceira in the Azores and then returning to Madeira	Cargo of tobacco was discharged at Le Havre. Cargo of rye was loaded in Vannes river. Cargo of wheat was loaded in Terceira.
The *Britannia*	c. Jul 1736	None, saw it at Lisbon lying in the River Tagus	A first-rate warship commanded by Sir John Norris with a fleet in attendance.
Unnamed Barbary cruiser	c. Jul 1736	None, briefly boarded by it off Lisbon	A frigate.
The *John Snow*	Jan–Feb 1737	From Funchal, Madeira to South Carolina	Cargo of wine. Secker had a venture of two quarter pipes of wine. Cargo of rice loaded in South Carolina to be taken to Lisbon.

Unnamed vessel	Feb 1737	None, anchored in South Carolina	Secker pressed on board a privateer schooner intended to patrol the Georgia coast, but he soon escaped.
Unnamed vessel	Feb 1737	None, anchored in South Carolina	Secker hid on board a merchant ship preparing to leave for Bristol in order to escape service on a privateer.
The *John Snow*	Feb 1737	South Carolina	Secker deserted, complaining of his captain's misbehaviour.
Unnamed vessel	Mar–22 Apr 1737	From South Carolina to Harbour, Eleuthera and Providence islands, then Abaco and Grand Bahama islands, all in the Bahamas, and return to South Carolina	A sloop commanded by Captain Petty, who had a brother in London. Secker was paid £12 per month Carolina currency (32 s.) Cargo of wood, oranges and limes loaded on Providence and turtles loaded on Grand Bahama.
Unnamed vessel	22 Apr–18 Jun 1737	From South Carolina to Cowes, Isle of Wight	A Gdańsk (Danzig) merchant commanded by Captain Powel of Bristol.
Unnamed vessel	Jul–Sep 1737	From Cowes to Philadelphia	A Palatine ship with a cargo of four hundred Palatine settlers.
Unnamed vessel	Nov 1737	From Philadelphia to South Carolina	A New England sloop loaded with passengers and horses.
Unnamed vessel	c. Dec 1737	From South Carolina to the Bahamas to South Carolina	Cargo of turtles and fruit loaded in the Bahamas.
Unnamed vessel	1738	Ashley river, South Carolina	Secker was master of a pettianger sailing the river, bringing wood to be sold in Charleston.
The *Agatha*	1738	From Charleston, South Carolina to Hellevoetsluis and Rotterdam	Dutch ship belonging to one Hope of Rotterdam, commanded by a Swede. Secker received £8 for the passage. Cargo of rum.
Unnamed vessel	Summer 1738	From Holland to Yarmouth	Vessel owned by John Sparshall and Richard Wright, mastered by John Jermin.

Name of Vessel	Dates	Secker's voyages on board	Secker's description of vessel and cargo
Unnamed vessel	12 Oct 1738	From Yarmouth to London	
The *Defence*, East Indiaman	1 Nov 1738–Jan 1739	From London to the Cape of Good Hope	Commanded by Captain Coates, a two-week stay at the Cape to re-provision.
The *Defence*, East Indiaman	Feb–May 1739	From the Cape of Good Hope to Al Mukhā (Mocha)	Three month stay in Al Mukhā, loading a cargo of coffee, drugs, rich gums and an Arabian horse.
Unnamed vessel	May 1739	None, sighted in the Red Sea	A French ship bound for Pondicherry to which Secker unsuccessfully planned to desert.
The *Defence*, East Indiaman	Jul 1739	From Al Mukhā to Mumbai (Bombay)	A two-week passage.
The *Defence*, East Indiaman	Sep 1739	From Mumbai along the Malabar coast to Tillicherry to Cochin to Anjanga	
The *Defence*, East Indiaman	Oct 1739–4 Jan 1740	From Anjanga, passing Diego Roys and Mauritius, to the Cape of Good Hope	Stayed at the cape for ten days to re-provision.
The *Defence*, East Indiaman	14–27 Jan 1740	From the Cape of Good Hope to St Helena	Waited on St Helena for a convoy to assemble.
The *Defence*, East Indiaman	10 Jul–15 Sep 1740	From St Helena to the Downs	Among a convoy of fourteen ships, Secker arrived in the Downs and travelled to London on foot.
The *East India Yacht*	Oct 1740–4 Jan 1741	From London to the Cape of Good Hope, via Gravesend, the Downs, Portsmouth and Spithead, crossing equator in Nov and spotting Anson's fleet in Dec 1740	An East India Company yacht commanded by Captain Gabriel Steward. Secker was paid 45s. and 6d. per month. Sailed from Spithead amongst Sir Chaloner Ogle's fleet, but was separated from them during a storm in the Bay of Biscay.

The *East India Yacht*	18 Jan 1741	From the Cape of Good Hope to St Helena	Commanded by Captain Robert Kellaway, with a cargo of 20 sheep.
The *East India Yacht*	Jan–Mar 1741	From St Helena to Ascension Island to St Helena	Cargo of fish and turtles caught on Ascension. The fish went off and the turtles died.
The *East India Yacht*	Jul–Oct 1741	From St Helena to London	Sailing in a convoy.
Unnamed vessel	Feb -Aug 1742	From Wells to Hull on several return voyages	Vessel of Wells engaged in the Hull trade, mastered by Thomas Parsons.
Unnamed vessel	1742–1744	From Yarmouth to Rotterdam, Amsterdam, London and Newcastle	Vessel bought by John Sparshall and Richard Wright from John Worsted of Yarmouth. Mastered by Secker.
Unnamed vessel	Jun 1744	From Newcastle to Ostend	Secker captured by a privateer of Dunkirk on a voyage carrying coals from Newcastle to Ostend. Imprisoned at Dunkirk.
Unnamed vessel	Sep 1744	From Dunkirk to Veurne	
Unnamed vessel	1744	From Ostend to Bruges	Passage in a boat.
Unnamed vessel	1744	From Bruges to Rotterdam	Passage in a scute.
Unnamed vessel	Dec 1744	From Rotterdam to Yarmouth	
The *William and Thomas*	Jun 1745	From Yarmouth via Harwich, Deal and Torbay to Waterford and Dublin	A large snow owned by Thomas Dawson and William Palmer of Yarmouth. Mastered by Secker and loaded with malt. Joined by three London privateers and a north country snow at Torbay.
The *William and Thomas*	Jan 1746	From Dublin to Milford Haven, Tenby, Sandersfoot, then Yarmouth	Cargo of Welsh coals loaded on Sandersfoot beach.

Name of Vessel	Dates	Secker's voyages on board	Secker's description of vessel and cargo
The *William and Thomas*	Feb–Apr 1746	From Yarmouth to London to Yarmouth	Cargo of Welsh coals sold in London. On his return Secker was sacked.
Unnamed vessel	Jul 1746	From Yarmouth to Sunderland	Secker was a passenger, hoping to find a vessel at Sunderland.
Unnamed vessel	Aug 1746	From Sunderland to London	Secker was a passenger, hoping to find a vessel at London.
The *Noble Ann*	4 Nov 1746–Feb 1747	From London to the Downs, and from Spithead by convoy to Virginia and then up the James River to Warwick Town	Secker enlisted as chief mate on a Scarborough ship commanded by Ralph Finch at £4 per month. Secker struck by the captain and discharged.
Unnamed vessel	26 Sep–28 Dec 1747	From Norfolk, Virginia by convoy to Plymouth sound, Margate, Deptford and London	A new snow built in Virginia, owned by John Hanbury of London. Secker enlisted as chief mate at £4 per month. Cargo of tobacco damaged off Margate.
The *Duke of Cumberland*	18 Jan–5 Apr 1748	From London to the Downs. Left Downs in convoy on 1 April, but taken in Bay of Biscay, 5 April	Secker enlisted for £4 per month as chief mate on privateer with 34 hands and a letter of marque, commanded by Captain Jefferson. Cargo was 220 last of wheat.
Unnamed vessel	Apr 1748	From Bay of Biscay to Morlaix	French privateer of 30 guns and 360 hands, owned by Granville, Normandy, and commanded by Dedesmain Hugen. Secker imprisoned at Morlaix and Dinan.
Unnamed vessel	Jul 1748	From St Malo to Plymouth	A cartel ship.
The *Duke of Cumberland*	7 Oct–17 Dec 1748	From London to the Downs, Spithead, past Lisbon, Cape St Vincent, Gibraltar, Balearic Islands, anchoring off the Laire of Mahon and then Marseilles	Secker enlisted as chief mate under Captain John Colwart of Scarborough, with a cargo of wheat.
Unnamed vessel	Oct 1748	None, sighted in Cowes Road	A London snow commanded by Captain Alcock.

Unnamed vessels	26 Oct 1748	None, sighted off Ushant	Three French West India men from St Domingo and Cape Francois.
The *Crown*	8 Dec 1748	None, sighted on the Laire of Mahon	A forty-gun warship commanded by Captain Cockburn.
The *Duke of Cumberland*	8–17 Dec 1748	From the Laire of Mahon to Marseilles	Unloaded cargo of wheat at Marseilles and took on ballast.
The *Duke of Cumberland*	8–17 Feb 1749	From Marseilles to Cagliari, Sardinia	Cargo of salt loaded in Sardinia after much trouble with onshore authorities.
Unnamed vessel	18 Feb 1749	None, sighted in Cagliari harbour	A brigantine from Curaco upon which a fight broke out with a Turk passenger.
The *Duke of Cumberland*	28 Mar–21 Apr 1749	From Cagliari via Malaga and Gibraltar to Cadiz	Secker argued with the captain and was discharged, 7 May 1749.
The *Lovely Peggy*	15 Jun–Jul 1749	Return cruise from Cadiz along the Portuguese coast	A small sloop mastered by Secker. The vessel was sold and Secker discharged on 29 July.
The *St Juan Babtista St Antonio de Padoua, Y de Las Animas de Purgatorio* alias *Grand Tuscany* (hereafter The *Grand Tuscany*)	29 Dec 1749–11 Jan 1750	From Cadiz to Santa Cruz, Tenerife	The ship was built in London for the South Sea Company and was 1,000–1,200 ton burden but was sold to Spain in 1748/9. It became a Spanish South Sea vessel commanded by Don Santo Mathias, a Corsican, and navigated by Monsieur Louis Louison a Frenchman, with the second pilot an Irishman, Gilles Swillevant. 160 hands speaking at least fifteen different languages.
The *Grand Tuscany*	13 Jan–28 May 1750	From Santa Cruz, Tenerife, crossing the Equator on 7 Feb, sighting straits of Magellan on 30 Mar, into the Pacific by 7 May and then anchoring in Callao, the port for Lima	Loaded at Tenerife: forty-eight pipes of water and four pipes of wine with greens, and pumpkins for the ship's use. Three English vessels and some Dutch vessels in Santa Cruz harbour.

Name of Vessel	Dates	Secker’s voyages on board	Secker’s description of vessel and cargo
The *San Pablo*	20 Nov–25 Dec 1750	From Callao to Chockow on the island of Chiloé	Vessel commanded by a Frenchman, Captain Colee. Secker was to be paid $12 per month.
The *Brilliante*	Jan 1751	None, seen at Chockow	A small snow belonging to Lima.
The *San Pablo*	21 Jan–12 Feb 1751	From Chockow to Valdivia, assisted through the narrows by a pettiago	A cargo of boards was loaded on Chiloé. Secker was arrested by the governor of Valdivia on arrival for espionage.
The *Christo*	Feb–Mar 1751	From Valdivia to Valparaiso	A ship of Lima. Secker was carried as a prisoner, but treated well by the captain and boatswain.
The *Christo*	3–22 Apr 1751	From Valparaiso to Callao	As above.
The *Grand Tuscany*	30 Sep–29 Oct 1751	From Callao to Valdivia	The ship was hired by the Viceroy at Lima to carry a cargo of stores and provisions for Valdivia. Secker was paid $25 in advance.
The *Trinidado*	16 Oct 1751	None, passed it on its way to Chiloé from Callao	
The *Grand Tuscany*	6–12 Nov 1751	From Valdivia to Valparaiso	Cargo of provisions loaded at Valdivia for Valparaiso.
The *Grand Tuscany*	Nov–19 Dec 1751	From Valparaiso to Valdivia	Cargo of provisions loaded at Valparaiso for Valdivia.
The *Grand Tuscany*	10–11 Jan 1752	From Valdivia to Pinco in the Bay of La Conception	
The *Grand Tuscany*	31 Jan–3 Feb 1752	From Pinco to Juan Fernandez	Cargo of provisions loaded in the Bay of La Conception for Juan Fernandez.
The *Grand Tuscany*	10–16 Feb 1752	From Juan Fernandez to Valparaiso	
The *Grand Tuscany*	29 Apr–13 May 1752	From Valparaiso to Callao	Cargo of wheat, jerkied beef and lard loaded at Valparaiso. A priest on board carried a venture of apples.

The *Grand Tuscany*	1–11 Jul 1752	From Callao to Punada and the island of Puna, for Guiyaquil	
The *Esperance*	Jul–Aug 1752	None, sighted at Guiyaquil	An old fifty-gun ship sent from Spain after Anson in 1740.
The *Grand Tuscany*	11 Aug–10 Oct 1752	From Punada to Callao	Cargo of cocoa nuts and some drugs loaded at Punada.
The *Grand Tuscany*	30 Jan–5 Jul 1753	From Callao round Cape Horn to the vicinity of the Azores	Cargo of 150 chests of money on board, gold, silver and wrought plate. Six hundred chests for the king of Spain and merchants.
The *Sainto Ann, Saint Reamondo, La Miserio* and *La Carmelo*	5–19 Jul 1753	None, sailed alongside in convoy from the Azores to Cadiz	Spanish ships from the West Indies.
The *Grand Tuscany*	5–19 Jul 1753	From the vicinity of the Azores to Cadiz	Cargo of 150 chests of money on board, gold, silver and wrought plate. Six hundred chests for the king of Spain and merchants. Secker was paid in Spanish dollars and a promisary bill he later redeemed in London.
Unnamed vessel	Aug 1753	From Cadiz to Faro	Secker was given free passage.
Unnamed vessel	Aug 1753	None, Secker went on board to view damage at Faro	An English brig sacked by pirates, Secker later found out in English newspapers it came from Dublin.
Unnamed vessel	Aug–26 Sep 1753	From Faro to London	Cargo of figs and some other articles.
The *Three Brothers*	22 Jun 1754–13 Sep 1755	From Yarmouth to Dublin to Yarmouth. Secker made six of these return voyages	A brig of Yarmouth owned by Charles Legrise and three of the Gurney brothers. Secker enlisted as chief mate, Richard Smith master. Secker was paid £3 per month and carried rum from Dublin in his cabin. Secker resigned when the vessel was fitted out with guns.

APPENDIX 2: THE WILL OF JOHN SECKER

NRO, ANW 1795, Will 83, *ff. 118r-119r* (MF 350)

[*f. 118r*] This is the last Will and Testament of me John Secker Shopkeeper of Holt in the County of Norfolk made this tenth day of the tenth Month [October] in the year one thousand seven hundred & ninety two. First I nominate <and> & appoint my Dear Cousins Joseph Haycock of Wells and John Ransome of Walsingham my Executors of this my last Will & Testament. Willing them to sell off all my effects <and> & Property both in House [*f. 118v*] & shop or any other part of the Premises belong to me excepting such Books & <and> Writings as hereunder mentioned. And with the amount thereof and what Money I may have by me or in the Hands of any other Person to pay of [*sic*] all my just Debts Funeral Expenses Probate of my Will and all other incident Charges Also satisfying themselves for their trouble. What remain after the above Deductions I would have distributed amongst my undermentioned Relations in the following manner. Videlicet. First I give <and> & bequeath to my Brother William Secker <and> & Wife of Swafield or either of them if living one half of what is left as abovementioned the remaining half to be equally distributed amongst my undermentioned Relations in manner following to my Niece Phebe Brett, <and> & Son Anthony Brett, to John Secker son of my Deceased Nephew Isaac Secker of Worsted, to my Nephew Barnard Beans of Thursford, to Mary, Elizabeth <and> & Christian Beans of Yarmouth that being their Maiden Names before married, to Mary Bransby Daughter of my Wife's Sister Mary Kirby deceased at Lammas, to all the above mentioned or as many of them as may be living at my decease or if dead leaving Children those children to have their Parents Share equally divided amongst them. But if dead not leaving Children their Shares to be divided amongst those living. All Friends Books, that are my own and also of my own writing, as my Spiritual Diary, a Narrative of my Travels, my Book of Memorandums A Book of remarkable Dreams & <and> Deliverances, Chartes of Harbours in the South Sea with other Journals papers &c I bequeath to my Brother William Secker if living But if dead to be disposed *of* at the discretion of my Executors. [*f. 119r*] Desiring also that after my Effects are disposed of the several Legatees may be paid their Shares as soon as conveniently can be. In Witness of the beforementioned and every particular herein contained I the said John Secker have set my hand & <and> seal the Day & <and> year above written.

John Secker (S[igned] S[ealed])
Signed sealed & <and> published by the abovenamed John Secker as & <and> for his last Will & <and> Testament in the presence of us whose

names are hereunder written who did each of us subscribe our Names as Witnesses thereto at his request in his presence and in the presence of each other. Witnesses Jos. Peckover John Ransome. Joseph Haycock.
August 20th 1795

The within named Executors duly made their proper affirmations before the Revd. Michl. Bridges Clk Surr[ogate] to the Comm[issary].

[In different hand] Effects about £30 Examd. 12th Augst 1808 Mr Rackham.

APPENDIX 3: THE SECKERS AND SPARSHALLS IN THE EIGHTEENTH CENTURY

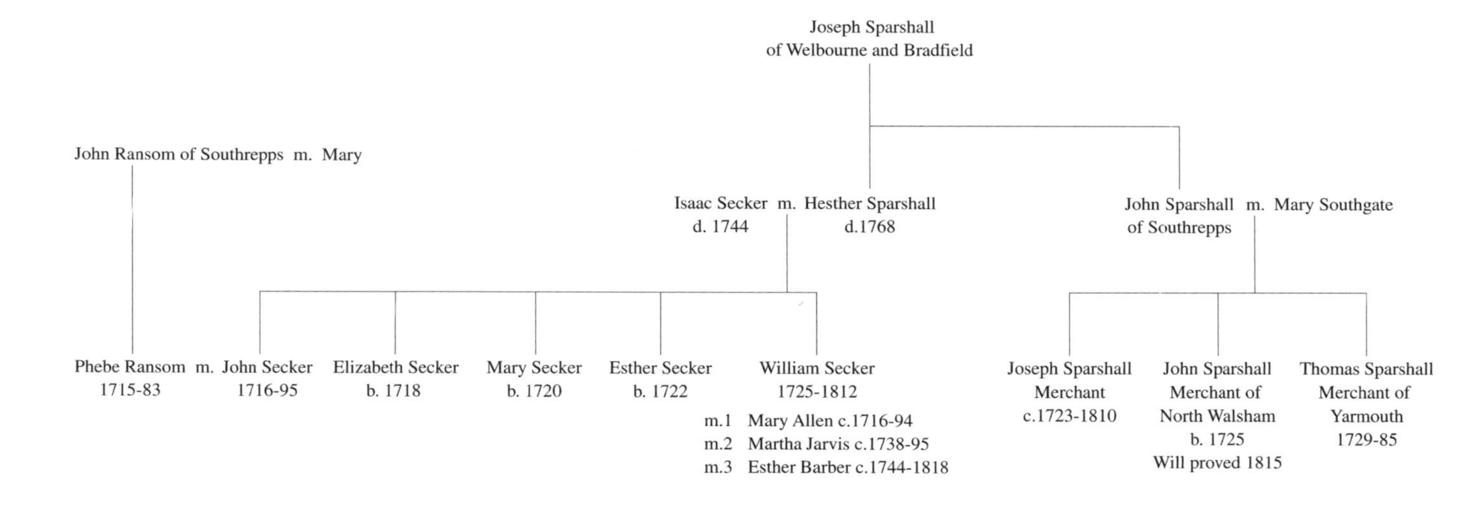

Sources: P. Palgrave-Moore, *Norfolk Pedigrees, Part Three* (Norfolk Geneology, XIII, 1981); NRO, SF42-45

APPENDIX 4: JOHN SECKER'S ATTENDANCE AT THE NORFOLK AND NORWICH QUARTERLY MEETING, 1757–1794

Year	Attendances	Year	Attendances	Year	Attendances	Year	Attendances
1757	2	1767	3	1777	4	1787	2
1758	1	1768	4	1778	3	1788	0
1759	3	1769	2	1779	3	1789	0
1760	2	1770	3	1780	3	1790	4
1761	3	1771	4	1781	3	1791	1
1762	2	1772	3	1782	2	1792	1
1763	2	1773	3	1783	1	1793	1
1764	3	1774	4	1784	2	1794	1
1765	3	1775	4	1785	2		
1766	3	1776	3	1786	2		

Sources: NRO, SF 4–6, Minute Books of the Norfolk and Norwich Quarterly Meeting, 1747–1794

SELECT BIBLIOGRAPHY

The place of publication is London, unless otherwise stated.

MANUSCRIPT SOURCES

British Library, Asia, Pacific and Africa Collections (BL)

IOR/L/MAR/B/645B Log book of *The East India Yacht* 1740–1741
IOR/L/MAR/B/647B Log book of *The Defence* East India Man 1738–1740
IOR/L/MAR/B/647E Pay book of *The Defence* East India Man 1738–1740

National Maritime Museum (NMM)

ADM/L/N/5 Navy Board, Lieutenant's logbook of *The Namur*, 1731–1733
ADM/L/S/511 Navy Board Lieutenant's logbook of *The Sunderland*, 1729–1737
ADM/L/S/512 Navy Board Lieutenant's logbook of *The Sunderland*, 1731–1736

Norfolk Record Office (NRO)

Rye MS 71 Memorandums collected and connected together in order to compile a short Narrative of the Life and Travels of John Secker written by himself, copied from the original Manuscript By Samuel Mason for D. Boulter, 1800.
Y/D 41/105 The original travel narrative of John Secker
ANW 1795, Will 83, *ff. 118r-119r* (MF 350) The will of John Secker
MS 4415, pp.519–27 A Short Narrative of the life of Daniel Boulter (1740–1802)
MS 4415, p. 531 Note of Edmund Sparshall, 1810
MS 21,393/3, Minute Book of the Monthly Meeting of Wells, 1738–1759
MS 21,393/4, Minute Book of the Monthly Meeting of Wells, 1797–1802
MS 21,393/8, Minute Book of the Monthly Meeting of Lynn, 1734–1775
MS 21393/51, 293 x 1 Indenture for Wells Meeting House, 14 November 1767
SF 3 Minutes of the Norfolk and Norwich Quarterly Meeting, 1739–46
SF 4 Minutes of the Norfolk and Norwich Quarterly Meeting, 1747–62
SF 5 Minutes of the Norfolk and Norwich Quarterly Meeting, 1763–81
SF 6 Minutes of the Norfolk and Norwich Quarterly Meeting, 1781–94
SF 7 Minutes of the Norfolk and Norwich Quarterly Meeting, 1795–1809
SF 42–5 (MF/RO 320/6) Registers of the Norfolk and Norwich Quarterly Meeting, including SF 42 Marriages; SF 43 Births, SF 44 Burials and SF45 Supplement
SF259 'Record for the People called Quakers in the County of Norfolk of all their Burying grounds, Meeting houses, and yearly profits of Charitable gifts and Bequests to their Poor, annually digested: Shewing by whom and when Purchased or Given, to whom & when since transferred in Trust; and with whom the several writings thereunto belonging are lodged.'

PRINTED PRIMARY SOURCES

E. Barlow, *Barlow's Journal of his life at sea in King's Ships, East & West Indiaman & other merchantmen from 1659 to 1703*, ed. B. Lubbock (2 vols., 1934)

B. De Chair, ed., *A Calendar of the Freemen of Great Yarmouth, 1429–1800* (Norwich, 1910)

D. Defoe, *A Tour Through the Whole Island of Great Britain*, ed. P. Rogers (Harmondsworth, 1971)

T. Lurting, *The Fighting Sailor Turned Peaceable Christian: Manifested in the Convincement and Conversion of Thomas Lurting* (1711), reprinted in L. Kuenning, ed., *Historical Writings of Quakers against War* (Quaker Heritage Press, Glenside, Pennsylvania, 2002)

E. H. W. Meyerstein, ed., *Adventures by Sea of Edward Coxere* (Oxford, 1945)

K. Morgan, ed., *An American Quaker in the British Isles: The Travel Journals of Jabez Maud Fisher, 1775–9* (Records of Social and Economic History, new series, xvi, 1992)

Museum Boulterianum: A Catalogue of the Curious and Valuable Collection of Natural and Artificial Curiosities in the Extensive Museum of Daniel Boulter, Yarmouth (c.1794)

J. Phipps, *A Summary Account of an Extraordinary Visit to this Metropolis in the Year 1753, by the Ministry of Ann Mercy Bell* (1754)

F. B. Tolles, ed., *The Journal of John Woolman and a Plea for the Poor* (New York, 1968)

R. Walter and B. Robins, *A Voyage round the World in the Years MDCCXL, I, II, III, IV, by George Anson*, ed., G. Williams (1974)

SECONDARY WORKS

D. Armitage and M. J. Braddick, eds, *The British Atlantic World, 1500–1800* (Basingstoke, 2002)

M. Hope Bacon, ed., *Wilt Thou Go On My Errand? Three 18th Century Journals of Quaker Women Ministers* (Wallingford, Pennsylvania, 1994)

C. Barringer, ed., *North Walsham in the Eighteenth Century* (North Walsham, 1983)

H. W. Bowen, M. Lincoln and N. Rigby, eds, *The Worlds of the East India Company* (Woodbridge, 2002)

J. B. Braithwaite, ed., *Memoirs of Joseph John Gurney* (2 vols. Norwich, 1854)

D. M. Butler, *The Quaker Meeting Houses of Britain* (2 vols. Friends Historical Society, 1999)

L. Colley, *Britons: Forging the Nation, 1707–1837* (2nd edn, 2003)

L. Colley, *Captives: Britain, Empire and the World, 1600–1850* (2002)

P. Crowhurst, *The Defence of British Trade 1689–1815* (Folkestone, 1977)

R. Davis, *The Rise of the English Shipping Industry in the Seventeenth and Eighteenth Centuries* (1962)

P. Earle, *The Pirate Wars* (2003).

P. Earle, *Sailors: English Merchant Seamen, 1650–1775* (1998)

A. W. Ecclestone and J. L. Ecclestone, *The Rise of Great Yarmouth: The Story of a Sandbank* (Norwich, 1959)

P. Edwards, *The Story of the Voyage: Sea Narratives in Eighteenth-Century England* (Cambridge, 1994)

P. Gauci, *Politics and Society in Great Yarmouth, 1660–1722* (Oxford, 1996)

D. J. Hall, 'The Study of Eighteenth-Century English Quakerism: From Rufus Jones to Larry Ingle', *Quaker Studies*, 5:2 (2001), pp. 105–19

D. Hancock, *Citizens of the World: London Merchants and the Integration of the British Atlantic Community, 1735–1785* (Cambridge, 1995)

A. J. C. Hare, *The Gurneys of Earlham* (2 vols. 1897)

R. M. Jones, *The Later Periods of Quakerism* (2 vols. 1921)

P. Langford, *A Polite and Commercial People: England 1727–1783* (Oxford, 1998)

P. Linebaugh and M. Rediker, *The Many-Headed Hydra: The Hidden History of the Revolutionary Atlantic* (2000)

A. Lloyd, *Quaker Social History, 1669–1738* (1950)

P. J. Marshall and G. Williams, *The Great Map of Mankind: British Perceptions of the World in the Age of Enlightenment* (1982)

P. Palgrave-Moore, *Norfolk Pedigrees, Part Three* (Norfolk Genealogy, xiii, 1981)

M. Rediker, *Between the Devil and the Deep Blue Sea: Merchant Seamen, Pirates, and the Anglo-American Maritime World, 1700–1750* (Cambridge, 1987)

N. A. M. Rodger, *The Wooden World: An Anatomy of the Georgian Navy* (1986)

D. J. Starkey, *British Privateering Enterprise in the Eighteenth Century* (Exeter, 1990)

R. T. Vann, *The Social Development of English Quakerism, 1655–1755* (Cambridge, Massachusetts, 1969)

N. Virgoe and T. Williamson, eds, *Religious Dissent in East Anglia* (Norwich 1993)

M. R. Watts, *The Dissenters: From the Reformation to the French Revolution* (Oxford, 1978)

C. Wilkinson, *The British Navy and the State in the 18th Century* (Woodbridge, 2004)

G. Williams, *Buccaneers, Explorers and Settlers: British Enterprise and Encounters in the Pacific, 1670–1800* (Aldershot, 2005)

K. Wilson, *The Island Race: Englishness, Empire and Gender in the Eighteenth Century* (2003)

K. Wilson, *The Sense of the People: Politics, Culture and Imperialism in England, 1715–1785* (Cambridge, 1995)

A. Winchester, 'Travellers in grey: Quaker journals as a source for local history', *The Local Historian*, 21:2 (1991), pp. 70–5

R. Young, 'The adventures of John Secker', in D. Joice, ed., *Bygones*, v (1980), pp. 34–55

UNPUBLISHED THESES

J. D. Murphy, 'The Town and Trade of Great Yarmouth, 1740–1850' (University of East Anglia, D. Phil. thesis, 1979)

S. Stevens, 'A Believing People in a Changing World: Quakers in Society in North-East Norfolk, 1690–1800' (University of Sunderland, D.Phil. thesis, 2005)

Index

Ships are given in italics and Secker's relationship to his kinfolk is given in brackets.